"This is a great book to learn about the early signs of borderline personality disorder in adolescent children in ways that increase awareness and might facilitate earlier interventions."

—Frederic Bien, Ph.D., president, Personality Disorder Awareness Network (PDAN), www.pdan.org

". . . empowers families with a wealth of information to better understand and help their loved ones."

—Lynn Courey and Mike Menu, co-founders of the Sashbear Foundation, "making waves for BPD," http://sashbear.org

## PRAISE FOR THE FIRST EDITION OF
### *BORDERLINE PERSONALITY DISORDER IN ADOLESCENTS*

". . . a long overdue book that eloquently and expertly addresses the wide-ranging issues surrounding borderline personality disorder in adolescents. This compassionate book is a must for parents with children suffering from borderline personality disorder, as well as clinicians, educators, pediatricians, and clergy trying to understand and help adolescents with this serious, chronic disorder."

—Perry D. Hoffman, Ph.D., president of the board of directors, National Education Alliance for Borderline Personality Disorder

"A must-have book for every parent with a borderline child."

—Randi Kreger, coauthor, *Stop Walking on Eggshells: Taking Your Life Back When Someone You Care about Has Borderline Personality Disorder*

"Families and their children with BPD will find this book a very useful guide as they struggle together toward a more fully realized life."

—Mary C. Zanarini, Ed.D., director, Laboratory for the Study of Adult Development, McLean Hospital, and associate professor of psychology, Harvard Medical School

# Borderline

# Personality

# Disorder

# in Adolescents

SECOND EDITION

## What To Do When Your Teen Has BPD

A COMPLETE
GUIDE FOR
FAMILIES

### BLAISE AGUIRRE, MD

Assistant Professor of Psychiatry, Harvard Medical School,
and Medical Director, 3East, McLean Hospital

FAIR WINDS

© 2014 Fair Winds Press
Text © 2007, 2014 Blaise Aguirre, MD

First published in 2014 by Fair Winds Press,
an imprint of The Quarto Group,
100 Cummings Center, Suite 265-D,
Beverly, MA 01915, USA.
T (978) 282-9590 F (978) 283-2742
www.QuartoKnows.com

Fair Winds Press titles are also available at discount for retail, wholesale, promotional, and bulk purchase. For details, contact the Special Sales Manager by email at specialsales@quarto.com or by mail at The Quarto Group, Attn: Special Sales Manager, 100 Cummings Center, Suite 265-D, Beverly, MA 01915, USA.

ISBN: 978-1-59233-649-4

Library of Congress Cataloging-in-Publication Data available

Cover design by Megan Jones Design
Book layout by Sporto

Printed in USA

*The information in this book is for educational purposes only. It is not intended to replace the advice of a physician or medical practitioner. Please see your health care provider before beginning any new health program.*

*To all the young people with BPD who fight courageously through the chaos of BPD to ensure that they have more settled lives and more harmonious relationships. You have taught me so much and know who you are.*

# CONTENTS

MY COLLEAGUES AND I interviewed a teenager and her family who sought treatment for her at McLean Hospital in Belmont, Massachusetts, where I practice. She had been referred to us for treatment of mood problems and bipolar disorder even though she had all the classic symptoms of borderline personality disorder (BPD): fears of abandonment and emptiness, self-injury, overidealizing and later devaluing her boyfriend, suicidal thoughts, reactive mood swings, and impulsivity.

The girl's parents wondered why she wasn't getting any better despite all the medication she had been on. We reviewed her symptoms and pointed out that she met criteria for BPD but not bipolar disorder. The father, a prominent psychiatrist who worked with adult patients, became very upset and asked for a meeting without his daughter.

"How," he asked after she left the room, "can you make the diagnosis of BPD in a child? Giving her that diagnosis means years of misery and hopelessness for her and for us. You forget I am a psychiatrist. I know borderlines. They're impossible!"

Years ago, I might have agreed with this father. Years ago, I myself saw firsthand the devastating suffering of a close friend who struggled with the disorder. I was a medical student at the time, and though I tried to find help for her, there was little useful treatment or understanding of BPD. My friend found no peace from her struggle or hope that she would ever get better. Like many others who have relationships with people who suffer from this disorder, I found I didn't have the strength to maintain our relationship, and we fell out of touch. But my friend's intense suffering made a lasting impression. Despite—or perhaps even because of—my inability to help her I developed a profound interest in this difficult and little-understood disorder.

A decade and a half later, in May 2000, I joined the staff at McLean Hospital, the largest psychiatric affiliate of Harvard Medical School, to work on its thirty-bed, adolescent residential psychiatric unit. I soon discovered that there was great disinclination to make the diagnosis of BPD in adolescents because of the concern that it would label these teens with one of the most feared, stigmatizing, and difficult-to-treat disorders in psychiatry. To make matters worse, of all the conditions in psychiatry, BPD has one of the highest suicide rates, with up to 90 percent of patients making suicide attempts and up to 10 percent completing suicide.

From the beginning, I felt an ethical obligation to diagnose adolescents with BPD when appropriate, regardless of the early reluctance of some colleagues. Despite being cautioned against making the diagnosis of BPD, I found that, for the most part, neither the patients nor their parents shied away from the diagnosis. The stigma of BPD was the clinicians' issue, not the patients'. In fact, the more parents read about BPD in adults, the more it seemed to fit the clinical picture of their children. Parents were frustrated, however, that there was so little information on the condition in adolescents, and they often asked for something to read on adolescent BPD.

Sadly, there was scant literature, despite the fact that many of the adolescents who come through psychiatric hospitals like McLean have BPD or traits of BPD. Furthermore, I was frustrated that our early attempts at treatment in adolescents did not appear to reduce their misery.

No amount of medication or talk therapy seemed to help. But soon after my arrival at McLean, some of our clinicians started to practice treatment known as dialectical behavioral therapy (DBT), and these sometimes highly self-destructive adolescents would dramatically reduce their self-destructiveness.

It took me a few more years to fully understand and accept the promise of DBT, but after seeing the outcomes I completed an extensive training in the therapy. It is a powerful and comprehensive treatment that helps patients, families, and the therapists who work with emotionally intense BPD, self-injurious, and suicidal kids. In September 2007, I co-founded, with my colleagues Michael Hollander, Janna Hobbs, and Cynthia Kaplan, a dedicated unit to treat adolescent girls and young women with BPD. The model of treatment we would use was dialectical behavioral therapy.

## NEW THERAPY, NEW AWARENESS FOR A RARELY RECOGNIZED YET COMMON DISORDER

It has always been a fairly straightforward matter to explain the use of lithium for bipolar disorder, or Prozac for depression, because these conditions have been talked about and written about for years. But it has been much harder to explain the use of DBT for BPD. Most patients or parents have never heard of BPD, let alone DBT, when we tell them of it. DBT is an excellent therapy and after many years its promise is being realized as increasing numbers of clinicians are trained in the practice.

Since the first edition of this book in 2007, we have learned a tremendous amount about BPD in adolescents, and increasingly it is more common for clinicians to make the diagnosis. Today, not only are we applying DBT, but we are also researching related best practices and outcomes. This book is a reflection of past to present; a collection of the stories of the adolescents themselves; a focus on what we know about BPD and how to treat it; and a guide for parents and patients, offering simple ideas and solutions that can be applied now.

My hope is that, with this book, parents and adolescents will have a more comprehensive understanding of BPD. This condition is widely recognized by the adult psychiatric community but reluctantly (though increasingly) recognized in adolescents, despite compelling evidence that BPD has its roots firmly planted in childhood and adolescence.

The right diagnosis guides treatment, and so I hope that therapists, too, will find accounts in these pages that resonate with their clinical experience. Beyond this, I hope that therapists will take on the challenge of working with these young people.

A young woman I have worked with for a few years recently had a fight with her parents and became angry and self-destructive. She used her newfound emotional regulation skills, a coping mechanism I discuss later in the book, to rapidly calm herself down. In her next session, she asked me why I would ever want to work with not just one, but a group of kids who are as needy, demanding, and potentially lethal as she was! The answer to this is complex. Some of it is remembering my friend's suffering and some of it is that I find many of these adolescents to be insightful, empathic, caring, and funny much of the time. Also, because these adolescents cannot tolerate their misery, many are truly committed to their therapies and to creating lives worth living. But most of all, new insights into BPD and the success of DBT have made the outcome of the condition far more promising than it has ever been.

I remember that when I first started to work with people with BPD I would often end up feeling as hopeless and defeated as I had with my friend. But after years of this work, I realize that it is not about how *I* feel. My feeling inept and hopeless for an hour or so pales in comparison to the years of pain and emptiness my BPD patients have felt. To be able to recognize that their anger, frustration, rage, and suicidality are often reflections of their feeling alienated and alone and say, "Okay, I get it.

I can handle that," helps kids with BPD feel they are understood, and the healing can begin. This, too, liberates me to persevere in the work of helping children live lives worth living. Increasingly, seeing kids live such lives is reason enough to continue in this effort.

# Understanding Borderline Personality Disorder

## CHAPTER ONE

# What Is Borderline Personality Disorder?

PSYCHIATRIC DIAGNOSES appear to be like cultural fads that come and go. There was a time in child and adolescent psychiatry when everyone had post-traumatic stress disorder (PTSD), and then everyone had bipolar disorder, then Asperger's syndrome, and surely the next big diagnosis will come and go.

Part of the perception of these conditions as fads stems from problems in diagnosing psychiatric disorders and the general absence of accurate diagnostic tools and procedures. Without such tools, any single behavior might be "claimed" by people researching a particular diagnosis. For instance, agitation with anger might be a part of bipolar disorder, or a symptom of PTSD, or a reaction in borderline personality disorder (BPD). The complexity of the brain and its functioning does not yield its inner workings or disruptions as easily as do the illnesses of other organs. An x-ray, a blood test, and a blood pressure cuff can confirm a broken leg, diabetes, or high blood pressure, respectively. Despite powerful imaging machines and a better understanding of gene and neural functions, though, we are still far from making diagnoses for most psychiatric disorders based on anything more than a description of behavior and functioning.

In that light, there is something particularly elusive about BPD, especially in adolescents. It seems to overlap with many of the behaviors of normal adolescence and also with PTSD, bipolar disorder, mood and anxiety disorders, attention deficit disorder (ADD) and attention deficit hyperactivity disorder (ADHD).

BPD is all of those conditions at once and then none at all. Yet sitting with adolescents with BPD is unlike sitting with any other group of kids. It is as distinct as being with someone with autism or Down syndrome, but trying to capture what makes it so is difficult at best. Adolescents with BPD don't have the social deficits of autism, the disheveled appearance of severe depression, the disorganized thinking of psychosis, the grandiosity of mania, or the cravings of addictions. Yet their suffering is all too real and, frequently, the scars on their arms bear testament to lives of misery and inner pain. When adolescents with BPD feel understood, they lighten up and talk profoundly and insightfully of their struggles and desires.

*Adolescents with BPD don't have the social deficits of autism, the disheveled appearance of severe depression, the disorganized thinking of psychosis, the grandiosity of mania, or the cravings of addictions. Yet their suffering is all too real and, frequently, the scars on their arms bear testament to lives of misery and inner pain.*

But when they feel threatened, unknown, or abandoned, they shut down or rage as if all their insights were nothing more than illusions.

Yet, adolescents with BPD are not alone. Depending on the research, between 2 and 6 percent of the general population suffers from BPD. That equates to somewhere between 6 and 18 million Americans. And BPD affects not only those afflicted but also the family members and friends who care for them.

According to the American Psychiatric Association and statistics from the World Health Organization, 10 percent of mental health outpatients and 20 percent of psychiatric inpatients have BPD. Of those diagnosed,

75 percent are women, although more recent data indicate that men may have rates of BPD similar to those of women.

## BPD AND SUICIDE

And then there are treatment challenges because although evidence-based therapies for BPD exist, such as dialectical behavior therapy (DBT), few with BPD are treated with such therapies. In addition, about 85 percent of people with BPD also meet the diagnostic criteria of another mental disorder. There are also physical health impacts; for instance, a thirty-year-old woman with BPD typically has the medical profile of a woman in her sixties, often because of the effects of smoking, metabolic and weight changes tied to medication side effects, and poor self-care. Thirty-eight percent of adults with BPD are prescribed three or more medications, and the majority of the young people admitted to our unit are on more than three medications. Also, 38 percent of those with BPD have substance abuse/dependence disorders.

BPD also has a significant economic and societal impact. For instance, up to 40 percent of frequent users of mental health services have BPD, and more than 50 percent of people with BPD are severely impaired in employability. Finally, BPD is implicated in 17 percent of the prison population.

Despite all these statistics, the greatest tragedy of BPD is that up to 90 percent of people with the disorder will attempt suicide, and up to 10 percent will complete suicide. We do not have statistics on suicide attempts or rates specifically in adolescents, and these data are desperately needed. On our unit, which can accommodate up to fourteen adolescent girls and young women, more than 95 percent of the young people admitted have either made one or more suicide attempts or thought about doing so. It is a well-established finding that suicidal thinking is found almost universally in people with BPD. Many people with BPD cite the hopelessness and pain of the suffering together with the loneliness and constant fear of abandonment as reasons for wanting to die.

## CHARACTERISTICS OF BPD

BPD in adolescents is typically characterized by struggles in the following five aspects of functioning. In the ensuing chapters I will expand on these concepts, giving examples from clinical practice, what research has to offer, and skills that can help target the symptoms.

## THE FACTS ON SUICIDE IN ADOLESCENTS

In 2010, suicide was the fourth and third leading cause of death for youths aged five to fourteen and fifteen to twenty-four years, respectively, according to the National Institute of Mental Health. Completed suicide is fortunately less common in children and adolescents than in adults: The one-year incidence rate for suicide in adolescents is 7.53 per 100,000 compared to 13.92 per 100,000 for adults aged twenty to twenty-nine and 16.69 per 100,000 for adults aged forty to forty-nine.

Different from completed suicide, suicidal ideation (SI)—that is, the contemplation of suicide—and suicide attempts (SA) are relatively common in youth. In the general population, nearly 20 percent of teenagers aged fifteen to nineteen years reported SI and nearly 10 percent reported at least one SA within a twelve-month period. Because one in three adolescents with SI go on to attempt suicide, and because past SI and SA are strongly correlated with future attempts and completed suicide, it is critical that this behavior be aggressively targeted in therapy. Clinicians and parents need to know that the strongest risk factor for SI and SA in adolescents is a psychiatric diagnosis. Up to 90 percent of adolescents who attempt or think about suicide have a psychiatric disorder. These can include BPD, as well as bipolar, anxiety, and substance use disorders.

1. Adolescents with BPD often display **behavioral dysregulation** or difficulty in controlling their behavior. The most worrisome of all BPD behaviors is suicidal behavior and suicidal thinking.

Adolescents with BPD commonly injure themselves (frequently in the form of cutting themselves), and most typically the reason they do so is that they are trying to regulate intense emotions. Other forms of injury include burning, branding, picking at scars, piercing, head banging, and punching walls.

Researchers are looking to see whether self-injury releases naturally occurring brain opiates that might provide a temporary sense of well-being. I am often asked whether self-injury is the same as making a suicide attempt and the answer is almost always no. It is important to make this distinction and to clarify further because parents often worry about how suicidal their children are.

## THE RELATIONSHIP BETWEEN RECURRENT SUICIDAL BEHAVIOR AND SELF-INJURY

Although suicide is not the same as self-injury, throughout the book I will often mention these two behaviors together. Research shows that people who self-injure have an approximately thirtyfold increase in the risk of suicide compared with the general population. This risk is substantially higher for women who self-injure than for men who self-injure, and suicide rates are highest within the first six months after the first self-harm episode. So even though suicide and self-injury are different behaviors with different goals, they are closely linked.

In research studies, the behavior of cutting is known as *non-suicidal self-injury* (NSSI). The studies show that although many people with BPD self-injure, many others do not. There are people who engage in NSSI who do not have a personality disorder but instead suffer from depression, anxiety, suicidality, and poor social functioning.

Impulsivity is another behavioral problem, and parents often describe how the adolescent appears to be "acting without thinking." We think of it as behaving quickly without evaluating the consequences of the behavior or even disregarding potential consequences. Impulsive behaviors often take place in the context of strong emotions and can include suddenly dropping out of school, driving recklessly, engaging in dangerous sexual encounters, and abusing drugs. Although impulsivity is not always dangerous, it can lead to situations that can seriously affect long-term health.

**2.** Adolescents with BPD typically suffer from problems in their **interpersonal relationships**, with sometimes profound fears of abandonment. This can lead to chaotic relationships, particularly with those whom they are close to, as they try to grapple with this fear.

The fear of abandonment might be triggered by what seems like a minor rejection: a friend canceling a plan to go to dinner or a therapist running a few minutes late for an appointment. Abandonment fears can lead to anger because the adolescent feels uncared for or unimportant. To others, the rage appears disproportionate to the situation at hand, but to the adolescent the ensuing suffering and fear are nearly intolerable.

When feeling abandoned, the adolescent can resort to *reassurance-seeking behaviors*, which is behaving in ways that will get others to reassure them that they will not be abandoned. An example of such behavior is calling or texting a boyfriend multiple times even at the risk of annoying the boyfriend. Ironically, sometimes the reassurance-seeking behavior can lead to the destruction of the relationship and the very abandonment the adolescent fears. Further, adolescents with BPD show instability in relationships particularly with their parents and close friends. This instability is manifested by rapidly changing intense anger and overidealizing and devaluing those closest to them.

**3.** Adolescents with BPD frequently have difficulty regulating their **emotions** and can be referred for treatment because of difficulty in controlling anger or very reactive moods.

For instance, they can appear perfectly happy one moment, quickly become explosive, weepy, or agitated, and then appear to calm down just as quickly the next moment. Unstable mood, along with difficulty controlling emotional extremes, is a defining problem for people with BPD. Unstable moods can be true of adolescents without BPD, but for people with this disorder, the emotional ups and downs are often triggered by frustration and interpersonal conflict, and the extremes of mood are intense. It is this intensity that sets them apart from typical adolescent mood swings.

Adolescents with BPD tell us that they feel emotions more quickly and more intensely, and they take longer to calm down than their friends who don't have BPD. They also recognize that when they are in a good mood they can get almost anything done, but achieve almost nothing when in a bad mood. This is known as *mood-dependent behavior.*

Another aspect of the powerful emotions associated with BPD is that, for adolescents, it can feel as if they have always felt that way. During interviews, when they say they are feeling miserable and we ask them how long they have felt that way, they say that they can't remember ever not having felt miserable. Having other people remind them that they seemed to be having fun a few hours earlier or that their bad mood won't last forever hardly seems to help, and in fact can perpetuate their worry that they are not understood.

4. Adolescents with BPD have trouble controlling their thoughts or **cognitions** and can have paranoid and irrational beliefs and dissociative experiences. Typically, adolescents with BPD experience these episodes during times of high stress and high emotions. They can believe that other people are intentionally trying to hurt them or make their life miserable.

Dissociative experiences can include feeling disconnected, feeling as if the rest of the world is not real, or disconnecting emotions from bodily sensations. These symptoms often appear particularly if there has been abuse or trauma in the life of the young person.

Another common belief is that they are not loved, that they are toxic or evil, or that they are loathsome despite no evidence to support these beliefs. These cognitive distortions are the most difficult aspect to treat in working with adolescents with BPD, and this is because the adolescent with these entrenched beliefs is certain that they are true.

5. Finally, adolescents with BPD have confusion about who they are or their **self**. They struggle with their own identity, feelings, morals, and values. They can show sudden and unexpected changes in life goals, interests, and romantic preferences and partners. Although confusion about self is typical in adolescence, adolescents with BPD and their families recognize that they are at times so devoid of a sense of self that they take on the emotions and behaviors of the people around them, at times almost as if appropriating others' identities.

Adolescents with BPD also sometimes describe profound loneliness, emptiness, or boredom. These sudden changes can lead to an erratic academic history, wreak havoc in relationships, and lead to confusing and unpredictable behavior toward others in their lives.

## DYSREGULATION DEFINED

Throughout this book, I use the term *dysregulation*. Dysregulation means an inability to or difficulty in regulating or controlling behavior or emotions.

**Emotional dysregulation.** People with BPD often display marked emotional sensitivity, feeling things "quicker" and for longer periods of time than other people, and then taking a long time to return to a calmer mood.

**Behavioral dysregulation.** Those with BPD have difficulty regulating their behavior and often display extreme and destructive impulsive behaviors—such as attempts to harm themselves; recurrent suicide threats; binge eating, drinking, or drug use; episodes of promiscuity; and gambling or spending sprees.

*continued on the next page*

**Interpersonal dysregulation.** Being in relationships can be difficult for people with BPD because of their intense fear of abandonment and their rapidly changing from overidealizing to devaluing the other person. These characteristics can make it difficult for the other person in the relationship, sometimes to the point that he or she leaves and then the feared abandonment becomes real.

**Cognitive dysregulation.** People with BPD can display episodes of disorganized and paranoid thinking to the point that they might lose all touch with the world around them and dissociate—a state in which their thoughts, feelings, and memories become disconnected from their current or actual experience They appear to have a hard time regulating their thought processes, especially under stress, and can resort to extreme, black-and-white thinking, all-or-nothing thinking, marked self-doubt, and indecision. They can have repeated thoughts that people do not like them, and this can bring on profoundly debilitating self-loathing.

**Self-dysregulation.** This inability to maintain a stable sense of self is common in people with BPD. It is not unusual for adolescents to say that they have no sense of self, feel empty, and do not know who they are or what they want. They often have difficulty expressing their needs, feelings, likes, and dislikes to others, and they can be easily influenced by the opinions and actions of those around them. They tend to be very concerned with outward appearances and frequently compare themselves and their situations to those of others.

## MULTIPLE MEDICATIONS AND DIAGNOSES

Time and again young people appear for treatment with variations of the symptoms discussed previously. Their stories are frequently similar in that they often have had multiple diagnoses—most commonly a mood disorder such as bipolar disorder (formerly known as manic depression), PTSD, or ADD/ADHD. They often arrive on our unit with multiple psychiatric medications, which have had little or no effect on their behavior.

Many psychiatric disorders have a disturbance in one or two of the previously mentioned areas. But when one person has a disturbance in all five areas, this is a diagnostic category in itself—even if for no other reason than that no one treatment type can treat all the problem areas—and further, that a comprehensive treatment approach is needed. Consider the following stories from parents seeking help for their children.

"My daughter Katrina is twelve, and she will be thirteen in June. She has been in therapy for about five years with everyone you could possibly think of. She has been evaluated by top doctors, and she has been on medication, all kinds of meds to control her behavior, even though I thought she was too young to be on meds and thought therapy was the goal. In any case, none of the meds worked at all. She's defiant, constantly angry, and very disrespectful to her peers, parents, and grandparents. It has begun to spill out to other [people], such as her teachers. I am at my wit's end and don't know what to do anymore. I cannot find a program anywhere or people who know about her problems. I don't think an outpatient program is in her best interests now. I almost think it's too late, although I am trying to stay positive. I am afraid of the future."

"My fourteen-year-old daughter has a four-year history of treatment for mental illness. She started with cutting her arms and her thighs and talking about death, and then she developed more extreme mood swings, mostly when she was angry at her friends or me. Her diagnoses have included BPD, mood disorder not otherwise specified, and attention deficit hyperactivity disorder from three different psychiatrists in our city. Then we took her to a university hospital's mood disorder clinic, and she was diagnosed with cyclothymia [a condition characterized by repetitive periods of mild depression followed by periods of normal or slightly elevated mood]. She continues to have impulsive, aggressive, unstable mood swings with an intense lack of self-worth. Currently, she is hospitalized in our city's acute care psychiatric hospital, which is able to provide only 'safety net' treatment."

"I have a daughter who has been in seven different hospitals for the past three consecutive years. Presently, she is in residential care, but they want her sent to another hospital. She has many diagnoses from many psychiatrists and many med trials. She will be seventeen in two months and time is running out. [Many parents of mentally ill adolescents worry about their children turning eighteen because their legal status changes, too; the law now considers them adults with far broader legal rights, including a stronger right to refuse treatment.] She is a client of the department of mental health. We are terrified for when she turns eighteen."

## A NEW THERAPY BRINGS NEW HOPE

There is hope for adolescents like those described here. A treatment called dialectical behavior therapy (DBT) has changed the prognosis of adolescent BPD, and the promise of this treatment means that far fewer adolescents will suffer from the ravages of BPD or continue to suffer with BPD as adults.

Although DBT was originally developed for adults with BPD, it has been adapted to the needs of adolescents who suffer from the early symptoms of BPD. For example, parents are included in treatment so that the DBT skills can be extended to the home. Also, DBT skills are modified to be more developmentally pertinent to adolescents. Finally, the therapy is adapted to address the dilemmas of the parent–child interaction.

DBT is composed of the following four parts, all of which will be explored in depth later in this book.

- Weekly individual psychotherapy
- Group skills training
- Phone consultation/coaching with the patient
- A support system for therapists who treat people with BPD

## DIAGNOSING BPD IN ADOLESCENTS

BPD remains a controversial diagnosis in adolescence, even though the *Diagnostic and Statistical Manual of Mental Disorders-IV (DSM-IV)*—the American Psychiatric Association–published manual that covers all mental health disorders—allows for the diagnosis of BPD in adolescents. The *DSM-IV* is the manual physicians, psychiatrists, psychologists, therapists, and social workers use to diagnose mental illness.

Therapists have historically given two major reasons for not making the diagnosis in adolescents. First, they say that it is difficult to distinguish between BPD symptoms in adolescence and normal adolescent behavior. Second, they say that the adolescent personality has not fully developed and that giving someone such a diagnosis means unfairly stigmatizing the adolescent. Most therapists wait until a person is eighteen years old before making the diagnosis.

Other clinicians who treat adolescents tell parents that they simply cannot diagnose an adolescent with BPD or that the kids will grow out of the behavior. Still others say that they don't want to say anything to the parents about BPD for fear of upsetting them, and that being diagnosed with bipolar disorder or ADHD will "look better," because they are so much easier to treat.

But here is the problem with not making the diagnosis as early as clinically evident: BPD is a complex and serious psychiatric disorder. If left untreated, a person with BPD has a one in ten chance of killing him- or herself. People who suffer from BPD can feel profoundly miserable and misunderstood, so much so that they would rather die than tolerate their suffering. Not diagnosing BPD or misdiagnosing it as something else prolongs the suffering of the children and their families. This can contribute to a cycle of multiple hospitalizations and at times unnecessary or unwarranted medication trials. Further, it can perpetuate the stigma that is often associated with BPD.

Two things are absolutely clear. First, adults with BPD almost always recognize that their symptoms and suffering started in childhood or adolescence. Second, some adolescents have symptoms that are so consistent with BPD that it would be unethical not to make this diagnosis and treat them accordingly.

*If left untreated, a person with BPD has a one in ten chance of killing him- or herself.*

Clinicians who are unwilling to make this diagnosis in adolescents do so in the face of increasing research, which has determined that the conditions necessary for BPD's development are found in the genes of the baby, in the temperament of the young child after birth, and in the environment in which the child is nurtured. I will discuss the causes of and contributing factors to BPD in depth later in the book.

## BPD'S ROOTS IN CHILDHOOD

It is enlightening to look at the history of BPD. The psychiatry books of the 1950s reflected the view that adolescence was a time of such emotional turmoil that it was difficult to decide whether a teen's behavior reflected a psychiatric illness that required treatment or normal adolescent development and that any strange behavior would subside. Treatment was not recommended.

In the 1970s, psychiatrist James Masterson, MD (a pioneer in the area of personality disorders), challenged this view when he treated a series of adolescents whose behaviors would be recognized as BPD today. He termed these adolescents as having borderline syndrome. He noted that these patients had a cluster of symptoms that included mood swings, terrible fears of abandonment, and self-destructive behaviors. Unfortunately, psychiatry at the time did not have the benefit of current research and Masterson concluded that the adolescents' parents almost universally had borderline syndrome themselves.

If it was believed that many of these behaviors would burn themselves out—but on the other hand, if the child had it the parents had it—then perhaps that is why therapists often decided to wait for people to turn eighteen before diagnosing them with BPD. In my early days working with adolescents with BPD, I asked a couple of my adult psychiatry colleagues why the diagnosis had not been previously been made in adolescents. One told me: "We all had kids who sometimes acted similarly to adolescents with BPD; we thought they would grow out of it and none of us wanted a kid with that label." Putting the diagnosis off until age eighteen allowed for the hopeful resolution of this adolescent turmoil until the parents could be absolved of any guilt or diagnosis.

So let's agree that adulthood begins at eighteen. What do these young people look like the day before they turn eighteen, and the day before that? I have seen kids as young as thirteen with such behaviors, and even in their younger days they were described as being emotionally intense and anxious children.

The enduring nature of the behaviors, the lack of clear boundaries between typical adolescent behavior and illness, and the patients' perceptions of the symptoms as being a part of them, and not necessarily something that is happening to them, make BPD-type symptoms and behaviors more difficult to conceptualize than the more typical, episodic mental disorders, such as bipolar disorder and major depression.

Even though researchers have very different ideas as to what causes BPD, with some looking at it from a genetic perspective and others feeling that it is a problem of poor parenting, most experts agree that BPD has its roots in childhood.

It is critical that comprehensive treatment start when the symptoms first appear to stop them from becoming an entrenched pattern of maladaptive and disruptive behaviors. At times it seems that clinicians focus only on the immediate problem. For example, a patient with BPD may complain of feeling empty and so, rather than looking at the whole picture, the psychiatrist diagnoses depression and prescribes antidepressant medication. This is especially unfortunate because while medication has a clear role in the treatment of BPD (especially in reducing anxiety and treating other co-occurring psychiatric conditions), medication plays no present role in treating the core features of BPD.

The recent surge of research reports dealing with personality disorders such as BPD in adolescents suggests that the reluctance to make the diagnosis in adolescents may be waning. In this book, I hope to make a clear case for making the diagnosis in adolescents. But if after the stories, the arguments for the diagnosis, and the research have been presented there is still doubt, then I argue that the degree of self-destructiveness, despair, self-loathing, and suicidal behaviors in adolescents who don't respond to conventional treatment needs more careful evaluation. The need for early and effective treatment is critical.

## A Parent's Story

The research in this book would make little sense if it didn't resonate with adolescents who suffer from BPD, and with their parents. Because of this, many parents and some patients have kindly allowed for their stories to be included in the book. However, to respect their privacy and with their agreement, I have changed all identifying details while retaining all clinical facts. The following is one mother's experience with her daughter with BPD.

"As a baby, Miranda always wanted to be held. No matter what we were doing, as long as my husband or I held her, she was fine. She seemed to have a hard time sleeping through the night until she was about two, but as soon as I picked her up and rocked her, she would go right back to sleep. That seemed okay with us, though.

"When she started preschool at about three and a half years old, she would get so upset that I was leaving her that she would throw up. It wasn't just in the beginning of the school year; it happened through-out the year, probably three to five times a month, and I would have to take her home with me—school rules. Her pediatrician said she was fine, that it was a ploy and it was working, so she kept doing it. The next year, she didn't go to preschool.

"As she got a little older, her temper tantrums seemed to be com-pletely out of control, nothing like with any of the other kids whom I saw. And it seemed as if the smallest thing would set her off, like if I wouldn't let her have a snack before dinner. She would throw herself on the floor and kick and scream bloody murder. She did this until she was about six or seven! As she got older, it seemed like there was a lot of emotional trauma happening with her at school over friends. She either loved her friends or hated them. We thought it was girl stuff; our two sons didn't seem to have those same issues with their friends. She seemed to go "through" friends a lot. She still does now at seventeen.

"I also noticed that she always seemed to act or behave like whom-ever she was a friend with—that is, laughing like them, speaking like them, and so on. I asked her why she did this, and she didn't think she did. We thought she seemed almost desperate to have friends, causing her to do anything to be accepted by them, which has gotten worse as she gets older.

"I started taking her to different therapists when she was about ten because she just didn't seem 'normal' to me compared with all of the other little girls that I knew, and I felt really sad for her having such a hard time emotionally. I thought if I understood her better and we could figure out why she always seemed to feel 'empty,' then I could help her. She gained about thirty pounds when she was eleven, and we fought about her weight. It broke my heart that she never seemed to have enough to eat and was always sneaking food when she thought no one was watching. The doctors said that it was my issue, and she was fine. At about this time she started to tell 'stories' to get what she wanted so she didn't hear 'no' as much. Her temper tantrums were becoming less frequent, but more volatile when they happened.

"At about age twelve, she discovered the 'power' she had over boys by using sex. We didn't want to believe this. Our older son tried to tell us. He was really angry that his little sister was a 'slut.' She would offer complete strangers a blow job if they would be her friend. That really broke our hearts; we figured she had to be hurting inside to act like that. We got even stricter with her after that; she never went anywhere without one of us or another adult. We even stopped sending her to overnight camp. Life got tougher. She started sneaking out in the middle of the night to meet up with boys—people she was meeting on the Internet, we found out later.

"One time, there were two cars filled with guys from a neighboring town, and they came and picked her up one night. I was awoken by a phone call from 'Tyndall' looking for his boys because his new sneakers were in one of their cars and they were at our house to see my daughter—this was at 1:30 in the morning and Miranda was thirteen. When she finally came in that morning, she was mad at me for finding out. Shortly after that, she tried to run away to Philadelphia to live with a bunch of guys who were going to help her become a 'famous singer.' Her dog alerted me that she had left; that dog was obsessed with her. The police came, and we were able to find her at the bus terminal as she was getting off of the bus.

"I had her escorted to a behavior modification program in upstate New York. She was there for twelve months, and she made the same mistakes over and over again, so she was never able to move up in levels to complete the program. It was almost like she forgot every time she was corrected for breaking a rule and losing points, because a week later she would do it again. She did start to behave like a robot, albeit one without a memory. That was where we learned a lot of the gory details of her past indiscretions. She kept a journal while she was there that is just amazing; there was so much emotion poured onto the pages that it made me cry to read it and feel some of her pain.

"When she came home, she was so beautiful and sweet. She said she finally believed that we loved her and she was really happy. Life was nice for about nine months, and then slowly it started to be just like it was before with the lying, stealing, and sneaking out. We couldn't believe it. And the temper tantrums were back worse than ever because not only was she out of control emotionally, but she had also started punching herself in the head over and over every time really hard, and we couldn't stop her. And if we would slap her to try and snap her out of it, we were 'beating' her up. If we spoke in an angry voice, we were 'screaming' too loud, and she had to block her ears. According to her, we all hated her, her life was miserable, and she hated us and wanted us out of her life. She started to break things and punch holes in the walls and also started threatening to 'shoot' me, if she had a gun. And these rages would happen if we said no to what she was asking. It didn't matter what it was, as soon as we said no, she would freak out.

"Two weeks before her seventeenth birthday last year, she was arrested at school with drugs and asked not to go back to school for the rest of the year. She was angry at the school for catching her; it was their fault. She was not remorseful in the least, which didn't surprise us; she has never seemed to be remorseful for anything that she does, because it is always 'everyone else's fault.'

"She started to see a psychologist on her own; she thought it would help get her out of the trouble she was in. I thought that maybe she would get something out of it because it was her decision to go, and at first the psychologist thought that she was a spoiled brat, which is something that we had been hearing her whole life, and we didn't spoil her at all. Then as time went on, the psychologist thought that maybe she had bipolar disorder. She sent us to a clinician who specializes in treating adolescents with this disorder. We started going to her every four weeks for about six months, trying different meds until we found some that seemed to help.

"It was around this time that I went to the bookstore to get some books on bipolar disorder, but nothing I read seemed to fit. I stumbled upon a chapter in one book that talked about misdiagnosis and borderline personality disorder. It described Miranda to a T. I bought the book *New Hope for People with Borderline Personality Disorder* by Neil R. Bockian, PhD. I was amazed how much it described Miranda. She seemed to have seven or eight of the criteria listed in the *DSM-IV* for BPD. So I called the psychologist, and she said that you can't diagnose an adolescent with BPD and that I shouldn't think of that because she will probably outgrow a lot of her behaviors. I called the clinician and told her what I thought, and she said, 'Oh yes, she does have BPD,' but she hadn't said anything because she didn't want to upset us! I was so angry. The more I read about BPD, the more I felt comfortable with this disorder because knowledge is power and I can handle Miranda so much better now that I know more. Her clinician is also more comfortable with it now. (The psychologist told me she went to a seminar about BPD and is trying to learn more about it.)

"Her clinicians have recommended that Miranda be on some kind of an emotional individualized education plan (IEP) at school because of her issues, but the school doesn't want to do anything for her because she is a 'bad' kid. We are fighting them right now. I was told that without a letter stating what Miranda had, they were not going to do any further testing on her. The clinician didn't want to write that she has BPD because it would look bad for Miranda, so she wrote that she has bipolar and ADHD, with borderline personality disorder traits. She didn't want Miranda to be stigmatized!

"I have now read several books about the disorder, and I keep thinking, if only I knew even half of what I now know when Miranda was younger, it could have made all the difference in the world for her. None of the psychologists whom we went to even hinted at any kind of a disorder. They all seemed to feel that Miranda was fine, just a little 'bratty.' I asked her to read the chapter on what the disorder is about and its symptoms in the book *Borderline Personality Disorder Demystified* by Robert O. Friedel, MD, and she was amazed how much it described her also. Better late than never; she will be eighteen next week."

## CHAPTER TWO

# Diagnosing BPD in Adolescents

I N THE FIRST EDITION OF THIS BOOK, I wrote: "Because of the lack of information about adolescent BPD, there are no formal criteria for diagnosing it in teenagers." A tremendous amount has changed since 2007. First, various research studies have shown that there is continuity between adolescent and adult BPD and that adult BPD looks very similar to adolescent BPD. Second, the authors of the new *Diagnostic and Statistical Manual of Mental Disorders (DSM)*, the *DSM-5* (see page 36), removed previous cautions about diagnosing BPD in adolescents while retaining all the diagnostic criteria of the previous edition. Hopefully, this should dispel the widely held myth that BPD can't be diagnosed in people younger than 18. In this chapter, I introduce some broad concepts and in later chapters, look at these in more nuanced detail.

The *DSM* describes BPD as a pervasive pattern of instability in relationships, self-image, and affects, and marked impulsivity beginning by early adulthood; these appear in a variety of contexts, as indicated by five or more of the criteria that follow. Throughout the book I will continue to expand on these criteria, but in this section I want to review it and give examples from my clinical practice that highlight the definition. The *DSM* criteria for BPD is:

**1. Frantic efforts to avoid real or imagined abandonment.**

Adolescents with BPD who are hospitalized often appear for treatment after a breakup with a boyfriend or girlfriend. Such breakups will often lead to desperation, and typically we see an increase in self-destructiveness. At times they will have considered or attempted suicide, feeling despair at the loss of a relationship they feel is essential to their well-being.

But such despair can happen even if the loved one had no intention of breaking up with the BPD adolescent. Simply the thought that they will be left, a thought that can be triggered by the loved one being late for a date or not answering a phone call, can lead to such desperate behavior. The fear of abandonment is not simply that some loved person will leave, but rather it's a profound sense that someone essential to their well-being will absolutely never come back.

*The fear of abandonment is not simply that some loved person will leave, but rather it's a profound sense that someone essential to their well-being will absolutely never come back.*

I remember struggling with this concept when one young woman told me: "Okay, imagine that you are a six-year-old at Disney World, and your parents suddenly disappear, and you cannot find them, and there are all these strange people around you. It is like that. The dread is terrifying, and when I fear being left, it is exactly that fear."

The fear can be so consuming that even if there is no basis to the fear, adolescents with BPD can behave in dangerous ways, and this behavior will often cause fear in parents, particularly when the adolescent makes a suicide gesture or self-injures. This in turn can cause the parents or loved ones to worry so much that they are terrified into inaction for fear that any wrong move will cause their child to act on suicidal behaviors. Unfortunately, this can have the effect of making parents ineffective in such situations by teaching the child with BPD that such self-destructive behavior gets the attention that they sometimes want. In clinical terms, we call this *reinforcing* such behavior.

## A NOTE ABOUT THE DSM

The *Diagnostic and Statistical Manual of Mental Disorders* (*DSM*) is the standard classification of mental disorders used by mental health professionals in the United States and many parts of the world. Clinicians and researchers use it to provide a common understanding of a patient's diagnosis. The fifth edition, the *DSM-5*, came out in May 2013 and is the most current edition. In this book, I mention the previous edition, the *DSM-IV-TR*. Because the criteria of BPD in the two editions are essentially the same, references from them are essentially interchangeable. In future editions of the *DSM*, the criteria might change, but for now, the clinical descriptions in the fourth and fifth editions are equivalent.

**2. A pattern of unstable and intense relationships characterized by alternating between extremes of idealization and devaluation, called "splitting."** Parents describe how at one moment their children tell them that they are the best parents in the world, and at another, they are the worst parents ever. During a recent family therapy call with the mom of Ingrid, a sixteen-year-old with BPD, Ingrid at first was happy to hear her mother and told her how much she loved her. Her mother seemed happy in return and said she was looking forward to an upcoming pass for Ingrid to go home for a visit but that she had to take her sister to skating practice and so she would be an hour late. Ingrid erupted and started yelling at her mother, telling her how much she hated her, that she had always hated her, and how she always picked her sisters above her. Her mother was clearly upset and said that she had intended to surprise her by bringing her dog on the pass. Ingrid apologized profusely and told her mother that she loved her and hadn't meant what she said. Her mother said that she was worried by how angry Ingrid seemed and that she had second thoughts about going on the pass. Ingrid again started to rage and we had to end the call.

In BPD, such behavior occurs repeatedly and tends to be reactive. On residential and inpatient units, adolescents with BPD can similarly divide the staff into good and bad staff, and these designations can easily change. It is often the case that what an adolescent is asking for is reasonable, but that the way she is asking for it is not. Parents and staff members often find themselves taking sides, which often leads to conflict between them. From a psychodynamic perspective, this conflict between parents or staff is considered to be a reflection of what goes on in the patient's sense of self. Sometimes they feel all bad, and other times they feel all good, leading to all-or-nothing or black-and-white thinking. In this theory the problem becomes integrating the good self and bad self into a complete person, or recognizing that we are all composites of "better" and "worse" qualities. From a behavioral perspective, an adolescent with BPD does not have the skills to manage interpersonal conflict, and because some of us are more lenient and tolerant and others are stricter and rule-bound, natural conflict arises.

One of our former patients emailed me to let me know how she was doing. As you'll read in her message that follows, the relationship quickly switches from a fulfilling one to a meaningless one. The torment and doubt about whether people care comes and goes rapidly in BPD, and this can be terrifying to an adolescent. The former patient also acknowledged that because of treatment she had become more self-aware.

"So things with my boyfriend are so good. I have accepted that he gets me even though he doesn't know a lot about my disorder, and that that's the way it's supposed to be. Maybe it's better because it's not that intense. Maybe we are supposed to ride in the car silently together with a little talking on the side. I do wish he knew my ideas, though. I will work on that. I have gone crazy here in Florida. I think he wants to talk to me when I get back. He called a couple of times, but I think it's just how he wants it to be, nothing bad. But there is still me giving in on some independence but him not at all because he does his own thing 100 percent. And also it's kinda like how he wants the relationship to be.

"Damn! It switches so fast from 'I know he loves me' to 'what the heck, I mean nothing to him.' And I think some of that is justified now. Will you give me advice on how not to be so self-absorbed? My best friend, whom I do not like except that she tells me things, told me that I talk about myself a lot (she said it when she was drunk), and now I can't stop thinking about it. Now if I say something about myself . . . well, I am constantly catching myself. My dad has always called me selfish my whole life and says that I think only of myself, and I think that it's true when it comes to my family, but what if not? What if I treat everybody that way? And even so, even in my head I'm constantly thinking about the good things or the bad things or events that all have to do with me. I don't know how to stop. What a mess."

### 3. Identity disturbance: markedly and persistently unstable self-image or sense of self.

Adolescents with BPD have a hard time defining a stable sense of who they are. Their values, morals, and identity seem fluid and changing and often, their sense of self is determined by their identification with the group of friends in that moment—"I am a very different person with different people or groups of people." This criterion is trickier in diagnosing adolescents with BPD because adolescence is generally a time of defining identity, and identity issues are common in adolescents without BPD as well. Nevertheless, it is an important criterion when taken into consideration together with the other criteria because it will remain a focus in treatment.

Parents who have kids with BPD tell me one of two things. Most commonly, parents say that they always thought that they knew their child, and that the behavior—say, self-injury—came as a complete surprise and was confusing to them. A significant minority of parents feels that their child was always a mystery to them. Parents who have more than one child often compare their child with BPD to their other children who don't have BPD. Their kids without BPD are generally more predictable and emotionally regulated, whereas the child with BPD is more impulsive and difficult to soothe and seems to—as one parent put it—change identities "with the wind."

"She wants to pretend that she is a 'rich girl' who couldn't be bothered with middle class people," complained one parent, or "she tells us that she is going be the next Paris Hilton" and then acts completely like what she reads about Paris Hilton in the magazines, or she acts "like a happy, fun, loving girl all the time, when deep down she is miserable." Other parents have said that their children change to be images of whoever the children's best friends happen to be at the time.

Adolescence is a time when popular culture and the peer group can have profound influences on behavior, but in cases of children with BPD, it is an extreme version of this phenomenon, often an attempt to grasp onto and then anchor into a more defined identity.

**4. Impulsivity in at least two areas that are potentially self-damaging— such as excessive spending, dangerous sexual encounters, substance abuse, reckless driving, and binge eating.**

In younger adolescents with little money or access to cars, extreme spending and reckless driving are unusual. However, dangerous and unprotected sexual encounters, sometimes with complete strangers, drug abuse—including sharing psychiatric medication—eating problems, and running away from home are quite common. Further, younger adolescents might go for drives with older drivers who are reckless, or alternatively they may take their parents' car without permission. Another example of potentially self-endangering impulsivity is "hooking up" with older adults whom they have just met on the Internet or elsewhere. We also see adolescents posting naked pictures of themselves on social networks, which can lead to online bullying and tarnished reputations.

**5. Recurrent suicidal behavior, gestures, or threats, or self-mutilating behavior.**

In adolescents, we most commonly see cutting of the wrists and other parts of the body, including the stomach, inner thighs, and breasts. On our unit we also see adolescents who have burned themselves, overdosed on drugs, tried to hang themselves, attempted to jump from high buildings or bridges, or made other suicide attempts. Because this is the main reason that families of children with BPD seek treatment and because it is a misunderstood and terrifying symptom, I will cover this much more extensively in the next chapter.

**6. Affective instability due to a marked reactivity of mood (e.g., intense episodic dysphoria [a type of "low grade" depression, or a low-mood state that is not as severe as depression], irritability, or anxiety that usually lasts a few hours and only rarely more than a few days).**

Adolescents describe (and parents agree) how they can feel perfectly normal one minute and the next they are "pissed off" or angry or depressed, and that this change in mood is a reaction to something that happened between them and someone else, generally a parent, close friend, boyfriend, or girlfriend. The mood is reactive in that it is often a reaction to a clear precipitant. Even when the precipitant is less than clear, we teach the adolescent to pay close attention to this symptom so that they can be clearer about what happens. At times, rather than the trigger being interpersonal, it can be intrapersonal. This means that the conflict is not between the BPD adolescent and another; rather, it is a conflict or an imagined conflict within the BPD adolescent. This type of moodiness does not reliably respond to mood-stabilizing medication.

**7. Chronic feelings of emptiness.**

Emptiness is often the feeling of aloneness. Adolescents also describe this as feeling bored a lot of the time. This emptiness can lead to difficulties in setting goals and expressing aspirations, which, in turn, can lead to judgment from others. Sometimes adolescents feel that being close to others alleviates this sense of emptiness and they will sometimes choose partners who are not ideal in exchange for simply being with someone. Adolescents can run into the problem of others possibly finding the need for closeness to be more than they can provide.

**8. Inappropriate, intense anger or difficulty controlling anger (e.g., frequent displays of temper, constant anger, and/or recurrent physical fights).** Fights occur most predictably with people with whom the adolescent with BPD is closest, including best friends, romantic partners, and parents. These fights might not be witnessed or experienced by casual acquaintances and can be a source of embarrassment and shame when discussed. Some adolescents and parents feel that although this criterion does not apply, that it would apply if the feeling were something other than anger. They say that their children might display, for instance, intense jealousy or intense self-hatred. In reaching five of nine criteria, any intense emotion that appears disproportionate to the circumstances should be considered.

## WHAT PARENTS CAN DO WHEN THEIR BPD CHILD RAGES

Generally, parents are not too concerned when a two-year-old has a temper tantrum. At that age, children might have a sense of what they want—say, a toy or cookie—but might not have the words to ask for it.

Adolescent temper tantrums, or rage episodes, however, are a source of serious disruption in a family, especially if they turn violent or lead to destruction of property. These events can terrify a family and wear them down to the point of exhaustion. Some adolescents with BPD say that they don't remember what happens during the rages, they black out, and these episodes are sometimes followed by an extended period of calm. For the family, though, there is seldom a sense of calm. Although

*continued on the next page*

many times adolescents and parents say that the eruption came out of nowhere, when we get the teens to pay attention by breaking down what happened in a chain analysis of the events, which is a technique used in therapy to understand step by step exactly what happened, the adolescents learn to recognize that more often than not, an interpersonal conflict led to intense emotions, which, in turn, led to the episode of rage.

This behavior can wear down parents to the point that they give in to the children rather than put up with the angry outbursts. When parents give in to nontrivial matters for fear of their child erupting, it has the effect of teaching the child that throwing a tantrum is what he or she can do to get a specific outcome. Later I will go into specific ways to address this common problem that occurs not only between parents and their BPD kids but also between parents and all kids.

Although on our unit we do not commonly see extreme violence toward others, it can happen. For instance, one young woman bit her mother hard enough on the chest that she bled. In another case, a boy assaulted his teacher at school. More commonly, anger is displayed by loud verbal and abusive fights or destruction of property and slamming of doors. When violence happens at home, we recommend parents call the therapist and the police.

**Preventing Rages Before They Happen**

The first step is prevention. Most importantly, BPD adolescents need to know which factors make them vulnerable to such events. Do these rages occur at night with lack of sleep? Under the influence of drugs? During arguments with certain friends? During final exams and high stress? Recognizing early signs of irritability and mood changes can be critical in preventing further escalation. In some ways, parents need to become scientists, noting data about these factors.

The second step is to teach children the skills necessary to get grounded or calm down once they notice that their emotions begin to escalate. I will get into far greater depth about these techniques later in the book, but some simple but effective methods include breathing deeply, listening to music, going for a jog, or taking a soothing bath—

ways that any person might use to reduce stress.

If the adolescent with BPD rages, the single most important rule that parents must know is to never reward teens by giving them what they want. There is no exception to this rule, no matter how violent the temper reaction. What they are asking for may be perfectly reasonable, and asking for what they want in a reasonable way is the behavior that should be rewarded. If safety is a real concern because of threat of injury to self or others, parents should call the police or an ambulance.

I want to underscore that parents should never give in to yelling, threats, throwing things, or even violent aggression, no matter how distressing or embarrassing it may be at the time. I realize that this is easier said than done, and as a parent of four teenagers, I know how hard it is to say no in the face of an upset child. An important corollary is that adolescents need to learn that, although angry reactions will not work as a way of getting what they want, you are open to more adaptive and effective communication.

My colleague Michael Hollander, PhD, the director of DBT Training on 3East, will often ask a teen during an interview, "Do you want to be right, or do you want to be effective?" Most kids recognize that they want to be effective to get their needs met. Learning how to be effective is important for both adolescents and their families.

Finally, if there is going to be a consequence for a rage episode, parents should be both calm and realistic when deciding on the consequence. In the heat of an argument, a parent might say, "Young man, you are grounded for a month." Generally, this consequence is hardly ever carried out because the teen might subsequently behave well and the parent does not have the emotional resources to maintain a month of grounding. Empty consequences like this teach children that there is never any substance behind a parent's threats.

Also important is to avoid using guilt as a response to an adolescent's unwanted behavior, though parents rarely do so intentionally. Adding guilt to anger will lead to further self-criticism and self-judgment in the child. In any case, adolescents with BPD often experience tremendous guilt, feeling that they are not good enough and that they have failed their parents.

**9. Transient, stress-related paranoia or severe dissociative symptoms.**
Dissociation is a psychological state in which certain thoughts, emotions, sensations, or memories are separated from the rest of the person. It is a symptom that frequently occurs in people suffering from post-traumatic stress disorder (PTSD). A significant minority of adolescents with BPD will have suffered physical, emotional, or sexual trauma. An important learning point is that sexual or other abuse is neither necessary nor sufficient to cause BPD. However, abuse is most definitely a factor in the development of BPD in at-risk adolescents. The most common dissociative experiences are depersonalization, which is when adolescents do not feel as if they are real, and derealization, when they feel as if the rest of the world is not real.

Given the tremendous amount of research into BPD since the publication of the *DSM-IV*, many experts believe these criteria alone fail to capture the full picture of BPD. As we will see later, research is taking place into all aspects of BPD functioning, including impulsivity, anxiety, shame, anger, attachment, genetics, neuroimaging, and relationships. In all likelihood, this research will change how we identify and define BPD in future generations; however, at this point in time the *DSM* criteria remain a fair and universally accepted starting point.

## AGE IS NOT A FACTOR IN DIAGNOSING BPD IN ADOLESCENTS

A chapter on diagnosing BPD in adolescents cannot omit a question that is asked by parents and therapists alike: "Isn't it impossible to diagnose BPD before age eighteen?" The answer is categorically *no*, and I argue that not making the diagnosis and directing the child into treatment before habitual patterns of maladaptive behavior have set in is unconscionable and inconsistent with compassionate and evidence-based clinical care.

Many people argue that the *DSM-5* does not allow for the diagnosis of BPD in people younger than eighteen, but that is not true because the *DSM-5* has omitted any reference to age of onset so as not to confuse the issue. In any case, the *DSM-5* allows for the BPD diagnosis in adolescents when "maladaptive traits have been present for at least one year, are persistent and all-encompassing, and are not likely to be limited to a developmental stage or an episode of an axis I disorder [a disorder that features acute symptoms that need treatment]."

I mention the *DSM* throughout this book and do so because it is the standard manual that physicians, psychiatrists, psychologists, therapists, and social workers use to diagnose mental illness. It spells out specific diagnostic criteria for depression, anxiety, and personality disorders. Also, it is used by insurance companies for billing purposes.

## DEFINING TERMS

Some of the concepts regarding BPD problems or BPD functioning vary among researchers. Here's the way that I define certain ideas. For the purpose of this book, I define **emotions** as mental states that arise spontaneously and generally as a response to certain stimuli, rather than through conscious effort. They are often accompanied by physiological or physical changes, such as agitation or excitement. They tend to by brief in duration, lasting from moments to a few days at most. Adolescents with BPD tend to attach powerful judgments to their emotions, often wishing that they didn't have emotions because they can be so painful and intense.

Once adolescents with BPD learn to regulate and effectively experience their emotions, the judgments of these and the self-destructive behaviors tend to diminish.

I define **affect** as a generalized feeling that by some is considered more persistent than an emotion but less so than a mood. Affect is the external, observable manifestation of an emotion. Affect is often described using terms such as *labile* (which means, for instance, observing a person change from weepy to happy to angry in a short period of time), *flat* (which means the general absence or reduction of expressiveness), or *expansive* (which means a lack of restraint in expressing one's feelings, frequently with

*continued on the next page*

an exaggeration of one's significance or importance).

In the context of this book, I use **mood** as a more prolonged state of emotional being, a more characteristic or habitual state of feeling. It is a feeling state that a person would generally recognize as his usual state of being or feeling. Examples are an irritable state, a happy state, or a depressed state of being.

Many people use these three terms interchangeably. People with BPD tend to be emotionally reactive and as such don't have a typical mood picture in that mood states tend not to be stable. This volatility is often difficult for a person with BPD to tolerate. Parents describe their children's moods as constantly changing and unpredictable, and this can also be difficult for a parent to bear.

## WHEN YOUR ADOLESCENT MAY HAVE BPD

Even though many adolescents with BPD appear for treatment with the criteria I've just discussed, some of these criteria can overlap with normal adolescence. So why are adolescents referred for treatment?

The following snippets are from a few typical emails from parents asking for help with their adolescents whom they suspect have BPD. In some cases we don't have enough information, but in others, the parents' descriptions appear consistent with adolescent BPD.

"I have a fifteen-year-old daughter. She has recently started cutting herself and may have depression. None of the medication has worked."

"My son has had problems since he was thirteen. He was diagnosed with bipolar disorder, but he seems to fit BPD more. He spent his teen years in and out of hospitals, residential programs, special classrooms, etc., and made our family's life a living hell. I have tried so hard to do the right thing for years, but his rage toward me has worn me out."

"My daughter got a diagnosis of ADHD and bipolar disorder. They tried several medications, which helped a little with the mood but not with her rage. Everywhere else she is loved—her teachers, classmates, sports coaches—but at home we are either loved one minute or are hated if she doesn't get her way."

"My fifteen-year-old daughter has attempted suicide four times, and I think she's heading down the road to number five. Cutting, sex, impulsive spending, drinking, and drama are all part of her story."

"My fourteen-year-old nephew has created so much trouble for our family, and he has caused a lot of strain and tension in the household. He throws unbelievable temper tantrums."

From these emails and from the phone calls and interviews of adolescents with BPD, it is clear that we need more adolescent-specific diagnostic tools. In thinking about the criteria to use in future diagnostic tools, we need to consider the behaviors that lead these adolescents and their families to seek help.

My colleague at McLean, Mary Zanarini, EdD, arguably the most published author on BPD in adults, published the McLean Screening Instrument for Borderline Personality Disorder (MSI-BPD) in 2003. Although it is an adult screening measure, we can tweak it a bit and come up with a symptom checklist that can alert you to the possibility that your adolescent may have BPD. Although the list is highly reliable in adults, it has not been tested in adolescents. Here is a modification of the MSI-BPD targeted more toward adolescents:

## McLEAN SCREENING INSTRUMENT FOR BPD*

1. Have any of your closest relationships been troubled by a lot of arguments or repeated breakups?

   Yes____ No____

2. Have you deliberately hurt yourself physically (e.g., cut yourself or burned yourself)? Alternatively, have you made a suicide attempt?

   Yes____ No____

3. Have you experienced more than one problem with impulsivity, such as eating binges, impulsive hook-ups, running away from home, or drinking too much?

   Yes____ No____

4. Have you been extremely moody, mostly because of your relationships?

   Yes____ No____

5. Do you feel very angry a lot of the time? Do you respond in a sarcastic manner toward others?

   Yes____ No____

6. Are you often distrustful of other people, especially adults?

   Yes____ No____

7. Have you frequently felt unreal or as if things around you were unreal?

   Yes____ No____

8. Do you feel empty and alone most of the time?

   Yes____ No____

9. Do you often feel that you have no idea who you are or that you have no identity?

   Yes____ No____

10. Do you fear being abandoned and need constant reassurance that someone important (romantic interest, therapist, etc.) won't leave you (maybe even begged them not to leave you or clung to them physically)?

    Yes____ No____

*modified for adolescents

Seven of these ten criteria should lead a parent to seek a professional evaluation. However, even if fewer than seven criteria apply to your child, it does not mean that your adolescent does not have BPD. This is a self-questionnaire and adolescents, whether or not they have BPD, are unlikely to let their parents into all of their thoughts, experiences, and feelings.

## CHILD AND ADOLESCENT PERSONALITY TRAITS AND THE DEVELOPMENT OF BPD

When we ask the parents of adolescents with BPD when they first became aware that there was something wrong or that they needed help for their children, some say they noticed a significant change in behavior when their child reached puberty. They attributed the difficult behavior to the hormonal changes associated with puberty. Many parents, however, say that they recognized that their children were different from other children soon after birth.

For instance, some parents say that their BPD child was more colicky or less cuddly, made less eye contact, was moodier, had more temper tantrums, and was more difficult to soothe than their other children. These symptoms do not necessarily mean that such a baby will go on to develop BPD, but if the symptoms persist and worsen over time, they may indicate that something is wrong.

I am certainly not advocating that young children be diagnosed with BPD. However, if it is clear that a child has marked emotional regulation problems, and that these difficulties cause social and educational damage to the child—and family stress at home—then addressing these problems as early as possible by providing the child with skills to deal with them is critical.

Even if children never go on to develop worsening problems, learning problem-solving skills at an early age will benefit them for years to come. For instance, relaxation techniques such as deep breathing exercises, physical exercise such as taking a fast walk or jog, or grounding exercises, such as counting slowly to five after being asked a question rather than impulsively blurting out an answer can go far to lessen the effects of stress and anxiety.

Acquiring these skills when young is like learning a new language earlier in life. The earlier children are introduced to these skills, the greater the chances are that they will become truly proficient in using them.

## DIFFICULT TO DIAGNOSE AND TREAT: TYPICAL CHALLENGES

Many parents tell me that their child has been in multiple therapies with many therapists and been on many medications. Therapists often call our unit saying that they are at a loss of how to treat these kids because they seem so complicated, with so many problems and so many needs. Here are some of the issues that challenge parents and therapists.

*Parents of adolescents with BPD often say that their children were diagnosed with ADD, bipolar disorder, or other disorders, but that these diagnoses never seemed to completely explain their children's behavior.*

**Misdiagnosis:** Parents of adolescents with BPD often say that their children were diagnosed with ADD, bipolar disorder, or other disorders, but that these diagnoses never seemed to completely explain their children's behavior. Often, when these parents come across the diagnostic criteria for BPD in online searches, they recognize their children. In some circumstances, taking these concerns to mental health experts leads to comments like "You don't want your kid to have BPD," or "The diagnosis cannot be made before eighteen."

**Overmedicated:** Parents say that all the medication in the world did not appear to reduce their children's symptoms. Medications have a clear role to play in many psychiatric conditions that affect children and adolescents. There is well-researched evidence for medication use in mood disorders, attention deficit hyperactivity disorder (ADHD), and anxiety disorders, but the parents we see at McLean Hospital are not simply describing mood or anxiety symptoms in their kids, but serious self-injury, impulsivity, and desperation in their children's lives. These are not symptoms that can be medicated away. Also, the ravages of the use of multiple medications, or polypharmacy, can contribute to the finding by Mary Zanarini that the health profiles of BPD women at age thirty are similar to those of sixty-year-old women. Many of the medications children are put on can lead to significant weight gain and increases in cholesterol and other blood fats.

**Fear:** Some parents feel that they can no longer trust their children, or that their children are outright liars. Other parents worry about going to sleep at night for fear that their children will kill themselves. Children feel that their parents don't understand them and slowly isolate themselves from their parents. Some adolescents feel that they have to threaten self-harm in order to get the attention of their peers. These chaotic interpersonal interactions will ultimately leave the children feeling lonely, misunderstood, and at times suicidal.

**Unhelpful Therapies:** The usual kinds of treatment will not work with BPD. For instance, when adolescents with BPD are simply diagnosed as depressed, psychotherapies that link their current depressive symptoms to conflicts that originated in their earlier years are not effective in reducing the self-injury or self-loathing that these kids exhibit. Treatment approaches such as DBT and cognitive behavior therapy (a form of psychotherapy that emphasizes the important role of thinking in how people feel and what they do, but does not include the validation strategies of DBT) are much more useful in this age group in dealing with the broad spectrum of disruptive behavior. Medication in many of these cases hardly seems to have an effect, and it is further unclear what consequence medications have in the developing adolescent brain, particularly when they are not indicated.

## PONDERING PERSONALITY TRAITS

In a 2006 article published in *Comprehensive Psychiatry* that looked at social, emotional, and personality development in children and adolescents, the authors felt that the following personality traits in adolescents were likely to be important in the development of BPD.

- They noted that children and adolescents vary in their experiences and expression of **trust of others, anger, rage**, and other intense emotions. Poor trust in others and high levels of anger are more likely to be important for the development of BPD than not having those traits.
- They explored the concept of **agreeableness**, where children can range on a spectrum of being highly agreeable to being antisocial. Low agreeableness—as shown by children being spiteful, hostile, manipulative, and defiant—is more likely to be associated with the development of BPD than being agreeable.
- There is the idea of **conscientiousness**, which is comprised of the capacity for attention and the capacity for self-control. Being less conscientious is more likely to be associated with the development of BPD, and, as we will see in later chapters, the capacity for attention is affected by the functioning of the frontal lobe of the brain.
- Children and adolescents who are by nature nervous and who worry excessively about things are often also more anxious, tense, easily frightened, and insecure. Many people who go on to develop BPD often describe a childhood filled with excessive worries and insecurities.

These personality traits are simply building blocks of the whole person, but it is now possible to imagine that these building blocks—under the right environment and with the right biological pressures—can develop into a more maladaptive and enduring way of functioning.

My composite view of adolescents with BPD is based on years of working with this group. The following symptoms broadly capture the majority of what I see clinically as adolescent BPD, although I think that many of the symptoms are accurate for adults as well. Not all of these symptoms have been validated by scientific research, but they are almost always seen in adolescents with BPD and are frequently part of their histories. It's important to bear in mind that the adolescents I work with have ended up on a residential unit, and so they may represent a more extreme version of BPD.

Many of the adolescent patients with BPD see themselves as loathsome, evil, or contaminated by some toxic poison, and they believe that they contaminate others with this poison. Sometimes they feel that they should not get close to others, despite wanting desperately to be close, for fear of being abandoned. They describe feelings of emptiness and of being intolerably alone. This pain can be so unbearable that self-injury or suicide is frequently seen as the only way out of their pain. This

profound sense of hopelessness and self-hatred seems to be unique to patients with BPD. In fact, I cannot remember a patient with this combination of symptoms who did not have BPD.

Adolescents with BPD tend to have trouble regulating their daily rhythms in activities such as sleeping, eating, exercising, studying, playing, and resting. A curious symptom is a marked lack of a sense of continuity of time. Adolescents with BPD have a difficult time telling a story sequentially and the timeline gets jumbled. For example, a young woman told me of a fight with her boyfriend, a fight she had had a week previously. She felt hopeless, that life was not worth living, and that this feeling would never change. When we examined the fight in a later session, she had nearly forgotten it and added details of previous arguments she had had with her boyfriend, putting all the details into one event.

Another classic finding is that at times the turmoil is so enduring that many kids with BPD have great difficulty consistently performing

*continued on the next page*

at school (or work) despite being intelligent and apparently able. They note that when they are in a good mood they can get almost anything done, but when they are in a bad mood they seem paralyzed and unable to accomplish anything. We call this "mood-dependent behavior."

The relationships of BPD teens tend to be chaotic, unstable, and rapidly changing, and their views of others tend to change dramatically, often depending on their own moods. These mood states tend not to last long and are often reactive to interpersonal conflict or fear. Reactive or impulsive aggression tends to be focused on the people—friends or parents—who are closest to them. Then, BPD adolescents frequently complain that they are misunderstood by their friends, their parents, and even by their therapists. In fact, it is easy to not fully understand BPD adolescents because their symptoms are confusing to those of us who don't get why the reactions appear so overblown.

Like adults with the disorder, adolescents with BPD fear rejection or abandonment to the point that when they perceive that they are going to lose a loved one, they suddenly devalue the person, be it friend, parent, teacher, or therapist.

Some adolescents with BPD can appear to be incredibly attuned to nonverbal communication by significant people in their lives to the point that parents and others remark on just how intuitive their child with BPD appears to be. There is increasing evidence that a brain network that contains what are known as *mirror neurons* gets activated and that these neurons capture the small changes in others' mood states. This capture of information by neurons gets adolescents with BPD to feel as if they themselves are experiencing the emotion. I will review the mirror neuron concept further in a later chapter. However, it is also true that given the amount of abuse that many BPD sufferers have experienced, it is possible that this ability to read nonverbal information is an adaptation to protect themselves from further abuse.

During arguments and fights, a time when the adolescent tends to be in a highly emotional state, arguments often have an "all-or-nothing" or "black-and-white" content. There tends to be little capacity to see others' point of view or to see a nuanced perspective.

Even though adolescence is a time of defining self and defining values, many adolescents with BPD have a particularly poorly defined sense of who they are—much more so than the typically developing teen—and they tend to describe themselves more as a composite of characteristics of their close friends or peer group. This pattern of changing self-identity continues as they move from one group to the next. Sometimes they say that people don't ever get to see their real self and that they mask who they really are.

Other than these core symptoms, there is frequent drug use, although even this appears to be qualitatively different from other adolescent drug use in that it is often in the service of reducing their emotional experience rather simply to get high. Frequent sexual encounters, if they occur, also tend to be to escape the misery of loneliness or to feel wanted rather than some rampant and wanton display of sexual indulgence.

Even though laboratory tests are not currently used in diagnosing BPD, as our understanding of BPD in adolescents continues to evolve, more comprehensive and definitive diagnostic tools will develop. These will include the use of brain imaging techniques, genetics, brain chemistry (which deals with the brain chemicals that allow the brain to function), and questionnaires—all of which together with the clinical history will lead to a far more reliable diagnosis of BPD. You will read more about how research is exploring all of these biological systems in chapter 4.

## THE SIMILARITIES BETWEEN REACTIVE ATTACHMENT DISORDER AND BPD

Some clinicians have wondered whether BPD is a variation of another condition, called reactive attachment disorder (RAD).

The *Diagnostic and Statistical Manual of Mental Disorders-IV* (*DSM-IV*) defines reactive attachment disorder of infancy or early childhood as follows:

**1.** Markedly disturbed and developmentally inappropriate social relatedness in most contexts, beginning before age five years, as evidenced by either (A) or (B):

**(A)** Persistent failure to initiate or respond in a developmentally appropriate fashion to most social interactions, as manifested by excessively inhibited, hypervigilant, or highly ambivalent and contradictory responses (e.g., the child may respond to caregivers with a mixture of approach, avoidance, and resistance to comforting, or may exhibit frozen watchfulness).

**(B)** Diffuse attachments as manifested by indiscriminate sociability with marked inability to exhibit appropriate selective attachments (e.g., excessive familiarity with relative strangers or lack of selectivity in the people they choose to become close to).

**2.** The disturbance in criterion 1 is not accounted for solely by developmental delay (as in mental retardation) and does not meet criteria for a pervasive developmental disorder.

**3.** Continued discounting of a child's needs and well-being, as evidenced by at least one of the following:

**(A)** Persistent disregard of the child's basic emotional needs for comfort, stimulation, and affection

**(B)** Persistent disregard of the child's basic physical needs

**(C)** Repeated changes of primary caregiver that prevents formation of stable attachments (e.g., frequent changes in foster care)

The American Academy of Child and Adolescent Psychiatry adds that RAD can be difficult to diagnose, but that most children with RAD have had problems or severe disruptions in their early relationships. Further, many have been physically, sexually, or emotionally abused or neglected. Others have had multiple traumatic losses or changes in their primary caretakers.

Although it is a stretch to make RAD a childhood version of BPD, it is possible that some traumatized and neglected children with RAD could go on to develop BPD given the common pathway of trauma, abuse, and neglect in many cases of BPD.

## WHY BIPOLAR DISORDER IS OFTEN THE WRONG DIAGNOSIS

When adolescents with BPD are referred to our unit, they most often come to us with the diagnosis of bipolar disorder (formerly called manic depression), and typically a type of bipolar disorder called bipolar not otherwise specified (NOS). Bipolar NOS is a mood disorder that fits no other category and includes fast cycling between manic (highs) and depressive (lows) symptoms. Often this diagnosis is made because mental health specialists have been reluctant to diagnose BPD, and because the adolescent with BPD has variable moods it seems like the best-fitting diagnosis. Bipolar disorder, just like BPD, occurs in adolescents, but the two are not the same illness. They are two very different entities whose main similarities are changes in mood states. Confusing BPD for bipolar disorder not only leads to a serious misdiagnosis but also an errant treatment approach.

Bipolar disorder is a mood disorder that involves one or more manic episodes alternating with major depressive episodes. A manic episode is a period of time where an elevated, expansive, or notably irritable mood is present, lasting for at least one week. A major depressive episode must either include a depressed mood or a loss of interest or pleasure in daily activities consistently for at least a two-week period.

As you see, the manic and depressive episodes each last for at least a week. In BPD, however, the mood states tend to last from minutes to only a few hours, and rarely a few days. Also, the moods tend to be highly reactive, which means that they are triggered as a reaction to a situation, usually an interpersonal conflict.

So while some people have bipolar disorder, and others have BPD, still other people have both. In chapter 7, we will look at the co-occurrence of BPD and bipolar disorder. In the next chapter I will review the behavioral differences between the BPD adolescent and the typically developing teen so as to further clarify that BPD behaviors are not simply extreme versions of adolescence.

## CHAPTER THREE

# Behavioral Differences between BPD and Typical Teens

IMAGINE IDENTICAL TWIN SIXTEEN-YEAR-OLD GIRLS. Both are moody, using drugs, engaged in sexual behavior with different boys, defiant of their parents' requests, and impulsive. One of them has BPD and the other doesn't. How can a parent tell? The short answer is this: Look at the function of the behavior. By this I mean, what is the reason they are behaving the way they are? It is possible that it is typical adolescent experimentation and development, but it is also possible that these behaviors are an expression of BPD. For instance, for the BPD adolescent, the function or reason for doing drugs is not for experimentation but as an attempt to regulate or control emotions. For the BPD adolescent, the function or reason for having multiple sex partners could be to feel better about herself, feel desired, and feel connected. Adolescent girls with BPD often tell their therapists that these casual sexual encounters provide little sexual pleasure.

In this chapter, I will expand on this idea of looking at the function of behavior as the way to differentiate between typical and BPD behavior. Because the behavior can appear like typical adolescent behavior, many parents and clinicians dismiss concerns about worrisome behavior, feeling that it is just a part of normal development. Parents might argue that they themselves were wild as teens and turned out okay.

Like typical adolescents, adolescents with BPD may drink, drive recklessly, use drugs, and defy their parents. However, adolescents with BPD often use drugs, self-injure, and rage against their parents as a way of coping with profound misery, intense emotions, emptiness, self-loathing, and abandonment fears. Although adolescents with BPD go through the same challenges and changes of normal adolescent development that non-BPD adolescents go through, recognizing the meaning or purpose of the behavior is critical.

Although the behavior of two kids may be identical, it may be far more concerning for one than for the other. For instance, I have interviewed adolescents who have told me that they have cut themselves once or twice. When I asked why they did this, they might say that it was because their friends were doing it. In some cases, they said that it hurt and that they didn't want to do it again, they cannot understand why their friends do it, and that it didn't do anything for them. Other children might cut themselves in an identical manner, saying that they had read about it online, or that some of their friends were doing it, and that they found that the cutting behavior led to a relief of misery, a reduction in intense emotions, a feeling of being more alive, a reduction in feeling numb, and that it did not hurt much, if at all. They also felt that they would repeat the self-injury behavior because it provided such relief. The children for whom self-injury works is a far more worrisome group than the group for whom it doesn't help because it can become a habitual behavior and might be a strong indication that the child has BPD. If they learn that cutting is an effective way to deal with their emotions, cutting will increasingly become part of their repertoire. The more they practice this behavior, the more it will become hardwired in the brain as a problem-solving skill.

## STAGES OF TYPICAL ADOLESCENT DEVELOPMENT

Before looking more closely at adolescents with BPD and the theories of BPD development, we should review the typically developing adolescent. Following are ways adolescents grow and mature physically, emotionally, mentally, socially, and sexually into adulthood.

### AGES TWELVE TO FOURTEEN

During the late middle school and early high school years, parents are often confused by the developmental changes in their teenagers. These children begin to move toward independence, and during this time adolescents often struggle with a sense of identity. They tend to feel awkward or strange about their bodies, especially during the marked changes that come with the onset of puberty. Many parents and patients with BPD identify this as the first time that they started to self-injure.

Teens in general tend to focus on self, alternating between high expectations of their capabilities and poor self-esteem. They focus on clothing style, which is often influenced by their peer groups as well as by popular culture. Typical adolescents are frequently moody. Up until this age, children tend to see their parents as generally right, but now the kids start to realize that their parents are not perfect, and they show less overt affection and at times rudeness toward them. Almost all adolescents, whether BPD or not, complain that their parents interfere with independence, but in times of stress they tend to regress to more childish behavior. There is also frequent rule- and limit-testing, both at home and at school.

It is typical during this stage for adolescents to be mostly interested in the present, with limited thoughts of the future. At times when I absent-mindedly ask a child in this stage how he imagines himself in ten years, he'll answer, "I don't know, I'm only thirteen!"

This time is also one of increasing interest in sexuality, and most typically display shyness, easy embarrassment, modesty, and an increased interest in sex. There is generally a move toward heterosexuality and fears of homosexuality, and they are frequently preoccupied with concerns regarding their physical and sexual attractiveness to others.

There also tend to be frequently changing relationships. Adolescents change their relationships for many reasons. These include factors such as changing from middle school to high school, changing shared common interests such as sports and extracurricular activities, a growing interest in dating or romantic realtionships after puberty, and a greater curiosity and interest in experimentation.

Teens have become more sexually active and experiment with more partners than before. The reason for this is also complex. An interesting study has suggested that adolescents who rely heavily on television for information about sexuality have high standards of female beauty and believe that premarital and extramarital intercourse with multiple partners is acceptable. They are also less likely to learn about the need for contraceptives as a form of protection against pregnancy or disease. Another interesting response I have heard from many teens who perform oral sex on multiple partners is that they do not believe that oral sex is sex.

Although many parents refuse to accept that it is normal, experimentation with sex and drugs is very common. For adolescents with BPD this is particularly true; however, as stated earlier, the reasons behind the behavior are different. Often they use sex as a way of holding on to partners who might otherwise leave them or as a way of coping with the fear of abandonment.

## AGES FOURTEEN TO SEVENTEEN

As teenagers grow, they move toward independence. They are more self-involved, alternating between unrealistically high expectations and poor self-concept, and more strongly complain that their parents interfere with independence. They continue to be extremely concerned with their physical appearance and use images portrayed in popular culture as the ideal, which is most concerning especially for young women, because emaciated models cover popular fashion magazines.

By now, they frequently have a lowered opinion of their parents, and they often withdraw emotionally from them, while redoubling their efforts to make new friends. They place a strong emphasis on the peer group and many of the friendships formed in this stage can last a lifetime.

Adolescents can exhibit periods of sadness, especially as the psychological loss of the parent takes place. I am often struck by adolescents' answers about what it is that has changed in their relationships between them and their mothers or fathers. I interviewed a teen who told me that she used to go fishing with her father, and an eighteen-year-old who said he used to watch the early Saturday morning cartoons with his dad while his mother was sleeping. Parents are often surprised, given how withdrawn and disdainful their adolescent has been, that their child is nostalgic for these times.

Teens in this age range often spend much time in the examination of their inner experiences, and they often keep diaries. They also tend to be more goal-directed and have a better sense of what they want to do with their lives.

At this age, relationships, both intimate and not, take on greater importance. Teens are increasingly concerned about their own attractiveness, and they show a clearer identification of their sexual orientation. They exhibit increasing tenderness and are less afraid to be vulnerable toward the opposite sex. They express feelings of love and passion, and the kids I see often tell me that they imagine that their current boyfriends or girlfriends are the people they will be with for the rest of their lives.

Drug and alcohol experimentation is extremely common at this age. Interestingly, there is increasing evidence that teens of this age have consciences that can consistently differentiate between right and wrong.

## AGES EIGHTEEN PLUS

By the time adolescents reach their eighteenth birthday, they normally show increasingly independent functioning and a far more consistent and cohesive sense of identity. They show a more developed ability for examination of inner experiences.

In adolescents with BPD, this ability for examination of inner experiences seems to develop much earlier than in typical adolescents. It is perhaps because adolescents with BPD suffer as they do that they begin to examine their lives at an earlier stage. On the other hand, although adolescents with BPD can seem more introspective, they often have a hard time naming and labeling emotional experiences. They are often exploring an inner world that has no words, and this can be bewildering and frightening.

Also at this age, typically developing adolescents show an ability to think ideas through, which is a reflection of a maturing frontal lobe, the part of the brain that deals with executive functioning, or decision making. Their conflict with their parents begins to decrease. Adolescents at this age begin to show an increased ability for delayed gratification and compromise, as well as better emotional stability, which again may represent maturation of the brain. Many brain imaging studies show that teen girls with BPD have immature prefrontal cortexes when compared with typically developing girls. Because the prefrontal cortex is the part of the brain that controls impulsivity and decision making, these brain images are further evidence that the impulsivity we see in BPD is likely due to delays in brain development.

In relationships, adolescents at this age show increased concern for others, and in their romantic relationships they express deeper feelings of love and passion. These relationships tend to last longer than the experimental relationships of earlier adolescence. Adolescents at this age gain a firmer sense of their own sexual identity and an increased capacity for tender and sensual love.

Older adolescents show increased self-reliance and place a greater importance on their own role in life and greater emphasis on personal dignity and self-esteem. At times, social traditions regain their previous importance, as they return to their religious or cultural roots.

After this, a typically developing adolescent is on adulthood's door, and his or her personality has almost fully developed.

## TYPICAL BPD SYMPTOMS IN ADOLESCENCE

I have never met an adult BPD patient who did not have symptoms in either childhood or adolescence. If we look at the previous description of typical adolescent development and we artificially contrive an adolescent by plucking out some of the descriptors of typical adolescence, we can create a hypothetical child who exhibits periods of sadness as the psychological loss of the parent takes place, struggles with sense of identity, is frequently moody, has self-perception alternating between high expectations and poor self-esteem, is extremely concerned with the appearance of his or her body, shows a tendency to return to childish behavior, particularly when stressed, experiments with drugs and sex with frequently changing relationships, and is self-involved. Given this picture, it is easy to see why normal adolescence could look like emerging BPD.

In this hypothetical child, and using the criteria in the *Diagnostic and Statistical Manual of Mental Disorders-5* (*DSM-5*), abandonment fears (criterion 1), identity issues (criterion 3), impulsivity with drugs and sex (criterion 4), and affective instability (criterion 6) are clear, so then only one more criterion is needed to meet adult criteria for BPD. Throw in some existential suicidal thoughts, which are common in adolescents, and there we are. Given this, it is easy to see why many mental health professionals are reluctant to make the diagnosis of BPD in adolescents.

Given that BPD occurs in an estimated 2 percent of the population, 98 percent of adolescents will not have BPD. Concerning and occasional behaviors, such as drug use, come and go in adolescents. However, when those behaviors persist in the context of broad emotional problems in an adolescent, clinicians must recognize the possibility that a personality disorder could be developing.

## THREE PARENTING STRATEGIES THAT WORK FOR TEENS WITH AND WITHOUT BPD

A major component of our DBT program is to get parents to recognize their kid's point of view and see how their teen's behavior makes sense from the teen's perspective. This is not to say that they agree with the behavior but that they simply understand that, at some level, the behavior makes sense. All of us who are parents were teens at one point and yet we tend to forget that we, too, behaved impulsively or even dangerously in our youth.

The BPD behaviors of suicidality and self-injury are not typical of adolescent behavior or development and so parents tend to have far stronger emotions, particularly fear, when these behaviors show up. In DBT we ask parents to think about balancing their response by considering the following three major ideas. These ideas are magnified in the presence of BPD behaviors but are ideas that all parents should consider for almost all adolescent behavior:

**1. Finding the balance between excessive leniency and authoritarian control.** In other words, balancing being too permissive versus being too strict. Setting limits with teens is a normal part of parenting. It not only teaches kids about what's acceptable and about what your values are, but also makes them feel loved and secure. It gives them something to struggle against, and struggling against rules allows children to develop their own internal sense of right and wrong. In BPD, however, behaviors like suicidality and self-injury are terrifying to parents and as a consequence they can be scared to set limits for fear that their child will do these very behaviors. On the other hand, parents have to learn not to be too strict by imposing too many demands and limits while being inflexible. Finding the balance between these two extremes is a common challenge in adolescent BPD treatment, and these are skills parents can use with their other, non-BPD children.

**Example:** A sixteen-year-old stays up past midnight on Facebook while sleeping at her boyfriend's house. In response to this behavior, her parents revoke all her Internet privileges and refuse to allow her to see her boyfriend.

**Practice: Finding Balance**
It is important to have clear rules and enforce them consistently, while at the same time being willing to negotiate on some issues. It is normal that a sixteen-year-old girl would want to see her boyfriend and be with her friends on Facebook. In the above situation rather than allowing their daughter to stay at her boyfriend's house (permissive parenting) or never allowing her to see him (too strict), her parents could allow her to spend time with her boyfriend

during the day and maybe being able to stay up late on Facebook if she finishes her homework first. The key to balance is to avoid extremes that lead to polarizing your relationship with your teen because you will lose any influence you ever had with him or her, and it will be hard to get it back.

**2. Finding the balance between minimizing the seriousness of problem behaviors versus overacting to typical teen behaviors.**
In other words, balancing taking things too lightly versus exaggerating the severity of normal steps teens take in forging an independent identity. This allows you to model that you are neither invalidating nor overdramatizing the effects of an adolescent's behavior.

**Example:** When their seventeen-year-old daughter became more irritable at home and her grades started to fall, her parents dismissed the behavior and felt that she was simply "going through a phase" and felt that they did not need to do anything about it. This minimized a serious change in behavior that had been brought about by their daughter's increas-

*continued on the next page*

ing depression and subsequent marijuana use. They eventually got her into therapy after she made a suicide attempt. Things started to turn around and she stopped smoking and her grades improved. Some months into her recovery she had a fight with a friend at school and came home and slammed her door. Her parents contacted me to say that they were worried that things were very wrong. They had swung from the extreme of under worrying to over worrying.

**Practice: Finding Balance**

Before reacting, put the situation in context. In DBT, mindfulness is the act of focused awareness in the moment and then broadening that focus to include all relevant information. By stopping, breathing, and contemplating the situation at hand, you can see where you might be stuck. Focus on the big picture and what your child needs. In the example above, noticing the increased irritability and being honest and direct with their daughter rather than dismissing her behavior as that

of a typical teen may have led to an earlier intervention. On the other hand, a single episode of door slamming in the context of a fight with a close friend does not constitute a major crisis.

**3. Finding the balance between forcing autonomy versus fostering dependence (or forcing children to be independent before they are ready versus holding on so tight that they are dependent on their parents way after they need to be).** Forcing independence means cutting the ties of dependence prematurely. Holding on too tight means preventing your child's movement toward independence.

**Example:** We worked with a twenty-year-old woman whose parents had protected and rescued her every time she got into trouble, never allowing life's natural consequences from affecting her. And then, after a wild night out, she subsequently discovered she was pregnant. Her parents insisted that she move out and take care of herself. This is an extreme example but captures the polar extremes accurately.

## WHEN YOUR TEEN CUTS

Many teens tell me that they started cutting themselves years before their parents ever found out. Parents sometimes say that looking back they "should have known" that something was wrong, but most say that they had no idea their children were injuring themselves.

You are definitely not alone if your teen cuts. A 2010 article in the *Journal of the American Board of Family Medicine* found that teens, in general, are at a higher risk for self-injury, and about 15 percent of teens have reported some form of self-injury. Typically, the behavior starts between the ages of fourteen and fifteen, and peaks during the early and late teen years.

Self-injury knows no intelligence barrier. A survey of students at Cornell and Princeton showed that nearly one in five students had self-injured while another study showed that nearly 6 percent of college students self-injure regularly. Self-injurers are more likely to be female and to have eating disorders. About half of the Ivy League students who harmed themselves said they'd experienced sexual, emotional, or physical abuse.

## WHY THEY CUT

Self-injury can occur as a fad. Most often this happens when someone in a group starts to self-injure and others follow. For typical, non-BPD adolescents, self-injury is very painful and so they soon stop harming themselves. BPD adolescents who cut are people who are generally very sensitive. They usually recognize that they feel emotions quicker and more intensely than other people do and that it takes longer for them to get their feelings back to normal.

The reasons why they cut vary, but here is what kids who come to our unit say cutting does for them: "It makes me feel real, alive, feeling something. It makes me stop feeling numb." "I can control the pain, not like what people did to me." "It makes me feel pain on the outside instead of the inside." "It makes me feel calm." "I cut myself because I hate myself. I deserve the pain for being such a terrible, disgusting person."

For most parents, self-injury in their child is the most confusing and terrifying of symptoms. A key concept is this: Most parents see cutting as a problem. For the teen, it is a *solution* to the problem. For them, the problem is not cutting but how they feel in the moment. Cutting provides relief. Feelings such as anger, loneliness, and sadness rapidly diminish when they cut. Others tell us that they cut to punish themselves for being bad people. We see many young women who have been abused cut themselves. When they have been sexually abused, the teens frequently tell us that when they cut they need to see blood after doing so. It is not completely clear yet why the phenomenon of needing to see blood occurs, but it is one that makes us wonder whether sexual abuse has occurred. If teens tell us that they need to see blood, we will then further explore the question of abuse.

Self-injuring is rarely done for attention-seeking reasons. Many parents, teachers, and clinicians think that this is why kids are cutting; however, research shows that this is true in only about 10 percent of cases. Frequently, the teens have been self-injuring for months, if not years, before they are found out. Certainly if attention seeking were the case, having it discovered after months or years does not seem like an effective way to get attention. Teens who hurt themselves tend to keep their feelings bottled up and have a hard time letting their feelings be known, often because they don't know what their feelings are. They just know that the feelings are intense, that they don't like them, and that they want to rapidly get rid of them. Cutting is a very effective way to do this.

*Most parents see cutting as a problem. For the teen, it is a solution to the problem.*

Why don't they do something other than cut? The reason is because they don't know what to do. However, there is good news. Dialectical behavior therapy is a powerful treatment that helps reduce self-injury because it teaches people how to identify and name emotions and then equips them with more effective, longer-term ways to deal with them. Typically developing, non-BPD kids acquire healthy methods as they mature, but in cases of adolescents with BPD, genetic and environmental factors prevent the typical development of emotion regulation skills.

## SIGNS OF ADOLESCENT SELF-INJURY

Some of the more obvious signs that adolescents are hurting themselves are frequent or unexplained scars, cuts, bruises, and burns. These are usually on the extremities, particularly the arms, but can be on the legs, thighs, chest, abdomen, or back. When parents see these cuts, teens often give implausible explanations for the injuries, such as a dog or cat scratched them or they fell.

Other signs include the consistent wearing of long-sleeve clothing, isolating behavior after a fight, excessive time spent in the shower, isolation from friends, and increasing substance abuse. These all could be signs of possible self-injury as well as symptoms of other concerns, such as major depression, anxiety, an eating disorder, or substance abuse. The hoarding of sharp implements such as razor blades, pins, needles, knives, and scissors would obviously be very concerning and a huge red flag of self-injury. Also, many teens ritualize their cutting behaviors, so a teen suddenly buying large quantities of antiseptic lotions, cleaning solutions, and clean dressings might also be concerning.

## THE RISKS OF SELF-INJURY

Although the vast majority of self-injury has almost nothing to do with suicide and even though most self-injury causes little permanent damage, it is not a riskless behavior. The following are the most common risks of self-injury:

- Infection from injuries or sharing razors
- Accidental severe injury such as life-threatening blood loss or infection
- Scars from healed injuries
- Shame, guilt, or other painful emotions, which in turn lead to more-self injury
- A 300 percent increase in the risk for suicide

Concerning the last item, there appears to be a contradiction here. If cutting has almost nothing to do with suicide, then why the increased risk? Researchers have hypothesized that self-injury makes the practice of self-destructiveness more habitual. Over years of practicing self-injury, the gap from self-harm to the ultimate self-destruction—suicide—appears to narrow, and so the leap from one to the other is easier.

## What to Do When Your Teen Cuts

Most adolescent self-injury doesn't require medical treatment nor does it mean the teen is contemplating suicide. However, some adolescents have done terrible damage to themselves. I have seen kids who have cut almost every bit of exposed skin, others whose cuts always need stitches, others who target arteries so that they bleed more, and yet others who have sliced their tendons. Some young women specifically target their breasts. One young woman told me that if she had not had breasts she would not have been sexually abused.

Certainly the first exposure to such self-injury is terrifying. Although it is generally difficult to be calm under these conditions, a calm approach allows for clearer and more effective planning.

Parents usually do not have medical training and so when presented with self-injury, the initial step is to address the teen's medical needs first by dressing the wounds or going to the hospital or doctor's office. Because it might be unclear as to what the teen used to self-injure, and if the cut is bleeding, the adolescent should receive a tetanus shot if he or she hasn't had one recently.

If the teen is in a type of therapy, such as DBT, which specifically targets self-injury, then follow the treatment plan as prescribed.

### Which Actions Do Not Work

Some parents act horrified, which is understandable; but because many teens who self-injure have a negative self-image and a negative body image, they can be very sensitive about their wounds. I have had kids tell me years later that they wish they had never cut, that the scars always remain as a testament to their past, and that when friends or intimate partners are curious about the cuts it can be difficult to talk about.

It is easy for parents to judge the self-injury behavior or the teen. More important, more effective, and more therapeutic is to work hard on understanding what is going on emotionally with your adolescent.

We have found that, rather than promoting self-injury, teens who know that others go through similar situations and use similar coping skills find it helps them to not think of themselves as alien, and that they, too, can be helped.

Just telling a kid to stop the cutting behavior will not work. Generally, cutting helps adolescents control their emotions, and unless there is another behavior that can replace the cutting, they will not stop. This is why a skills-based approach is essential to adolescent self-injury.

## HOW TO COPE WITH AN "EMOTIONALLY INTENSE" YOUNGER SIBLING

The mother of an eighteen-year-old boy with BPD told me that she was beginning to see some of the "same emotional intensity" in her ten-year-old daughter. She wondered whether her daughter, too, could have BPD, and whether there was anything she could do to handle her daughter's anxiety and outbursts.

Even though from what the mother told me there was no indication that the child had any psychiatric problems, using strategies to deal with such intensity is helpful at many levels. It teaches the child at an early age that there are ways to deal with being very upset, and it helps the family feel less hopeless about the situation. In some cases, such a

low tolerance of stress can become problematic if left unchecked and can morph into a broader problem, so using the following strategies might prevent the child from spiraling out of control.

- Recognize behaviors that signal that the child's stress level is rising, such as increased irritation, frustration, or annoyance.
- Provide activities that are soothing, such as a warm bath, massage, quiet music, or familiar stories.
- Help the child learn to recognize cues that signal his or her intensity is rising. Doing routine, yet simple, mindfulness exercises will teach the child to monitor mind and body. An easy example is teaching

slow breathing techniques while watching the body relax. Also, find a quiet space that a child can always use when he or she needs a time-out or a place to calm down.

· Avoid escalating the intensity of the child by reacting intensely in response to the child's behavior.

· Work with the other kids in the family about not escalating their sibling's anxiety during these moments. Help them recognize that this leads only to chaos and a prolonged situation. Including them in the mindfulness exercises can make it a fun family routine.

· Finally, after an outburst, give calm, clear, brief feedback and the commitment to continue to find ways to help the child and family as a whole.

## THE SINGLE MOST IMPORTANT CAPACITY FOR COMMUNICATION: VALIDATION

If you had only ten minutes to read this book and then had to throw it out, I would want you to read this section most of all. This is because the skill of validation is one that is not intuitive, can be difficult to put into practice, and yet brings vast benefit.

Simply put, validation is the recognition and acceptance of another person's internal experience as being valid. Self-validation is the recognition and acknowledgment of your own internal experiences as ones that are valid. Many people get tripped up because they equate validation with agreement. It does not mean agreeing with or supporting feelings or thoughts, it does not mean that you love someone, and it does not even mean that you like what the person is doing. It is not saying, "I know how you feel," especially when you don't. It simply means that you accept that your child has a point of view that might be different from yours and that his or her point of view is valid.

Parents often wonder how to know whether their adolescent is using drugs. Certainly the smell of marijuana on clothes or alcohol on the breath is a pretty clear sign. Short of drug testing, there is no fail-proof test, but there are many signs that should warn parents that substance abuse could be an issue.

At school, work productivity might have declined and grades might have slipped or even dropped dramatically. Adolescents can seem to lose their motivation to complete work, or be disinclined to do anything other than being with their friends. Teens sometimes miss school altogether, or walk off campus during breaks or free periods. They often drop out of their usual activities such as sports or music. Typically, this is simply because they would prefer to do drugs than do the activity, although at other times it is because the drug use has severely affected their ability to participate in these activities.

In relationships the teen might suddenly change friends, and be secretive about these friends.

Often they don't want their parents to meet these friends and refuse to invite them over.

At home, teens can become more moody and irritable, might begin to take less care of their appearance, and may become increasingly secretive in their behavior. They might spend more solitary time, such as by going to the basement, keeping their bedroom door locked, not responding when called, or taking a long time to answer. They can appear hostile and defensive when asked about apparently unimportant matters.

Parents have told me that a sure sign that their child was doing drugs was when money began to disappear from their purses or wallets, or when valuables went missing. These are often sold to pay for a drug habit.

Finally, sudden changes in sleep habits, and being overly exhausted despite apparently adequate sleep, might signify the use of tranquilizers in particular.

Because self-injury and drug use are particularly worrisome to parents, knowing the signs can give you a fighting chance

Without understanding another's point of view it is nearly impossible to see where he or she is coming from. If a person is a vegetarian, it is understandable that he doesn't want to eat meat and why he is rejecting the bacon you made for breakfast. Validation does not mean that you agree with vegetarianism, that you accept that it is the way to live, that the other person is good or bad or lovable. It is acceptance that the person is not a meat eater.

With emotions, if your BPD daughter is upset about breaking up with her drug-abusing boyfriend, you might be ecstatic that they broke up and not understand what she ever saw in him or why she is upset. Validation is to recognize that she is sad and that it is painful for her, even if you don't get it.

## WHY IS VALIDATION IMPORTANT?

Validation communicates acceptance. When children feel accepted, they feel understood, which has a calming effect on them. In the previous example, telling your daughter that there is nothing to be upset about because her former boyfriend was a no-good drug user without recognizing that she loved him and is in pain at his loss will lead to further emotional upset and move your daughter further from you at a time when you are trying to get closer. Validation transmits your recognition that what your child is experiencing is real to her. It does not have to be real to you.

Validation is actually a very early interaction, although most of us are not aware of it. Every time a parent soothes a hurting child who has just fallen off her bike, this is validation. It says: "You are hurt and I recognize it and your feelings are valid." This may seem trivial and obvious, but the same thing can be done with more complex feelings and emotions. When a child feels misunderstood—and many adolescents with BPD say that they are misunderstood—it creates thoughts of isolation or not fitting in. Those thoughts can lead to fear and sadness, to more worrisome behavior, such as self-injury and drug use, in an attempt to manage the suffering.

An adolescent needs to self-validate. Doing so helps create a sense of identity, an issue that many adolescents with BPD struggle with. Their values and patterns and choices become manifest, and this in turn allows others to see them more clearly as individuals.

Probably most important is that validation builds understanding and effective communication. As parents, we cannot possibly know everything that our child is doing or feeling. Even a mother and father can watch exactly the same event occur and yet see it differently or remember important details differently. The bottom line is that validation is a way of understanding another person's point of view. In adolescents with BPD, it tells them that they are important.

Effective communication between parents and their teen is essential to get through the developmental challenges of adolescence. This is true not only for the typically developing teen but for the teen with emerging BPD symptoms as well. Old patterns of communication will probably have to change to fit the growing needs and capabilities of the child. Multiple studies have shown a connection between a child's overall well-being and parent-adolescent communication.

The first step is to create an environment or expectation that allows for the free and safe interchange of ideas. All family members should feel free to bring up questions, worries, achievements, and perceived failures. Set aside time daily for the family to be able to share, even if this is just a few minutes. On weekdays, a shared dinner might do it. On weekends, a drive to a sports game or a walk in the park could provide the time necessary for a teen to share. Over time this will allow for discussion of the sensitive issues that arise during adolescence, such as sexuality, relationships, and drug or alcohol use. Studies have shown that adolescents who openly communicate with their parents are less likely to abuse substances.

It is important for teens to know that their perspective is both recognized and valued, although not necessarily shared. This helps build self-esteem in the adolescent and the understanding that people can have varying points of view, and, at times, disagree amicably. This is where the concept of validation is key.

Effective communication involves both listening and speaking. Listening with curiosity and interest is most effective. Parents should ask for clarity if they don't understand, or at least not assume that they understand what their adolescent is saying. Asking clarifying questions can help achieve this, although many teens and parents get frustrated at the "twenty questions" in which communication is broken down into and a parent asks multiple questions to find out information. The teen tends to answer these with "maybe," "no,"

*continued on the next page*

"yes," "I don't know," or a grunt. With the practice of curiosity must come the loss of certainty. It is so easy to be certain that you "know" why your child did what she did. You may be right but you can also be wrong. Practice being not certain.

Teens also often get frustrated when advice is offered without being asked. Even therapists fall into this trap. Often adolescents want to work out a situation by themselves or just know that they have been heard. Also, as the times change, so do behaviors. This is true of all generations.

For instance, at the turn of the twentieth century, children and adolescents were far more likely to adhere to rules and wear school uniforms; they were to "be seen but not heard." At the end of the twentieth century, children were encouraged to express themselves, wear whatever they wanted to school, and question authority. Kids often do *not* want to hear about what it was like in their parents' time, and so it is important to listen with as little judgment as possible, trying to recognize and understand the culture of the times. Being judgmental, or not recognizing that one is being judgmental, will often shut the teen down and not allow for the full understanding of a situation.

## CHAPTER FOUR

# How BPD Develops:
# Genes, Biology, and Environment

A S WE GAIN KNOWLEDGE and understanding and harness the promise of more powerful research tools, the causes of BPD will prove to be a complex combination of genetic makeup, how these genes express themselves under conditions of stress, the environment (including family interactions), brain maturation, development, and psychological constitution or temperament.

I am often asked whether there is a brain scan, blood test, or genetic test that can be used to diagnose BPD. At this time there is no such test; however, there may be brain scans and other tests that, when combined with observable behavior, could be useful in making the diagnosis of BPD. It is unlikely that there is a single cause for BPD, but rather that it is a product of the accumulation of risk factors expressing themselves in a vulnerable individual.

I'll make this clearer by pointing to specific research that looks at each of these areas. Although most of this research involved adults, much of it points to trauma or other factors in childhood or adolescence.

# BRAIN STRUCTURES AND BPD

"When we adopted James as a six-month-old, the adoption agency told us that he had a skull fracture, but that he didn't have any neurological problems. But now he is impulsive, angry, and manipulative. Do you think that it is possible that he had a brain injury that is causing all his problems?"

This was what the parents of a seventeen-year-old boy with BPD wanted to know. Unless a child develops typically and then displays behavior changes after a head trauma, there is no easy answer as to whether a head injury in infancy, such as James experienced, caused the behavior changes. However, because the brain ultimately controls the behaviors and symptoms found in BPD, a basic understanding of brain anatomy is useful.

Some researchers believe the behavioral problems of BPD lie in the abnormal functioning of two main regions in the brain—the frontal lobes and the limbic system—and in one network, the hypothalamic–pituitary–adrenal axis. We'll talk about each in turn.

## A Quick Anatomy lesson

The brain weighs about 3 pounds. It connects to the spinal cord through the brain stem, which contains bundles of nerve cells, or neurons. The largest part of the brain is called the cerebrum. The outer layer of the cerebrum is called the cerebral cortex, and although it's only a few millimeters thick (like the skin of an apple), it contains nearly one hundred billion nerve cells. The cerebrum is divided into four individual lobes, which are known as the frontal, parietal, temporal, and occipital lobes. Each lobe handles specific behaviors.

Deep inside the brain, below the temporal lobe, are the hippocampus and the amygdala. The hippocampus is primarily responsible for learning and various forms of memory, and we'll describe the role of the amygdala later. The temporal lobe itself contains the part of the brain that deals with hearing as well as processing sound and speech.

In the back of the brain is the occipital lobe, which contains the visual cortex, where signals from the eyes are processed and interpreted. We will focus on the two areas of the brain that get the most attention in BPD: the amygdala and the prefrontal cortex (PFC).

## THE FRONTAL LOBES AND TRAUMA

The frontal lobes are the part of the brain entrusted with executive function. This includes the ability to accomplish the following:

- Recognize future consequences resulting from current actions
- Choose between good and bad actions
- Hold and weigh opposing viewpoints
- Override and suppress unacceptable social responses
- Determine similarities and differences between things or events

One theory of the development of BPD is that if a child is traumatized (physically, sexually, or emotionally) in childhood, this can lead to damage to the frontal lobes, which in turn leads to diminished executive function. People who have had accidents or trauma that have damaged their frontal lobes often display irritability, impulsivity, and angry outbursts.

## THE LIMBIC SYSTEM: MEMORY AND EMOTIONS

The limbic system is a part of the brain that is often referred to as the "emotional brain" because it controls many of our emotions and motivations, particularly those that are related to survival. It is also the part of the brain that controls the fight-or-flight response.

The two main parts of the limbic system are the hippocampus and the amygdala. The amygdala plays an important role in emotions, such as fear, anger, and those related to sexual behavior. The amygdala is also involved in the making of memories—in particular, memories tied to strong emotions.

When Kathleen, a very sensitive seventeen-year-old with BPD, started therapy, she seemed engaged and chatty, but whenever her mother came to the therapy session, Kathleen refused to talk. In individual sessions she expressed deep love for her mother, so her behavior when her mother was in the room was confusing. Her mother said that she and Kathleen had been extremely close until Kathleen turned fourteen. That was when Kathleen's mother had lost her own mother to cancer. She noted that Kathleen had been close to her grandmother but had appeared to have dealt with her grandmother's death as well as could be expected. In therapy Kathleen was working on being able to experience and tolerate her emotions without becoming self-destructive.

One day in therapy, we wondered about her mother's idea that Kathleen's problems had started around the time of her grandmother's death and how before then, Kathleen and her mother had been very close. She agreed that she and her mother had been close.

"Then what happened?"

"When my grandmother died," she said, "I went to my mother and gave her a hug. My mother was crying and was so sad. As she was crying, she talked about her mother and about how empty she felt, that she had lost everything and that now she had no one." Kathleen said that when she heard her mother say that she had no one, she felt more hurt than ever before. How could her mother feel that she had no one? She had her, Kathleen. How could she possibly say something like that?

Whenever Kathleen saw her mother cry, it would trigger the memory of her mother saying that she had no one. That memory was tied to powerful and intolerable feelings of loneliness and sadness, which had led Kathleen to engage in self-destructive behaviors as a way to manage her pain. She had never told her mother, and held on to the memory and associated emotions for more than three years of suffering. When she was eventually ready to tell her mother, her mother broke down and cried, "You suffered for so long! Why didn't you ever tell me? Of course, I didn't mean that I was alone from you. I'm so sad that you thought that." At fourteen, Kathleen's amygdala and hippocampus had stored the memory of her mother's words, and that memory was attached to feeling hurt, sadness, and suffering.

The most consistent finding in imaging studies of people with BPD, compared to those without it, is increased activity in the amygdala, particularly if they also experience suicidal thoughts. Finding a way to reduce this activity is critical to reducing the flow of unrelenting emotions in BPD.

## THE INTERPLAY

The frontal lobes and the limbic system are generally in constant communication. The problem is that during highly emotional states, the frontal lobes, which govern decision making, shut down; and the limbic system, which is involved in emotions, takes over.

This reaction works against people with BPD—or any person, for that matter. In BPD, for instance, stopping to think what the future consequence of repeated self-injurious behavior, such as cutting, will be during an episode of feeling overwhelmed and self-injuring is nearly impossible. Techniques aimed at both recognizing and reducing high emotional states are essential in BPD therapy. Using them, adolescents with BPD can spend more time in their frontal (rational) brains, and as a consequence train them to better deal with conflicts.

## THE HYPOTHALAMIC–PITUITARY–ADRENAL AXIS

The hypothalamic–pituitary–adrenal (HPA) axis is a complex group of nerves that acts among the hypothalamus (which controls body temperature, hunger, thirst, and body rhythms), the pituitary gland (which secretes hormones, including oxytocin—considered important in attachment between mother and child), and the adrenal glands (which are responsible for stress regulation through the functioning of the hormones cortisol and adrenaline). The interaction among these three organs, which takes place by way of neurotransmitters and hormones, governs reactions to stress, controls early attachment between mother and infant, and regulates mood and sexuality.

Many studies have shown that this nerve network does not function properly in people with BPD, so some treatments are targeted at these problems. For example, some people with BPD who become stressed can take medication that partially blocks the effects of adrenaline, which can reduce stress.

## What the Brain Reveals about BPD

In 2006, researchers from the University of Freiburg in Germany looked at all the published studies on neuroimaging and BPD. They noted that neuroimaging had become one of the most important tools for investigating the biological causes of BPD. All the studies regarding imaging and BPD found abnormalities in the limbic system and frontal lobes, which the researchers considered to be consistent with the idea that problems in these areas of the brain led to BPD symptoms.

People often ask me whether any such brain scans or blood tests will "prove" that a person has BPD or at least show that the person has "something wrong with her brain," as one parent put it. The short answer is that there are no current tests that will diagnose BPD. The longer answer is that researchers are looking at information from various types of scans to see whether they can detect differences between the brains of people with BPD and those without BPD. So far, these scans have shown what researchers hypothesize—that the frontal lobes and limbic system play an important role in BPD.

## How BPD Brains Are Different

Charles, a sixteen-year-old junior in high school, came in for treatment because he had a hard time controlling his rage. He did well in the classroom, but with close friends and out on dates, he would explode when he felt things weren't going his way or that people weren't being fair. He admitted that on a few occasions, he had yelled at friends and, in desperate moments, physically attacked his girlfriend. He is not unlike many adolescents who come to see us because of impulsivity or aggression that's directed toward others or themselves.

In research, behaviors such as self-mutilation, physical violence, assault, destruction of property, and drug use fall under the category of impulsive aggression, which is the one area in BPD that is well researched. In a 1996 study of violent offenders and impulsive fire setters, 47 percent were found to have a personality disorder diagnosis—in particular, borderline and antisocial personality disorders. In another study, male perpetrators of domestic violence were more likely to have a diagnosis of BPD than men who did not engage in domestic violence.

Brain scans show that people with impulsive aggression have lower levels of activity in the prefrontal cortex (PFC). What this means is that the PFC is not as active in people who display impulsive aggression. Most brain-scanning studies demonstrate that people with BPD show disordered functioning in the PFC, compared to people without BPD, and this is particularly true if the person with BPD also suffers from post-traumatic stress disorder (PTSD). As I noted earlier, having a less-active PFC means having a more difficult time with regulating emotions (such as anger) that arise in the amygdala.

Essentially, all neuroimaging research points to abnormalities in the amygdala and the prefrontal cortex in people with BPD. Whether these abnormalities cause BPD, or if having BPD leads to these abnormalities, remains to be seen.

## BIOLOGY AND ENVIRONMENT

Dialectical behavior therapy (DBT) works on the theory that the cause
and maintenance of BPD are rooted in a hypersensitive neurobiological
system interacting with environmental factors. In BPD, the hypersensitivity
becomes complicated when the person is not able to control her emotions.
The biological causes of hypersensitivity could be due to genetics, intra-
uterine factors before birth, and/or traumatic events in early development,
including all forms of abuse.

The environmental factors include any set of circumstances that perva-
sively punishes, traumatizes, or disregards this emotional vulnerability, and are
termed *the invalidating environment.* The DBT model hypothesizes that BPD
results from a transaction between the biology and the environment over
time that can follow several different pathways. In some cases, there is more
of an environmental influence; in others, more of a biological influence. The
bottom line is that the final result, BPD, is caused by the interaction of these
factors, leading to the person never learning to regulate her emotions while
the environment continues to become more invalidating.

## THE ROLE OF PARENTING

The mother of a seventeen-year-old with BPD who had moved out of her
parents' home after she had had an abortion once told me: "I'm so sad
that my family is broken. My daughter hasn't spoken to her dad or me in
months. He gets angry at how she treats me. My two younger children are
also angry with her. I'm tired and depressed, and I don't feel like I have any
fight left in me. I want my daughter to be happy. I want to reach out to her
and help her with her pain. I failed her as a child, and now I'm failing her
as she becomes an adult. I am worried about what will happen to the other
kids as well."

Getting into a "blame game" is not helpful in the treatment of adolescents with BPD or their families. There is often plenty of blame being

thrown around by various people when it comes to BPD, and it is easy to get caught up in the "bad parenting" argument. In almost all cases, parents did the best they could. It should be clear by now that BPD has many risk factors and underlying causes.

Having said that, parenting *can* play a role—sometimes a big role—in the development of BPD. Understanding the role of parenting helps us recognize the risk factors and further help the family change whatever contributing parenting style might be pertinent.

A recent study recognized that inadequate parenting and traumatic experiences could negatively affect mood regulation. The researchers found that people who perceived their parents as having poor parenting styles had a harder time describing their emotions and had increased levels of depression. However, a positively perceived maternal parenting style was found to help adolescents express emotion, even if sexual abuse had also taken place.

The researchers concluded that the perception of parenting skills appeared to be of significance in the development of an inability to express emotions. They further found that optimal parenting of one parent could protect against the development of alexithymia (the inability to describe emotions, or how a person is feeling, in words) when the parenting of the other parent was perceived as nonoptimal.

## TEMPERAMENT AND ATTACHMENT

The concept in psychology of temperament is generally thought of as that part of the personality that is genetically based—the innate, inborn aspect of a person's personality. For example, parents will describe how their children were different from one another and recognize these differences as early as the first year.

In addition to temperament, a lot of research and thinking is taking place now on attachment deficits in the childhood of adults with BPD. Attachment is essentially the tendency to seek closeness to another person and feel secure when that person is present. It is the emotional tie that endures over time that binds a person to another, and in this particular context, a child to his mother, father, or other early caregiver.

A fundamental theory of attachment is that sensitive and attuned response by a parent to an infant's needs will result in secure attachment, and that the lack of such sensitive response will result in insecure attachment. Whether poor parent–child attachment is one cause of BPD, or whether disrupted brain wiring leads to poor attachment, remains to be seen. Poor attachment, nevertheless, is an almost universal finding in BPD research.

## THE PARENT–CHILD BOND

The quality of maternal care has been repeatedly shown to predict infant security. The parent's sensitive responsiveness is considered to be the most important determining factor in whether an infant feels secure. Studies have shown that negative parental personality traits are associated with child insecurity. Negative parental traits include, for example, rigidity, black-and-white thinking, being non-empathic, externalizing blame onto others (especially the child), and *always believing that all* their actions are in the best interest of the child.

Research suggests that parents' empathy and sensitivity to their children make it easier for the children to empathize with others and that this is made all the easier by a secure attachment.

Disturbed attachment may have a significant role in the development of BPD, but together with all the genetic and neurological findings, studies have shown that up to 87 percent of patients with BPD who required hospitalization for their symptoms had a history of severe abuse and/or neglect and that 81 percent of those patients experienced abuse at the hand of their parents. The issue of trauma is significant because studies have shown that childhood trauma affects the functioning of the frontal lobe, which is implicated in the pathology of BPD. Nevertheless, the role of parenting is important to look at.

## Why Early Attachment Is So Important

Karlen Lyons-Ruth, PhD, of Harvard Medical School at Cambridge Hospital has spent a career looking at how very early attachment between infant and caregivers pertains to later personality development. Her research has included looking at the relationship between the quality of early attachment and care and borderline symptomatology in adults.

Lyons-Ruth has stressed the significance of mother–child interactions that lead to the capacity of emotion regulation in the infant. She theorizes that disruption in the "attachment–exploration balance" interferes with a child's development of cognitive and social skills. The attachment–exploration balance is the idea that if an infant is to competently explore her environment, she must be confident that her mother will be there if a threat arises. A child who is not confident that this will happen will focus on the attachment relationship with her mother rather than exploring the environment around her. The fear that her mother might not be there if a threat arises is consistent with later abandonment fears in patients with BPD.

In 1991, Lyons-Ruth and her colleagues reported a number of studies that demonstrated that maternal and family risk factors such as child abuse, parental stress, and mothers' depressive symptoms consistently produced children who had difficulty forming secure attachments to their caregivers.

In addition, a 2004 review of thirteen attachment studies of patients with BPD found that every study concluded that there is a strong association between BPD and insecure attachment. The types of attachment found to be most characteristic of BPD subjects are unresolved, preoccupied, and fearful attachments. The review showed that in each of these attachment types, patients demonstrated both a longing for intimacy and a concern about dependency and rejection. The authors concluded that the finding that adults with BPD have insecure attachments is consistent with the finding of disturbed interpersonal relationships in people with BPD. They also concluded that people who have insecure attachment are vulnerable to developing BPD.

## ON GENES AND INHERITANCE

Many parents feel that they are to blame for their child's BPD, that they either did something wrong in their parenting or passed on a bad gene. Further, few adoptive parents are aware that serious behavioral and personality problems can occur in adopted children. When such problems manifest themselves, parents are often guilt-ridden, believing that they are to blame.

Symptoms of BPD—in particular, inappropriate anger, mood swings, paranoia/dissociation, impulsivity, and intense, unstable relationships—are more common among the relatives of borderline patients than among patients with other personality disorders. It also appears that BPD traits—rather than BPD itself—are more common in the first-degree relatives (i.e., parents, siblings, and offspring) of BPD patients.

Family and twin studies of BPD suggest that while BPD itself might not be inherited, some behaviors such as impulsivity, suicidality, mood instability, and aggression do appear to be inherited. For instance, many parents recognize that they were moody as children, but not as moody as their child. Some parents admit that they had suicidal thoughts but never acted on such thoughts.

It will probably be true that given the incredible variation of BPD behavior, the underlying cause of the disorder will include many genes as part of the complex puzzle. No gene study has found that there is one gene that causes BPD; however, studies show that variations of genes can be strongly associated with certain behaviors. These gene variations, when put together with brain anatomy and the effects of the environment on an individual, will represent a more complete answer.

### Genes and Behavioral Symptoms

One of the largest studies on BPD and genetics looked at 92 identical and 129 nonidentical Norwegian twin pairs. Identical twins share the same genes and the same environment. Nonidentical twins share the same environment but not the same genes. The researchers found that genes accounted for 69 percent of the symptoms of BPD and that environmental factors accounted for the other 31 percent. Most researchers consider BPD to be roughly 60 percent genetic and 40 percent environmental.

At McLean Hospital in Belmont, Massachusetts, John Gunderson, MD, and his fellow researchers have initiated a large study to look at the genetics of BPD. His group has divided BPD patients into three subtypes based on the major problems each group displays. The first group has marked mood swings, the second group has behavioral problems such as self-injury, and the third group has interpersonal problems such as difficult relationships. The researchers are studying whether any of these subtypes has a stronger genetic component than the others. The study hopes to provide results that will help us further classify BPD and develop a gene bank (where DNA is collected and stored) for future BPD research. One study of BPD found a variation in a gene that affects the functioning of dopamine, the brain chemical that regulates movement, emotion, motivation, and feelings of pleasure. Patients with BPD with this gene abnormality tend to be more depressed than those without it.

## OTHER FACTORS IN THE DEVELOPMENT OF BPD

If it were only bonding issues or low serotonin levels that influenced BPD development, a few parenting classes and a serotonin-boosting drug would be all that was needed, but many other life events affect the emergence of BPD, including substance abuse, trauma, maltreatment, and sexual abuse.

## Substance Abuse

A 2005 study by Dawn Thatcher, PhD, and colleagues looked at adolescent alcohol use and other adolescent characteristics as predictors of adult BPD symptoms. The researchers recruited 355 adolescents with a history of alcohol abuse and 169 adolescents without any history of alcohol abuse into their study.

Six years later, they measured symptoms of BPD in the now young adults. They found that the adolescents who abused alcohol and had other psychiatric disorders were more likely to develop adult BPD than adolescents with psychiatric disorders without alcohol abuse.

## Trauma, Maltreatment, and Sexual Abuse

Many studies have shown that the majority of people diagnosed with personality disorders have a history of trauma, abuse, and maltreatment. This is particularly true of people diagnosed with BPD. Also, adults with BPD and a history of childhood and adolescent physical abuse are twice as likely to develop post-traumatic stress disorder (PTSD) as those without BPD or an abusive history.

Clinicians who treat BPD are often on the lookout for childhood abuse, and upon finding it, tie it in as the cause of BPD in a patient. This assumption is strongly supported in the BPD literature, which shows that the majority of individuals with BPD have suffered emotional, physical, and sexual abuse. Research shows that up to 75 percent of patients with BPD have been sexually abused, and it is important to recognize that many do suffer abuse. However, a significant minority has not suffered childhood sexual abuse. Gunderson has pointed out that sexual abuse is neither necessary nor sufficient to cause BPD.

Research has also found that sexual abuse by a parent is significantly related to suicidal behavior in the child, and both parental sexual abuse and emotional neglect are significantly related to self-mutilation. The following four risk factors pertaining to abuse have been found to be significant predictors of a BPD diagnosis:

- Female gender
- Sexual abuse by a male noncaretaker
- Emotional denial by a male caretaker
- Inconsistent treatment by a female caretaker

Of patients with BPD who were sexually abused, more than 50 percent report being abused both in childhood and in adolescence, on at least a weekly basis, for a minimum of one year, by a parent or other person well known to the patient, and by two or more perpetrators. More than 50 percent also report that their abuse involved at least one form of penetration and the use of force or violence. It stands to reason that the severity of reported childhood sexual abuse is significantly related to the overall severity of BPD and general functioning.

## CHILDHOOD MENTAL DISORDERS

Almost all the adolescents referred to our unit at McLean Hospital have been diagnosed with other mental disorders such as an anxiety, depression, bipolar disorder, PTSD, attention deficit disorder (ADD), and many others. Childhood mental disorders, such as ADD, attention deficit hyperactivity disorder (ADHD), or bipolar disorder, might increase the risk that the affected child develops a personality disorder when he or she grows up. This can happen in various ways.

First, the disorder itself could directly influence personality development. For example, a child who is depressed might feel that she is worthless, and over time this belief could become a core belief that she has about herself.

Second, the symptoms and behaviors of a condition might lead to a response by others, which could affect personality development. For instance, a hyperactive child might be physically punished or abused by a parent or might receive differing responses to his behavior, sometimes getting punished, sometimes being ignored. Third, it is possible that the childhood mental disorder is simply a manifestation of personality problems in the first place.

Australian psychiatrist Joseph Rey, MD, one of the foremost researchers of personality development in adolescence, has conducted various studies over the years. His group found that 40 percent of patients who were diagnosed with a "disruptive disorder" (such as ADHD) during adolescence were later diagnosed with a personality disorder. By contrast, only 12 percent of patients who had emotional (or mood) disorders—such as depression—had a personality disorder. When he continued to follow this group of kids into adulthood, he found that having a personality disorder was associated with poor functioning. Issues included problems with the law, a poor work record, early cohabitation, social isolation, and problems in interpersonal relationships.

Other research has found that personality disorders are more than twice as common in individuals who had mood, anxiety, and substance abuse disorders in adolescence than those who had not; and further that the more axis I diagnoses a person has, the more likely he or she will go on to develop a personality disorder.

## ONLINE DANGERS

The Internet clearly presents an incredible benefit to society, but on it lurk many dangers, and adolescents with BPD are particularly vulnerable. Online sexual predators, information about drugs and suicide methods, friendships created without context, the formation of instant peer groups, and rapidly disseminated anonymous bullying are just a few of the hazards.

For example, research from 2014 shows that cyberbullying is more strongly related to suicidal thoughts in children and adolescents than traditional bullying. Today, there are many platforms on which cyberbullying can take place, including blogs, social networking websites (e.g., Facebook,

Instagram, and Twitter), online games, and text messaging. The number of children and adolescents who experience cyberbullying varies, ranging from 10 to 40 percent, depending on the age group.

In April 2006, the American Psychological Association (APA) published a series of articles titled *Children, Adolescents, and the Internet.* The APA noted that between "75 and 90 percent of teenagers in the United States used the Internet to email, instant message (IM), visit chat rooms, and explore other sites on the World Wide Web," and that, "a lot of time on the Web can have both negative and positive effects on young people, e.g., the sharing of self-injury practices by some and the improvement of academic performance and health awareness by others."

Another study found that the use of social media increased the number of relationships that an adolescent has. The study also found that the frequency and tone with which adolescents received feedback on their profiles affected their self-esteem. Positive feedback enhanced adolescents' self-esteem and well-being, whereas negative feedback had the opposite effect.

The Internet may be particularly important for adolescents who feel marginalized. It provides a venue that they perceive to be low risk for finding others who share their differences (both perceived and real) and for exchanging information that may be difficult to share in person. Further, the Internet offers anonymity; adolescents can hide behind assumed identities. Studies show that the main reason for joining an online forum is to find social support and reprieve from isolation.

Sadly, adolescents with psychological problems are much more likely to share personal information on the Internet with total strangers than those without such problems. For example, studies have shown that females between twelve and twenty years of age populate most self-injury message boards and forums. They log on to ask for and share information related to cutting and other self-injurious behavior. It's true that these outlets provide social and emotional support for isolated adolescents, but they also normalize cutting, other self-injurious behavior, and potentially lethal "problem-solving" options. The following message was anonymously posted on an Internet forum:

> "Thanks guys. I sign in whenever I'm going nuts. Even my friends don't get it. It's nice to chat with some of you. It helps me to understand and I relate to what some of you guys have been through. This BPD is a horrible thing to be diagnosed with and I do feel alone most of the time. Someone said cutting, but I don't cut. Instead, I burn myself and feel empty most of the time, but burning helps sometimes. I have been in the hospital and in emergency rooms throughout my life and have isolated most of my family and friends. I really want to find some people who share my diagnosis. I'll be back soon."

In the article "The Virtual Cutting Edge: The Internet and Adolescent Self-Injury," researchers looked at the role that Internet message boards played in creating communities centered around self-injury. They found that in 1998 there was one message board, with nearly 100 members, that dealt with self-injury. By 2005 there were 168 boards with nearly 10,000 members. The boards provided anonymous forums yet places where people felt they were understood.

An important question is: What happens to emotionally vulnerable children who are hooked on the Internet or an electronic lifestyle that provides little structure or consistency? Whom do they turn to when they are having a hard time? Online forums are an impersonal substitute for friends and family. The Internet is not filled with people who understand the situation or know the total misery of a person asking for help. One of the major fears of people with BPD is abandonment. When you're online, for example, it is easy to simply log off when the conversation gets too intense. This can trigger abandonment fears if a person with BPD is seeking help and the online peer logs off. One sixteen-year-old girl told me that whenever she would tell a support peer on an online forum about cutting that she was thinking of suicide, the person would simply not respond or would disconnect. She felt abandoned by someone she didn't really know. "I was cyber dumped," she said.

However, the Internet does offer benefits. Because online forums and blogs can, in theory, be a place where less socially skilled adolescents share experiences anonymously, they also can be a place for adolescents to practice social interaction. Researchers have found that such online exchanges decrease social isolation among adolescents and help them connect with peers as well as explore their identity. This helps explain how the Internet can be a virtual peer support group for adolescents under stress, a place where they can express their feelings and exchange information about modes of coping. Online groups can not only normalize but also encourage self-injurious and potentially lethal behaviors. They provide a powerful vehicle for bringing together self-injurious adolescents. (Self-injury is not the first behavior that has spread because of and through the media. In the 1980s, anorexia nervosa became widespread soon after it was exposed by the mass media as a problem. For instance, in a 2002 study of Fijian girls, disordered eating was significantly more common following exposure to mass media. This was aggravated by portrayals of feminine beauty by increasingly emaciated fashion models.)

Many of the adolescents we treat talk about how the Internet has provided a community that they needed. One told me that after she had posted that she was going to kill herself, she was saved from an overdose when a peer poster, "a sponsor" as it was explained, talked the girl into telling her mother that she had taken an overdose of pills. Some adolescents, though, say that the idea of hurting themselves would never have occurred to them had they not read about it online.

Besides using self-injury as a coping skill, many other online discussions are worrisome, including those about drug use, sexual behavior, purging of food, and normalizing suicidality. Another popular topic of adolescent discussion is frustration about parents whom, they claim, don't understand them.

Although it is increasingly difficult to monitor and restrict Internet and social media content and access, parents and caregivers need to know that these are powerful sources of information for adolescents. Some online resources are invaluable, but others are biased, misinformed, and potentially lethal. An adolescent needs a forum, whether in therapy or with a parent, to be able to question what he or she is reading or being told. For parents, the single most important skill to acquire is to be curious without being judgmental. It's a skill that requires tremendous practice.

## BPD AND CULTURAL AND SOCIETAL CONCERNS

You just need to go to the check-out aisle of any grocery store to see that what sells is a culture promoting a "false self" with emaciated cover models, beauty over brains, and sex without commitment. (The false self occurs when people are forced to comply with external expectations, such as being polite or looking attractive, when such expectations might be inconsistent with who they really are and how they would ordinarily act or feel. Over time, living in a perpetual false-self state can become extremely unhealthy as the person loses his or her sense of genuine self.)

Yet another concern is that generally our culture caters to the need for instant gratification and quick fixes and disdains the idea of people looking for long-term help. One catchphrase is "better living through chemistry," or the idea that taking a pill can make things better. Although this is certainly true for many conditions, it does not work for many others. Telling people with BPD that there is a simple answer or to "snap out of it" invalidates their experience; even worse, it will not solve their problems.

Another component of contemporary life that contributes to the development of BPD is the pressure and stress put on students (by themselves, parents, and institutions of higher learning) to perform and compete. Many clinics report that they are seeing a marked increase in self-injury in response to stress. A large study in 2011 on this topic found that of the

11,529 students who responded, 15.3 percent reported a history of self-injury and 6.8 percent had self-injured within the previous year. Most of the students who had self-injured had done so more than once and nearly half reported self injuring more than 6 times. The average age for starting self-injury was 15.2 years of age.

Many of these cultural factors combine with family environment and individual biology to set up the conditions for the development of BPD.

## THE BOTTOM LINE

BPD is a multifaceted illness with many components that contribute to its formation. Studies present a variety of connections and possibilities. They implicate genes in impulsive aggression and mood instability, show abnormal neurotransmitter levels in the brains of BPD and abuse victims, and reveal certain brain regions to be either damaged or underdeveloped in BPD. Then there is the effect of poor parenting, disrupted attachment, sexual abuse, invalidation, the effects of drug abuse, and finally the pressures of contemporary culture.

Thus, BPD is not caused by a single factor. Rather, the cumulative effects of the environment and genes acting upon the developing brain, its structures, and chemistry come together to produce the clinical picture. The downside is that BPD develops over time and often takes years of treatment to heal. What is encouraging, however, is that there are multiple points at which to intervene, and these interventions will continue to improve over time.

## CHAPTER FIVE

# BPD Myths and Misunderstandings

I N THE 2007 EDITION OF THIS BOOK, my main goal was to get the idea that BPD exists in adolescents into broad public awareness. Since that time, there has been a rapid growth in accepting the diagnosis, and there have been conferences dedicated to the topic, including well-attended conferences in New York in 2012 and Los Angles in 2013 sponsored by the National Education Alliance for Borderline Personality Disorder (NEABPD).

Although there is increasing acceptance, the nature of the questions asked at lectures and conferences I've attended shows that many myths and misunderstandings persist that need to be addressed. There is also a lot of misinformation on the Web and in online forums and blog posts. This chapter is dedicated to clarifying old beliefs and highlighting the research on these various topics.

I want to address the main myths and misunderstandings that come up over and over again in discussions with clinicians and family members. Here are the twelve biggest myths:

1. BPD does not occur in people younger than eighteen.

2. Adolescents with BPD are manipulative and attention seeking.

3. BPD is a rare condition.

4. BPD is a form of bipolar disorder.

5. Bad parenting causes BPD.

6. Adolescents with BPD don't know how to love.

7. BPD only affects women.

8. There are high-functioning and low-functioning forms of BPD.

9. Adolescents with BPD are unbearable to be around.

10. Adolescents with BPD don't really want to kill themselves.

11. There are no treatments for BPD and adolescents with BPD won't get better.

12. BPD is caused by trauma.


## 1. BPD DOES NOT OCCUR IN PEOPLE YOUNGER THAN EIGHTEEN.

I received the following email from the concerned mother of Maggi, a sixteen-year-old girl and the older of two children. She writes:

"We started seeking mental health help when she was six. Even at that time she was very emotional and would throw tantrums. She was diagnosed as ADHD at six, depression and anxiety at age nine, oppositional defiant disorder at age ten, and then bipolar at thirteen. She has been on every medication in the book and even some homeopathic drugs but none of them made a difference. We just had all the meds removed but I blame myself for the medications and now she is about 40 pounds overweight and more miserable than I have ever seen her.

"More about her: She is extremely sensitive. She explodes in anger with no provocation. She is always bored and it seems to cause her so much pain. Sometimes when she is struggling she binges on food and that seems to calm her for a bit. She is extremely needy. She craves love and affection and seems to make friends as quickly as anyone I know but then she pushes everyone away with her extreme demands and need for everything to be just her way. She can love her aunt—my sister—idealize her one minute and push her and yell at her the very next.

"Here is my problem: I am at a loss. She is in therapy and has a good relationship with her therapist, although she never displays her most problematic behavior in her presence so her therapist doesn't get the brunt of it. I truly think that she has BPD from everything I have read, but her therapist says she can't have it until she is eighteen years old. Do I really have to wait that long for a diagnosis? Does she have to suffer that long to get the right kind of treatment?"

This email is typical of the kinds of correspondence I have with many parents. It is simply not true that adolescents cannot be diagnosed. The new *DSM* does not prohibit it and even the earlier edition, the *DSM-IV*, clearly states that BPD can be diagnosed before age eighteen when the symptoms have been present and consistent for at least one year. The age distinction is a false barrier to diagnosis, and it would be unconscionable for a clinician to not diagnose BPD when a person was seventeen years and 364 days old and then diagnose it the next day when he or she turns eighteen.

Finally, research that we at McLean and others around the world are doing shows that BPD is persistent from adolescence through adulthood.

## 2. ADOLESCENTS WITH BPD ARE MANIPULATIVE AND ATTENTION SEEKING.

Caroline was a fifteen-year-old whose parents forbade her from seeing her boyfriend, a young man who had introduced her to cocaine. Her parents spoke to his parents and agreed that neither child could visit the other and that both sets of parents would enforce this ban. Further, the children could not email, text, or telephone one another.

One evening Caroline asked her mother whether she could go visit a friend and do her homework at her house. Caroline's mother checked with her friend's mother, who assured her that it would be fine. Caroline's mother took her to her friend's house and said she would pick her up after a few hours. During the visit, Caroline's boyfriend showed up at the house, and they both used cocaine. Caroline had used her friend to organize the rendezvous, and had used her mother to transport her to the meeting with her boyfriend. Caroline argued that her mother had never said anything about meeting up with her boyfriend at somebody else's house.

"She is so manipulative," her mother said.

I hear this assertion about nearly all of the patients with BPD who come to us for treatment. The charge is made as both a judgment and an accusation, as if not needing further explanation. Many parents and siblings of adolescents with BPD say that they end up feeling manipulated constantly by the child, and eventually the label of manipulative sticks.

A father told me about his fourteen-year-old "going on twenty" daughter:

> "Boys were always attracted to her. All she had to do was look at them, and they would come running. She could get them to do whatever she wanted, like take her places in their cars, especially the older boys. Or she would get them to do her homework. She would pit them against each other, to let them think that they were the ones. But eventually the boys would get discouraged, and she would move on to a new group. She manipulated them so easily."

The idea that people with BPD are manipulative is so widespread that it is important to spend time examining it. Consider, for example, the following definitions of *manipulate* from *Merriam-Webster's Collegiate Dictionary,* Eleventh Edition: "To control or play upon by artful, unfair, or insidious means, especially to one's own advantage; to treat or operate with or as if with the hands or by mechanical means, especially in a skillful manner."

Generally, when someone with BPD is accused of being manipulative, the implication is that the person uses shrewdness, deviousness, and cunning to get what he or she wants at the expense of another. But the concept of manipulation also includes the idea of the skillful use of the environment or the ability to adapt and change in order to survive. For example, babies learn that when they cry they get fed and held. Or a young girl learns that when she smiles sweetly at Daddy, he buys her the toy she wants. Or a boy realizes that if he learns how to skateboard, he will be more readily accepted into a group of friends. These are all examples of skillful use (whether conscious or not) of understanding the environment and adapting to it to get needs met.

The reality is, we are constantly manipulating others and our environment for our own well-being. In many cases, such as the previous examples, these manipulations are either mutually beneficial or don't cause others to feel that they have been taken advantage of.

In BPD, the concept of manipulation takes on a sinister connotation. In large part, it is because many people feel that the gains in the transaction between adolescents with BPD and their parents are all in favor of the adolescents. It is also because on further reflection, parents often feel that they should never have "caved in," and they feel duped.

## Manipulation and BPD

Marsha Linehan, PhD, the developer of dialectical behavior therapy (DBT), has spoken frequently about her dislike for the word *manipulative* as commonly applied to people with BPD. She has pointed out that this implies that they are skilled at managing other people, when precisely the opposite is true. I personally think that this is a well-thought-out perspective and agree with its core sentiment, even though earlier in my clinical practice, I concurred with the more sinister or "malicious intent" definition of manipulation.

The fact that therapists, parents, or others may feel manipulated by the adolescent does not necessarily imply that this was the adolescent's intention. It is more probable that the adolescent does not have the skills to deal with the situation more effectively. Usually their "manipulative" behavior is an impulsive action driven by fear of abandonment, loneliness, desperation, and hopelessness—not maliciousness. It is an ultimately maladaptive attempt to get others to care for them, which initially has that effect, but leaves caregivers feeling burned out in the long term.

Here's an example: James was a sixteen-year-old boy whose parents were separated. He was admitted to our unit for suicidal thinking, which he said was because he was profoundly alone. His relationship with his parents appeared to have a major impact on his life. He told us that they had a fair relationship with each other, but that their separation was still fresh enough in their minds that they were affected if the other was dating another person. James loved clothes and his parents had agreed on a monthly clothing allowance for him. However, whenever he felt that his parents were not buying him what he wanted, he would say something like, "Well, Dad's new girlfriend bought me this shirt the other day." This would get his mother upset and her impulse would be to buy him whatever he wanted, despite the agreement, as she felt that she needed to prove that she was a more loving parent than her ex-husband's new girlfriend.

James's mother recognized that she was doing the wrong thing by buying him clothes. James's father said James was simply manipulating his mother. What probably happened was that at some point in the past James had said something about his father's girlfriend. His mother had become upset and bought James clothes. Whether conscious or not, James now linked talking about his father's girlfriend with his mother becoming upset and buying him things. His behavior (talking about his father's girlfriend) was rewarded (his mother bought him clothes). Pointing out this pattern of behavior and teaching the parents about learning theory (which we'll talk about in more detail later) helped the parents change their own behavior. James's father was a little more mindful of when he invited his girlfriend over to the house, and his mother learned not to respond when James mentioned his dad's girlfriend.

The point is that James had learned to get a desire met. He loved his mother and at no point did his thought process appear to be: "Okay, I know Mom gets upset when I talk about Dad's girlfriend. All I have to do is talk about her and I will get what I want, even if Mom is terribly upset afterward."

Many parents feel, however, that their children calculate exactly what they are going to do in a premeditated way by preying on the parents' own vulnerabilities. Worse for parents is when their kids threaten to tantrum in public or have an angry outburst to get their parents to do what they want. Parents often give in rather than endure the behavior. All this does is teach children that they can get their way by behaving or threatening to behave in a certain way. Here's what one mother told me:

> "When my daughter turned fourteen, she became increasingly impossible to live with. She would rage, hit, spit, and throw things if she didn't get her way. In self-defense and to keep her from hurting herself, I would at first just try to hold her until she would become quiet. Later I was too terrified and I would just leave the house and listen to plates being thrown about. Then, just as soon as it had started, maybe fifteen minutes later, she would come out all happy and as if nothing had happened. Sometimes she would see me shaking and crying, and she would say that she was sorry. Sometimes I would just give in to her, even if I didn't think it was right, because I was so afraid of her tantrum. I would always feel so manipulated by her."

From my perspective, given the behavioral dysregulation this adolescent with BPD displayed, her awareness of herself and her mother during her out-of-control behavior is so distorted that what appears to be a manipulative intent cannot be, as she could not possibly be considered "skillful" during these moments. In this case, it was clear that the mother was both traumatized and terrorized by her child. The child required long-term residential treatment, and the mother went into therapy for herself.

Explaining manipulation, here's what one bright adolescent told me: "My parents think I am so manipulative. I am not aware of it. They tell me they feel manipulated, but I don't spend my time consumed by thoughts of how to get back at them. Everything I do, I do to survive, to belong, and to be heard. I can learn how to do things better, but my actions are not some preplanned way to get people to hate me. It's ridiculous."

The term *emotional blackmail* is sometimes used instead of manipulation and also implies some sort of devious, planned intent. Although this may be true for some people, people with BPD who appear to be "blackmailing" others usually act impulsively out of fear, loneliness, desperation, and hopelessness, but rarely malice, and the thing that they want most is to be understood.

## MANIPULATION: WHAT PARENTS CAN DO

Whether we define an adolescent's manipulation as an active and conscious behavior used to get his or her way at any cost or as an adaptive behavior that comes about because it is the only effective way he or she knows how to do something; parents clearly don't "like" manipulation!

The manipulative adolescent needs to be given the opportunity to identify unfulfilled needs, which he or she is trying to meet through their manipulative behavior. Once these needs are identified, it is important to explore alternative, less alienating methods of having these needs satisfied.

When I ask parents why they think their child is manipulative, or what the purpose of the manipulation is, the answers fall into the following general themes:

- The child simply wants to be liked by everyone and so will do whatever he thinks will get the other person to like him.
- The teen fears forming close relationships only to be abandoned and manipulates situations so the other person won't get close.
- The child simply wants people to feel guilty, or that by having people feel sorry for her, people will pity her and take care of her.
- Some parents feel that they are pitted against each other as the teen capitalizes on parent disagreements about how the child should be handled. They describe behavior such as "sucking up," whining, begging, or being profoundly earnest in their requests.
- Parents feel at times that the manipulation is a method to seek revenge and that the teen does this by pitting people against each other.

There is no instant way to stop behavior that we don't like, but it is crucial not to reward the behavior by giving in to it. The "manipulator" will simply learn that such behavior is rewarded and continue acting this way.

Parents, on the other hand, need to consider their parenting styles. Some parents say "no" simply just to dominate or control their adolescent without a broader perspective on the situation. This typically happens when a parent is exhausted or at a loss for knowing what else to do, but at times parents know no better.

Allowing for a dialogue to explain a decision sets a precedent for how things will be approached. It also allows children to know that they have a say in the discussion even if they don't get their way.

Another technique is for parents to explain how they see the behavior as manipulative. For instance, if the adolescent says, "Jen's mom is the nicest mother in the world. She lets her kids stay up until midnight and have sleepovers with boys," a parent might feel jealous of the other mother, or feel that she would like to be the best mother in the world. Saying instead that it is okay to ask to stay up late at night, or have a sleepover, even if the answer is no, is more effective for the parent in the long term.

If the point of the adolescent's comments is to make the parent feel guilty and shame him or her into allowing the later bedtime or sleepover, it is important for parents to point out that they feel as if they are being manipulated and that this behavior will not be effective.

If parents sense manipulation, they should ask their teen what he or she is really seeking. A statement such as, "Being honest takes courage, and it helps us trust you, whereas being sneaky or deceptive creates a lack of trust," can be useful. The child then needs to be rewarded for taking the courage to be honest. This does not necessarily mean giving in to the teen's request. The reward is the parent recognizing the child's honesty and promising to continue to work hard at understanding where the teen is coming from.

Another situation is when an adolescent asks for something that the other parent has already vetoed. A statement such as, "That's between you and your mother (or father). Leave me out of it," makes manipulation less likely to occur. If a parent sets a rule and the adolescent challenges it, saying the other parent has allowed a certain behavior, then saying that until the issue is clarified with the other parent the current rule sticks allows for clarity and less possibility of future manipulation.

Parents should generally not have disagreements or arguments about rules or child-rearing issues in front of their adolescent. Nor should they sabotage the other parent's authority in any way. If parents do argue, children then know which parent is on "their side," and consistently go to that parent to get their needs met. The "agreeable" parent can then be stuck in a situation where the child now demands to be allowed to do some high-risk activity, does not know how to say no, and ends up feeling manipulated. Careful, considerate parental teamwork can help reduce the chance of manipulative behavior.

### 3. BPD IS A RARE CONDITION.

BPD is not a rare condition. Many people have heard of schizophrenia, which occurs in more than 2 million people in the United States alone. BPD, however, occurs more than seven times that amount: It is estimated that more than 14 million Americans have BPD, according to a 2008 study in the *Journal of Clinical Psychiatry*. It is more common than not only schizophrenia, but also bipolar disorder. An estimated 11 percent of psychiatric outpatients, 20 percent of psychiatric inpatients, and 6 percent of people visiting their primary health care provider have BPD. In adolescents, the numbers are even higher: 22 percent in outpatient clinics and 26 percent in inpatient clinics have BPD, according to a 2012 study.

### 4. BPD IS A FORM OF BIPOLAR DISORDER.

When adolescents are referred to our unit, they are most commonly diagnosed as having bipolar disorder, often a type called bipolar not otherwise specified (NOS). Bipolar NOS is a mood disorder that fits no other category and includes fast cycling between manic (highs) and depressive (lows) symptoms.

Bipolar disorder, just like BPD, occurs in adolescents, but the two are not the same illness. They are two very different disorders whose main similarity is a change in mood states. Confusing the two leads to a serious misdiagnosis and an errant treatment approach. Many adolescents who are mistakenly diagnosed as bipolar are placed on powerful medications in an attempt to reduce the mood swings; however, because the mood swings of BPD are not the same as those of bipolar disorder, the medications simply don't work. If they do work, then they are treating a co-occurring bipolar disorder and not BPD. I cannot overstate this concern. Adolescents being treated with powerful mood stabilizers and antipsychotics they don't need get no benefit from the medications, and often get side effects such as weight gain and changes in liver function and blood fats. Also, the medications can lead to significant cognitive dulling.

Bipolar disorder is a mood disorder that involves one or more manic episodes alternating with major depressive episodes. A manic episode is a period of time in which an elevated, expansive, or notably irritable mood is present, lasting for at least one week. A major depressive episode is characterized by either a depressed mood or a loss of interest or pleasure in daily activities consistently for at least a two-week period.

As you see, the manic and depressive episodes each last for at least a week. With BPD, however, the mood states tend to last only a few hours. Also, the moods tend to be highly reactive, which means that they are triggered as a reaction to a situation, usually an interpersonal conflict. On the other hand, in a person predisposed to bipolar illness, the trigger for mood swings are typically not interpersonal but rather factors such as stress, substance abuse, the effects of medication, seasonal changes, and sleep deprivation. Although some adolescents have bipolar disorder and others have BPD, some have both and it is very important to distinguish between the two so that the appropriate treatment can be provided.

## 5. BAD PARENTING CAUSES BPD.

There is absolutely no data that bad parenting causes BPD, so I am just going to say a few words about this. Parents are all too often blamed for all kinds of problems in their children. I don't doubt at all that there are individual cases in which parents have aggravated their child's underlying vulnerability. Having said that, the vast majority of parents I meet are loving, caring people who are at a loss for what to do. No parents I know get up in the morning thinking about how they are going to turn their child into someone with BPD. Most parents have enough on their plate than to worry about making their own lives even more complicated than they already are. In the absence of any research data or clinical experience to support this idea, it is time to stop blaming parents for causing BPD in their children.

## 6. ADOLESCENTS WITH BPD DON'T KNOW HOW TO LOVE.

Adolescents with BPD have difficulty controlling their emotions and feel them too extremely at times. As with other emotions, feelings of love are complicated. At times, people with BPD would rather be numb or avoid feeling love altogether because, like other emotions, feeling intense love can be painful. However, adolescents with BPD do have powerful feelings of love. In many instances we have seen that having a pet can be therapeutic because they can channel the love toward another being without the messiness of interpersonal relationships. Also, having a pet requires the adolescent to take responsibility. Although it can be exhausting at times, it is absolutely possible for adolescents with BPD to develop and sustain loving relationships.

## 7. BPD ONLY AFFECTS WOMEN.

This is simply not true. In early studies of BPD, research found that women were disproportionately affected by a ratio of 3:1, or 75 percent. More recent studies have shown the distribution between men and women to be about equal, or 50:50.

Part of the reason this myth persists is that there is little research on BPD in men. There are a number of theories that try to explain the discrepancy among studies. Some people believe that clinicians have a subtle gender bias toward females with regard to BPD diagnosis, but others have disputed this. Another attempt at explaining the gender difference is that research on BPD is often conducted in psychiatric settings, and because more women than men engage in self-harming behaviors, there tends to be more women than men with BPD in mental health settings, making it appear that more women suffer from this disorder.

On the other hand, men with BPD exhibit symptoms such as substance abuse or aggressive behaviors that place them in treatment or correctional settings, which are less likely to diagnose BPD. One thing we know for sure is that more girls and young women than boys and young men seek treatment for BPD. Although future research may show that there is an even number of females and males with BPD, in this book you will find more case examples with girls than boys. I hope that you will view the case examples less as gender-specific but rather as an illustration of the challenges facing adolescents with BPD.

## 8. THERE ARE HIGH-FUNCTIONING AND LOW-FUNCTIONING FORMS OF BPD.

First, let me say that there is no validity to this idea. There is no supportive research or serious clinicians in the field who think about BPD in this way. Sadly, most people who use the adjectives *low* and *high* to qualify the term *functioning* do so in unkind ways. For example, I have heard the term *low functioning* used in the same sentence as "train wreck, needy, demanding, hospital-seeking, unproductive, suicidal, self-destructive, and manipulative."

"High functioning" people with BPD are often considered more capable of managing their lives and of being more civil, productive, capable, and "normal" than others. All of these labels are mischaracterizations of BPD. People with BPD can have good days and bad days just like everyone else, so by that definition we are all high functioning and low functioning. Another way to view this idea is to say that high functioning and low functioning can apply to many conditions, such as asthma, diabetes, Alzheimer's, life, and so on. Rather than the concept of high functioning, I would consider "effective functioning" or "skillful functioning."

This is not to say that there are not varying degrees of severity, which is true of almost all medical and mental health conditions, and like any condition, the more severe the manifestation, the more aggressive the treatment. Certainly the person's ability to function can be affected, and the manner in which a person with BPD manages aspects of his or her life can either be skillful or not. This concept of skillfulness is more useful and descriptive than high or low functioning. These latter ideas, though frequently reported in the lay press, are neither defined nor are they measurable.

## 9. ADOLESCENTS WITH BPD ARE UNBEARABLE TO BE AROUND.

In lectures I give, I often have people tell me that they feel sorry for people who have a child with BPD. When I ask them why, they give me a surprised look as if I were missing the obvious. "Well, those kids are unbearable, aren't they? All those rage attacks, and manipulation and threats to kill themselves and they are cutting all the time." It is true that some teens with BPD behave in this way, but the majority struggle with self-loathing, depression, and difficulty controlling their emotions and maintaining friendships.

I have met adolescents with BPD who are unbearable, but I have to say that as a father of four, I find that my own adolescent children are sometimes unbearable, too, and I know that they find me unbearable at times! The majority of my interactions with adolescents with BPD (and my own children!) are not only bearable but also desirable, engaging, pleasant, and thought-provoking.

## 10. ADOLESCENTS WITH BPD DON'T REALLY WANT TO KILL THEMSELVES.

BPD is one of the most lethal of all psychiatric conditions. Not taking suicidality seriously can end in tragedy. Statistics show that up to 10 percent of people with BPD will kill themselves and between 70 to 90 percent will make a suicide attempt. The idea that suicide attempts are manipulative or attention seeking is a tremendously misguided if not dangerous idea, and any suicidal adolescent, no matter what the diagnosis, should receive immediate medical and mental health attention.

## 11. THERE ARE NO TREATMENTS FOR BPD AND ADOLESCENTS WITH BPD WON'T GET BETTER.

Unlike schizophrenia and bipolar disorder, medications don't help people with BPD. Despite this, there are many therapies that can help an adolescent with BPD. The one I practice is DBT; however, there are many treatments that are being shown to be effective, including the STEPPS program, mentalization-based therapy, and cognitive analytic therapy. I will review these and others later in the book.

In addition, people with BPD do get better. My colleague Mary Zanarini, EdD, at McLean has shown in a large study that BPD is actually what she calls a "good prognosis diagnosis." She has followed a group of 290 people with BPD for nearly twenty years and has found that 88 percent of people with BPD achieve remission (they no longer meet the criteria for a BPD diagnosis) over ten years. In addition, about one-third of people with BPD achieve remission within two years. This means that only a small subset of people with BPD (about 12 percent) continue to meet criteria for the disorder for more than ten years. Although those studies are in adult populations, we are hoping to have data from our upcoming adolescent BPD study, but my clinical experience is that the results will be even more promising than the adult data.

## 12. BPD IS CAUSED BY TRAUMA.

My colleague John Gunderson, MD, at McLean likes to say that "trauma is neither necessary nor sufficient to cause BPD." I am often asked at conferences whether BPD is not just a form of the consequences of childhood sexual abuse, physical or emotional trauma, or bullying. On our unit we have evidence that between 30 and 50 percent of all our patients have experienced some type of trauma. However, at least 50 percent of these adolescents have experienced no trauma and still suffer with BPD symptoms.

What we do know is that if adolescents with BPD have experienced trauma and, as a consequence, post-traumatic stress disorder, their level of BPD tends to be more severe and they take longer to recover. Also, they will need a specific type of therapy known as prolonged exposure (PE) in order to address any enduring symptoms of their trauma after their BPD symptoms are under control. In our work it is clear that DBT plus PE in traumatized adolescents with BPD leads to the best outcomes. So even though abuse itself does not cause BPD, it certainly complicates the BPD picture. For instance, if you recall, an adolescent with BPD needs five to nine criteria to meet the diagnosis. In our preliminary research, adolescents on our unit without PTSD have six criteria of BPD, and those with PTSD have, on average, seven criteria of BPD.

## CHAPTER SIX

# When BPD Isn't Your Child's Only Psychiatric Disorder

COMORBIDITIES ARE the psychiatric conditions that co-occur with BPD, and research has found that they are common in people with the disorder. These conditions, which include mood disorders such as depression and bipolar disorder, substance abuse–related problems, eating disorders, post-traumatic stress disorder (PTSD), anxiety, dissociative identity disorder, and attention deficit hyperactivity disorder (ADHD), can complicate both diagnosis and treatment. Of these, depression and anxiety are particularly common in patients with BPD. Further, when PTSD co-occurs with BPD, the PTSD needs to be addressed if the teen is to make sustained gains in treatment.

It is not only depression and PTSD that complicate the course of BPD. On our unit, many of the kids with BPD who appear after multiple failed previous hospitalizations and treatments do not arrive with a BPD diagnosis. Most come in with a diagnosis of depression (because they have been suicidal in the past), bipolar disorder (because they have had episodes of rage and anger alternating with hopelessness), anxiety, ADHD (because they are impulsive), PTSD (because they have experienced trauma and abuse in the past), and substance abuse disorders.

Following is a discussion of what the research shows regarding other co-occurring conditions.

## DISORDERS THAT CO-OCCUR WITH BPD

In a 2004 study, researchers looked at the co-occurrence of psychiatric disorders among patients with BPD older than sixteen. They interviewed the patients at two-year, four-year, and six-year follow-up periods, and found that adolescents with BPD experienced high rates of mood and anxiety disorders. In patients whose BPD remitted over time (that is, former BPD patients who no longer had symptoms of BPD), they experienced a substantial decline in all other disorders, but those whose BPD symptoms did not improve over time reported ongoing symptoms of other disorders.

It is important to note that the BPD symptoms of patients who did not abuse substances were far more likely to go into remission than the symptoms of patients who had substance abuse problems. Adolescents with ongoing substance abuse problems were much less likely to get better than those who stopped using illegal substances or stopped drinking. This finding makes clinical sense, because abusing alcohol or drugs can lead to worsening depression, increasing paranoia and impulsivity, worsening relationships, greater difficulty in retaining learning, less compliance with therapy, and potentially dangerous interactions with medications. Given the findings of how much substance abuse affects the clinical outcomes in BPD, it makes sense to look at this co-occurring condition first.

### SUBSTANCE ABUSE

One of the kids with BPD who had been with us for months had finally turned the corner, started doing well, began getting along with her parents, graduated from high school, and got a job. Six months after her discharge her mother emailed me asking for help because the now eighteen-year-old had fallen back into a destructive pattern of marijuana abuse.

She wrote:

"Amy was largely absent most of the week, preferring to spend several nights with her friends. When she was here, she was civil, mostly distant, and nothing spontaneous. She initiated no conversations. It is what I would consider to be like living in a demilitarized zone. She is increasingly disheveled. I am quite concerned that the tide of depression is rising rapidly. Avoidance behavior has abounded this weekend. Finally, we invited her to the dinner table tonight. She was reluctant to engage, many questions from us, monosyllabic grunts from Amy, and she seemed ready to snap at any moment.

"Unfortunate circumstances occurred in Amy's transportation world. The family car, which she has shared with us for the past few months, is now in the shop and will be for quite a while, due to major undercarriage damage, which occurred while she was driving it (although she can't seem to remember where, when, or how this occurred). No apologies, no remorse, no curiosity about how and when it's going to be fixed. I am wondering if she is even able, at this point, to think more than a day in advance. [This is] symptomatic of how she appears to be living most facets of her life.

"Anyway, at dinner, we told her that we absolutely want her at home along with specific praise for the progress she has made these last six months. All we wanted to know is what she is going to do after she finishes her job at the local bookstore. She only makes $8.50 an hour, yet she wants to move out and get a car. Stonewalled. None of our business, the usual. Her dad kept trying from a number of different tacks. We kept our cool, stayed in validation mode, but the longer this went on, the tougher it became for her.

"There exists such a wide semantic gap between us. Amy's version: We are kicking her out because she won't give up smoking dope. Our version: Amy is welcome to live here within the terms of the contract that we all agreed to. That includes no drugs. This is a marijuana-free household. Her choice."

Almost every adolescent we see at McLean Hospital has had some experience with drugs, and drug experimentation is certainly developmentally normal for adolescents. Among the adolescents with BPD, drug use ranges from the rare kid who has never used to those for whom drug use is potentially lethal. Most typical is the adolescent with BPD who uses recreational alcohol, tobacco, and marijuana. When it comes to the hard-core drugs such as heroin, we find that it is so addictive that standard DBT does not work well unless the adolescent has been clean for about six months. Other substances of abuse include the taking unprescribed stimulant drugs such as Ritalin and Adderall, which the adolescents sometimes get from their friends or dealers at college. Parents are not always aware of how drug use affects their child's ability to cope, particularly when the drug use is recreational. When the drug use is heavy, however, the effects on overall daily functioning can be easier to see. In particular, relationships, academic performance, and work opportunities begin to suffer.

On our unit, whenever we consider any self-destructive behavior, such as self-injury and drug abuse, we look at what we call the "function"—the reason or purpose—of the behavior. For a child who is simply addicted, for instance, the function of the behavior is to get high. BPD adolescents, too, can become addicted, but the meaning behind their drug use will sometimes differ from other teens in that the drug use can serve as a way to change how they feel in the moment, or a way to treat emptiness, or to induce numbing and remove pain—rather than for the pure pleasurable effects of the drugs. In other words, the drug use in BPD adolescents functions as an emotion regulation strategy.

Research shows that substance abuse disorders are common among patients with BPD. Studies put the number at anywhere from 14 to 56 percent in BPD patients. Given the finding that substance abuse disorders significantly delay recovery from BPD, substance abuse treatment should be a main focus of therapy. Although treatment of substance-abusing BPD patients has historically not been optimistic, a recent study showed that DBT was more effective for women with BPD and opioid dependence than a regular 12-step program.

The type of drug use has significant consequences on overall functioning. For example, most non-substance-using BPD patients graduate from high school, whereas only half of stimulant-abusing BPD teens graduate. Prostitution and/or frequent and dangerous sexual encounters are also correlated with substance abuse in BPD teens.

Studies have found that women with BPD who abused substances were at a much higher risk for STDs than women with BPD who did not abuse substances. Gonorrhea, trichomoniasis, and human papillomavirus were of significant concern. The risk was made even worse by poverty, prostitution in the past year, recent unprotected sex with two or more partners, and more than twenty lifetime sexual partners.

One study found that in adolescents who abused alcohol, the alcohol abuse put the child at risk for physical and/or sexual abuse, and in some children this was associated with the later development of adult BPD. In a 2006 study, researchers compared adolescents with BPD who abused alcohol with adolescents with BPD who didn't. The researchers found that those who abused alcohol were more impulsive than those who did not. Further, these adolescents went on to make more serious suicide attempts during their lifetime than their counterparts who did not abuse alcohol.

Drug abuse is a dangerous co-occurring condition to have with BPD. It can ruin relationships, academic success, physical and mental health, and the eventual hope that BPD will go into remission. Because of this, substance abuse treatment should be prescribed along with other therapies in substance-using BPD adolescents.

## Major Depression

Depression, like substance abuse, is common in adolescents with BPD. Many clinicians like the simplicity of diagnosing depression because it is a psychiatric condition that is fairly easy to treat with medication and therapy, is readily accepted by insurance companies when seeking reimbursement, is easy to explain to parents and kids, and does not carry with it the stigma that the person is going to be difficult to treat.

Many clinicians hide behind the diagnosis of depression to get approval for treatment of a suicidal adolescent with BPD. That's because saying the person has BPD is sometimes met with a statement by insurance companies that "BPD is a chronic mental condition and we don't cover chronic mental conditions." Because depression occurs in adolescents with BPD, careful screening using validated assessment techniques for depression is essential in establishing whether an adolescent has this co-occurring condition.

Following is an email from a mother of a fifteen-year-old with BPD, co-occurring depression, and ongoing suicidality. She had until recently been a straight A student and had realistic hopes of attending an Ivy League college. The email was prompted after yet another failed medication trial. The mother wrote:

> "She still seems preoccupied. She is not as motivated about school as she was a few weeks ago, and she still has not written her psych paper. She hasn't done much with friends either. She's had more trouble sleeping at night. Sometimes she sleeps during the daytime. The sleep issue appears to have worsened when Luvox [a drug used to treat a number of conditions, including depression] was started—she thinks that the Luvox is sedating. She still looks depressed and is becoming less energetic."

This email is consistent with co-occurring depression. The teen has many classic symptoms of depression, including sleep problems, motivation problems, isolation, and loss of energy.

## SUICIDE RISK

One of the major reasons the treatment of BPD is so critical is because of the high suicide rate. Although rates of suicide in BPD may finally be coming down as more comprehensive treatment approaches are provided, about 90 percent of BPD patients will make at least one suicide attempt, and about 10 percent will succeed in killing themselves.

A 1997 study found that impulsivity in patients with BPD was associated with a higher number of previous suicide attempts. It also found that people with BPD who have been abused as children will make more suicide attempts than those who hadn't been abused. At McLean, we find that impulsivity tends to be high in the adolescents whom we treat, and nearly 50 percent of them have histories of childhood abuse—physical, sexual, emotional, or any combination of those three—and this abuse puts these kids at high risk for suicide. This speaks to the need for early intervention, especially to address the symptom of impulsivity and trauma associated with early childhood abuse.

A 2000 study found that co-occurring BPD and major depression increased the number and seriousness of suicide attempts, and that hopelessness and impulsive aggression increased the risk of suicidal behavior in both patients with BPD and those with major depression.

Researchers in a 2005 study reported that the severity of BPD was associated with self-mutilating behaviors and that co-occurring depression and BPD were more serious and impairing than co-occurring depression and other personality disorders.

In a 2007 study, researchers interviewed 188 people who had attempted suicide and gone to their local emergency departments for help. Those interviewed had a greater severity of depression, hopelessness, suicidal thinking, and past suicide attempts, and had poorer social problem-solving skills than those without a BPD diagnosis. These findings again underscore the seriousness of BPD and that patients diagnosed with BPD will attempt suicide.

## Post-Traumatic Stress Disorder

PTSD is a common but not universal co-occurring disorder among borderline patients. Studies have found that than 55 percent of patients with BPD also meet criteria for PTSD. On our unit, 33 to 50 percent of the adolescents have co-occurring PTSD. The reason I don't give a more specific number is that the 33 percent figure is specific to early childhood abuse and the 50 percent figure refers to all trauma, not just in childhood. Although trauma can be due to a number of events, the kids we see who also have PTSD have most commonly experienced physical or sexual assault or abuse, as well as family and domestic violence. The symptoms of PTSD we commonly see in adolescents with BPD and a history of trauma include the following:

- Disturbing memories or flashbacks of the trauma
- Repeated nightmares, difficulty sleeping, or dreams of death
- Pessimism about their future lives
- Avoidance of doing anything, being somewhere, or being with someone who will remind them of the trauma
- Fear of re-experiencing traumatic anxiety
- Emotional numbness, in which they seem to have no feelings
- Physical symptoms, such as stomachaches and headaches
- Feeling constantly on guard, nervous, and jumpy

The high degree of co-occurrence between BPD and PTSD is not unexpected, given that many studies have found that borderline patients often report traumatic childhood experiences. But what's also interesting is the finding that a substantial number of abused and traumatized BPD patients do *not* suffer from PTSD. This finding also puts into question older thinking that used to consider BPD as simply a chronic form of PTSD. What we have discovered in our work is that when we treated only the BPD symptoms with DBT, our patients got better, but if we did not also treat the co-occurring PTSD, they would go back to many of their former behaviors following discharge.

We also discovered that the level of illness in our patients with BPD is much higher when they also have PTSD, and that although they recover at the same rate as those without PTSD, they remain sicker. Because of this finding we have now started to use a dedicated protocol to treat trauma once an adolescent with BPD has not been self-injuring for more than eight weeks. The treatment is known as prolonged exposure, and it is a therapy that has been shown to be successful in people with BPD and PTSD. In prolonged exposure therapy, adolescents repeatedly confront the trauma-related thoughts, feelings, and situations that they have avoided in the past because of the distress these symptoms cause. The evidence is that repeated exposure to these thoughts, feelings, and situations over time reduces the power they have to cause distress.

## DISSOCIATION: A TEMPORARY MENTAL ESCAPE

An important symptom in many patients with BPD, PTSD, and other disorders is dissociation. Also found in people who have been abused or traumatized, dissociation is a psychological state in which certain thoughts, emotions, sensations, or memories are separated from the rest of a person's experience. During a dissociative episode, these thoughts, emotions, and memories are not necessarily connected to what is actually going on in the moment and so the person appears to temporarily disconnect from himself or the world around him. Dissociation serves to create a temporary mental escape from the fear and pain of a traumatic recollection. At times, it may lead to a complete loss of memory of the traumatic event.

Dissociation begins in the amygdala, a small, almond-shaped structure within the limbic system in the brain. The amygdala plays an important role in learning, social language, detecting fear, and emotional processing. When the amygdala shuts down, a person dissociates.

*continued on the next page*

However, at times, the exact opposite can occur—the amygdala works overtime. When that happens, a person becomes emotionally moody or experiences rapid ups and downs. At this time, you might also see a startle response, or startle reflex. This is the response of the body to a sudden unexpected stimulus, such as a flash of light, loud noise, or quick movement. The reaction includes physical movement away from the stimulus, a tightening of the muscles of the arms and legs, skin changes, and blinking. It also includes blood pressure and heart rate increases and breathing changes.

Both situations are common in people with BPD. Seeing both dissociation and high emotional states in a person suggests BPD or trauma, and that the limbic system is either over- or underreacting.

## BIPOLAR DISORDER

The relationship between BPD and bipolar disorder, formerly called manic depression, has been examined ever since BPD was added to the *DSM-IV* in 1980.

Studies that used strict *DSM-IV* definitions of bipolar disorder have found that about 13 percent of patients with BPD also have bipolar disorder. Studies that used looser definitions—such as "mood swings"— or included patients who had family histories of bipolar disorder show that 80 percent of patients with BPD also have bipolar disorder. If all the studies that have looked at the co-occurrence of BPD and bipolar are averaged out, it seems about 40 percent of patients with BPD also have bipolar disorder.

It can be especially tricky to treat people with both BPD and bipolar disorder. This is because antidepressants are frequently used in the treatment of BPD. If the person also has bipolar disorder, antidepressant treatment could potentially make the patient manic.

Some clinicians have asked whether BPD is a type of bipolar disorder. Studies show that typical bipolar medication treatments do not work for BPD patients; that even when bipolar symptoms are successfully treated in BPD patients, many of the BPD symptoms remain; and that patients with bipolar also have other types of personality disorders, not just BPD. These findings have led to the conclusion that BPD is its own entity and not a type of bipolar disorder.

## ADHD

A 2002 study that looked at the relationship of childhood ADHD and BPD concluded that there was a strong association between the two conditions. The impulsive, erratic, intense temperament of ADHD children and their low self-esteem, interpersonal problems, and moodiness are characteristics shared with BPD.

Consider this email from a mother in New Mexico who wondered about the similarities between the two conditions:

> "My daughter Krissy, who is fifteen, began her troubling behavior when she was an infant. She is the youngest of four kids. She was the most colicky and fussy and yelled more than the others. The three others are doing well. Nothing ever changed in our family during her early life. My husband is still at his same job and until very recently we have been happily married for twenty-three years.

> "When she was very young, Krissy would get so upset that she would hold her breath when she was crying. She would writhe her body, holding her breath, and her lips would turn blue. Eventually she would start to breathe again. It scared the heck out of me and I would hold her and try to soothe her but that did not seem to work when she was in that state.

> "My neighbor is a psychologist and he said that even at eighteen months she was manipulating me for attention. He suggested I

ignore her. I couldn't do that to a child so young. I ask myself if I did wrong in not listening to him. She was always needy and wanting my attention. She was very impulsive and I had her evaluated at age eight. The psychiatrist said she had ADHD and put her on Ritalin, which seemed to work for a few years, but she was always seeking thrills. We tried Adderall, Wellbutrin, Concerta, and Strattera. They all seemed to help with her school[work], but not with impulsivity and her being hyper. The doctors said that she would grow out of her ADHD and be like our other kids.

"Her early adolescence has been a nightmare for me. Here is where my husband and I started to argue after twenty-three years of an essentially conflict-free marriage! Krissy was extremely materialistic during this time. She would talk my husband into buying things she wanted. Of course, we didn't get these things for the other kids. They never complained! I overheard her telling her cousin how easily she could manipulate her dad.

"We were referred to a new psychiatrist because the so-called ADHD did not really get better, and he suggested she had BPD. I agree with the BPD diagnosis, but ADHD also seems accurate. Are they similar?"

The connection between ADHD and BPD can have several explanations. First, some researchers have considered that the two conditions are simply variations of one another. Second, ADHD in some children can be so disruptive that caregivers can sometimes resort to abusive or variable responses to this behavior. Children do not learn what to expect, or they learn that they will be punished for behavior that they cannot truly control. This caregiver behavior in turn results in an increased risk for BPD in the child. Third, both conditions may have some other common causative factor. For instance, people with both conditions have been shown to have significant deficits in the frontal lobe of the brain, in executive function, and in impulse control.

An interesting point is that whereas BPD is more often diagnosed in females by a ratio of 3:1 over males, the opposite is true for ADHD. In the previous chapter I mentioned that BPD is probably evenly split between males and females, but the BPD diagnosis is more commonly made in women. Joseph Biederman, MD, professor of psychiatry at Massachusetts General Hospital, has said about ADHD in females: "In [kids who are seen in treatment], the ratio of males to females is 10 to 1. In real life, it's maybe 2 to 1." This means that we are missing the opportunity to treat many girls with ADHD. One of the reasons some researchers have postulated why we are missing these girls is that boys with ADHD engage in more rule breaking and behaviors more likely to get noticed by teachers than girls with the disorder do. ADHD may be one of the pathways leading to BPD, particularly in girls, so clinicians need to keep in mind this possibility when assessing and treating ADHD patients, particularly if they are female.

## EATING DISORDERS

How often personality disorders occur among those with eating disorders is a matter of great debate. Some clinicians feel that many patients with eating disorders have personality disorders, whereas many clinicians who treat those with eating disorders feel that when the disorder resolves, so do any personality disorder features. At McLean, my research colleague Mary Zanarini, EdD, has found that up to 50 percent of the young women on our eating disorder unit have clinically diagnosable BPD.

A 2005 review of all of the studies on eating disorders and personality disorders found that BPD is the most common personality disorder in binge-eating/purging type anorexia nervosa and in bulimia nervosa. On our unit, if a person with BPD arriving for treatment also has a serious eating disorder, particularly anorexia, he or she must complete eating disorder treatment first because anorexia is among the deadliest of all psychiatric disorders, and anorexia will kill a person quicker than chronic suicidality will. Furthermore, the starved brain cannot learn DBT.

## THE BOTTOM LINE

BPD clearly co-occurs with other psychiatric conditions. This makes the treatment all the more difficult because it involves considering these other conditions in decision making. Are medications necessary if there is a mood disorder? Should certain drugs be used if there is substance abuse? Does the patient have medical complications from an eating disorder? What happens in family therapy if incest has led to PTSD? These are a few of the many possible questions that must be addressed if the adolescent with BPD is to be accurately diagnosed and treated.

# Treatment

## CHAPTER SEVEN

# Advice on How to Find Treatment

TWO IMPORTANT QUESTIONS COME UP regularly for parents desperate to find help for their adolescents with BPD. The first is where and how to find appropriate treatment, especially when many clinics and therapists are not willing to consider treating kids who self-injure or are suicidal. The second is what parents should do when their child refuses to go to therapy or get help. This email from a parent in crisis speaks to both needs.

> "We live in St. Louis, Missouri. Unfortunately, lots of programs say they can help, but if the patient is suicidal or self-injurious, they say that they cannot help. But that is my fifteen-year-old daughter's actual problem, that she is suicidal, so these clinics cannot really help. My daughter says she doesn't need therapy or drugs to get better. She has no respect for our authority and will not conform to the rules of the house. She says that she just doesn't want to live with us and proposes living with her friends. She is not really trying in school. She threatens us by bullying and screaming if we confront her on her lack of responsibility for her actions and shows no interest in doing her minimal chores. No consequence will make her do them either. We have tried it all.

"Because she is under eighteen, she hasn't been diagnosed per se, but her counselors and psychiatrist believe she has borderline personality disorder. Everything we have read about BPD describes her to a T. She also cuts herself, has low self-esteem, and is belligerent. Despite knowing that she has a mental illness, it makes it no easier to live with her. I worry about her younger brother, and we try to do things outside the house so that he won't be exposed to the behavior. We don't trust her to be home alone, and so we have no downtime.

"If patients under eighteen don't want to be treated, what are we parents supposed to do? Wait for her to kill us or someone else, or even just harm us? The system seems messed up. She talks about death a lot. If we send her to a wilderness program, her suicidal thoughts would make her ineligible, and she might even try it. BPDs have 10 percent suicidal success rate according to the National Institutes of Health. What are we to do?"

## FINDING TREATMENT

By the time that BPD is full-blown, it is likely that the teen is on the mental health system's radar. As BPD begins to evolve in the early teens, the child's pediatrician may be the first person consulted; research shows that between 24 and 50 percent of pediatric office visits involve a behavioral, an emotional, or an educational concern. Most pediatricians do not have expertise in identifying or treating complex behavioral health disorders such as BPD, but many pediatric practices can recommend or are affiliated with mental health specialists.

A word of caution: Don't diagnose your own child as having BPD. If you are worried that your child has many of the symptoms of BPD, have a mental health professional make that determination because an accurate diagnosis will inform treatment. One concern, though, is that even within the child mental health field many clinicians are not comfortable either making the diagnosis of BPD or working with kids with the disorder.

We recently had a referral of an adolescent from a small town in the Midwest. The town's only psychiatrist did not feel that he was qualified to work with people with BPD, and further did not feel capable of treating anyone who was actively suicidal. We must recognize that this professional knows his limitations. Would parents want their child to work with someone without expertise in a particular area of mental health? On the other hand, his stance perpetuates the stigma that people with BPD are hard or impossible to treat because all too often such professionals feel comfortable treating almost any other major mental disorder. It brings into question the ethics of refusing to work with suicidal patients. In addition, given cases in which the symptoms of BPD are severe, it often takes more than one over-stretched clinician to provide adequate care. So what is a parent to do?

Even if a clinician refuses to diagnose BPD in adolescents, one immediate question that a parent can ask is whether the clinician has expertise in dialectical behavior therapy (DBT), in post-traumatic stress disorder (PTSD), or in working with suicidal and self-injurious teens. If they have some expertise, they will generally be comfortable in working with adolescents with BPD. Sometimes the resources simply do not exist, or sometimes, sadly, parents are not believed when they tell their child's story. In such cases we have seen families uproot their lives (by, for instance, moving across the country) to get help for their kids.

Consider this email, which speaks to the frustrations of parents seeking help for their child with BPD or suspected BPD.

> "We are struggling what to do with our sixteen-year-old. We think she has BPD, but we want to rule it in or rule it out if she has it. Our first thought was to get her into intensive therapy, so we went to our hospital for a consult. All they did was pass her along to a doctor who administers her meds for ADD, who in turn passes us on to another list of therapists for her to see. We are so frustrated.

All we want is to have her fully evaluated and get help for whatever is wrong with her. We don't feel that we have the expertise to help us."

In the previous edition of this book, I had a resources section that included clinics and residential treatment facilities that work with kids with BPD. This time I have not included specific clinics or groups because there are many clinicians now being trained in DBT and any resource section trying to catalog all of these would be outdated by the time it was published. If a group or clinic states that it is doing DBT for adolescents, it is committing itself to working with high-risk kids. Unfortunately, these resources are few and not very convenient geographically for everyone. These days, when I am called by out-of-state people looking for resources in their area, either I know someone and recommend them, or use an online search engine to look for providers. The terms "BPD, borderline adolescent, DBT, therapist" followed by the town name and state will usually identify providers in a geographical area if there are any. One site that has many resources is run by Behavioral Tech, the group that trains DBT therapists. The Web address is http://behavioraltech.org/resources/crd.cfm.

If that site is not helpful, consider contacting the National Alliance on Mental Illness (NAMI) at www.nami.org. Many towns have local affiliates of NAMI, the largest consumer-driven mental health advocacy group in the nation. In June 2006, it placed those with BPD on its list of "priority populations," recognizing the seriousness of BPD and including BPD as a focus diagnosis. If even this does not help, strongly advocate that your local mental health clinician consider becoming familiar and comfortable with BPD by attending DBT training. This might not immediately help an adolescent in distress, but it may get the clinic to consider the possibility.

Here is a tool kit for how you might approach getting expert therapy if you suspect that your child has BPD. I use the acronym RIPEN.

## Before You Search

**1. Read:** People learn about BPD from many different sources. Ultimately, a mental health specialist will be your best guide. Nevertheless, reading well-researched books on BPD will give you a sense of what you are dealing with and the kinds of questions to ask a specialist.

**2. Insurance:** Your insurance company will typically provide a list of mental health specialists who take its insurance. This does not mean that that person treats BPD. Also, the work can be difficult and lead to the clinician spending more than the number of hours authorized by the insurance company in working with the person with BPD. Consequently, some clinicians won't take insurance because they will not be fully reimbursed.

**3. Psychiatric history:** Create a list of the concerns you have for your child, targeting specific behaviors that will help guide the evaluation. Also, having a list of all medication trials and doses of medications, hospitalizations, and past therapies will be useful for the evaluating therapist.

## Evaluating Your Professional

**4. Expertise:** Once you've identified a candidate or candidates, ask yourself: Does the therapist have the clinical skill set and expertise to deal with someone with BPD? Have they been trained in one of the therapies that have been validated in the treatment of BPD? Do they have adolescent experience? Are they comfortable dealing with co-occurring disorders? What are their views on the use of medications? What is their availability? How often will they see your child? Do they take after-hours calls? How will they work with you as a parent? Some of these questions might be found on the therapists' websites but others you will have to ask the therapist directly.

**5. Network:** If you have found a therapist who is comfortable working with your child, find out whether there is anyone else in the practitioner's network. Does the therapist run groups? Who covers for emergencies and vacations? Where will your child go if he or she needs to be hospitalized?

## WHEN OUTPATIENT THERAPY IS NOT ENOUGH

Sometimes, even if a local clinic or practice works with adolescents with BPD, outpatient services are not enough, and the child needs more intensive treatment. Hospital stays are often covered by insurance. However, when the child's behavior is unrelenting, longer term, and at times very costly, residential treatment care is necessary. I am very aware that these centers can be very expensive and that in many circumstances parents go through great financial sacrifice to help their child.

The choices that parents of suicidal children with BPD face are sad to hear. A father told me that his son's college funds were "of little use if he kills himself. We would rather use this money on treatment." Some parents have successfully lobbied their state departments of mental health, insurance companies, or school districts to help foot the bill for the cost of care for this serious and chronic mental health issue. These agencies face a rise in teen suicide and self-injury and have become more realistic about what they can and cannot provide within the limits of their services and will sometimes work with parents to find a reasonable resolution.

## SEEKING STATE ASSISTANCE

In the first email in this chapter, the parents felt bullied and terrorized by their daughter. This may not have been the daughter's intention, but the family felt that way nevertheless. Her behaviors were not necessarily enough to have her hospitalized. In the event that parents have lost hope that they assert any effective authority over the adolescent, they should investigate whether their state has the capacity to help.

For instance, Massachusetts has a Child in Need of Services (CHINS) petition in which the juvenile court tries to help parents and school officials deal with troubled youths. The person filing the CHINS petition must show the judge that the child regularly runs away from home, constantly disobeys the commands of a parent or legal guardian, misses school on a regular basis, or constantly fails to follow school rules. If a teen has untreated BPD, he or she may well have many of these behaviors.

A parent or guardian can file a CHINS petition on a child who is younger than seventeen, runs away, and/or does not or cannot follow the rules at home. A school district may file a CHINS petition on a child who is younger than sixteen, is absent a lot, or seriously misbehaves at school. The police may file a CHINS petition on a child younger than seventeen and a runaway. Once the CHINS petition is issued, it is up to the judge, not the parent or the school, to decide when to dismiss the petition.

When a petition is filed, a judge decides whether there is merit to the case. If there is no merit, the case is dismissed. If the judge feels that there is enough concern, a probation officer is assigned to the case to decide which specific services a child needs (such as protective services, mental health services, social services, and so on). If a teen refuses to attend therapy, the court can mandate that the teen go to therapy. If the adolescent continues to refuse and remains at risk, the department of social services can be contacted to determine whether an out-of-home placement is necessary.

Other states may have similar services, and clearly such drastic measures are not always necessary, but when parents feel that without such help they might lose their child or be driven to measures that will put the child at risk, such intervention is worth considering.

## FAMILY CONNECTIONS

The National Education Alliance for Borderline Personality Disorder (NEABPD) has developed an exciting initiative known as Family Connections (FC). FC is a twelve-week series for family members with a relative who has BPD or symptoms of the disorder. It provides education for the family on the latest understanding, research, and treatment of BPD. The idea is to provide the foundation for a better understanding of this complex disorder and practical ideas from other families who have had to face similar challenges.

What is different in these groups is that they are led by trained family members (parents, spouses, children, and siblings) and have no formal "professional" presence. It is a skills training model based on DBT and used in the context of a supportive group environment.

Because it is hard to establish an FC group in smaller communities, they have added a virtual class group and families can "meet" for the course weekly via teleconference or video conference.

## GETTING AN ADOLESCENT TO AGREE TO TREATMENT

Okay, so you finally found a qualified therapist! The next major challenge is getting your teen to therapy and what to do if he or she refuses to go. We often see that therapy refusal most often has to do with giving up hope. Many teens say that they have been going to therapy for years and have not found it helpful. Why would they want to try yet another therapy?

The young women who are admitted to our unit sign themselves in on a voluntary basis. It stands to reason that people who want and attend therapy are more likely to get better than those who do not want to or don't attend therapy. Still, some teens who don't "really" want therapy recognize it as a way to get their parents off their backs. Many adolescents who complete a course of DBT feel that it was very different and more helpful than any other treatment they have ever had before. Once the teen meets with the DBT therapist, we tend to be able to get almost all of them to commit to therapy because the treatment is targeted at their specific problems and they feel understood. But how do you actually get them out the door to come to that first appointment?

## Seven Steps to Getting Your Child into Therapy

At times, parents find that deception is the only way to get their child in for an appointment. I have had young people show up at my office for an appointment their parent scheduled only to find out that they had no idea they were going to be evaluated by a psychiatrist. "My mom told me I had a doctor's appointment," they tell me, or, "My dad said that this was to help me with my schoolwork." These steps will make it easier.

1. Is this for you or for them? Generally, people will only want to go to get help if they think that they have a problem. Your concern that your teen is staying up too late at night, for instance, might not be your teen's concern. Your wanting your child to see a therapist can be loaded with your own views of what constitutes normal behavior. For instance, I met a devoutly religious family who wanted their son in therapy because he had "homosexual feelings," so I could help "straighten" him out. The child did end up in therapy but not for his "homosexual feelings,"—which was his parents' problem, not his—but for how to deal with the intolerance of his parents. Check with others to see whether they agree that your concerns merit your child getting help.

2. If you and others agree that the problem is interfering with your child's ability to function and warrants further evaluation, talk to your child clearly about your concerns. This is not the time to go into all the problems they have ever had. If your child has been self-injuring, stick with just that concern. Saying ". . . and your grades have been dropping and your room is

a mess, and I don't like how you are treating your siblings," and so on, will leave the child more isolated and shut down. Tackle the major concerning issue. Also, suggest that your child would benefit from having the opportunity to talk through his or her feelings with a trained professional bound by confidentiality.

3. Once you have talked with your child, be patient. Many teens with BPD will hear your offer for help but will need time to digest what you have told them. It is not typical for them to jump up and agree that they will go to therapy; however, they will think about it. Sometimes adolescents with BPD see it as a win–lose proposition. If they agree to therapy, that means they have acknowledged they have a problem, and then you win and they lose. Your offering to get them into therapy but giving them the time to decide whether to go allows them some say in their treatment.

4. If they agree, recognize that they might not be a match for the therapist or the therapist might not be a match for them and that they are not necessarily locked into therapy with the first person you find. Further, if they are not a match, then tell them that after a few sessions you will help them find a different therapist.

5. Know something about therapy. It helps to do research on the type of therapy you are recommending to your teen. They are often more curious than you will suspect and do their own research. This will help the adolescent better understand why the therapy will be good for them. You don't want to make promises about how therapy will help improve things, especially if you know nothing about the therapy. For instance, knowing that DBT targets self-injury and suicidality and that the therapy is specific to their problem is more likely to encourage them to agree to treatment than not knowing anything about the treatment at all.

6. Encourage them to keep up with the therapy. Once they enter therapy, the initial sessions may be bumpy because they are getting to know their

therapist and starting to change old and familiar habits, which can be hard. Recognizing that they are doing very hard work will let them see that you are paying attention, even when they slip, which in BPD often happens.

7. Accept that if, despite everything you have tried, your teen continues to refuse treatment, you might need to either a) let natural consequences take their course (for instance, if their behavior is destroying relationships, they may need to hit rock bottom and realize they have no friends left) or b) involve the authorities and call 911 if the behavior is so dangerous that they need hospitalization. Often if a child is hospitalized, having outpatient therapy will be a prerequisite of being discharged.

### THERAPY

On our unit, teens have told us, "I don't need to be here, but my parents are crazy." This may or may not be true, but treating adolescents with BPD means treating the entire family because many of the interactions are trans-actional—that is, emotions and behaviors such as anger and physical harm often affect more than just the child. In consequence, even if the adolescent refuses treatment, it may be helpful for the parents to go into therapy.

Often parents have been burned out by behavior they see as manipula-tive, by constant badgering by the teen, or by worrying about their child's safety. Parents getting therapy might not necessarily get the adolescent into therapy, but it will help the parents deal with their own suffering. Some-times, though, if the parent accepts therapy, the teen will follow.

Certainly if the adolescent has gotten to the point of severe self-injury or acting suicidal, such as taking an overdose, then there can be no compromise and a hospital admission might be indicated to assess lethality.

Many of the kids who come to McLean Hospital have recently been suicidal, have made suicide attempts, or have ongoing thoughts of completing suicide. What we know of teen suicide is that of teenagers who eventually attempt suicide, about 80 percent have shown up at doctors' offices at some point in the few months before making their attempts, and the suicidal behavior will often be accompanied by other symptoms such as an inability to sleep, exhaustion, or problems at school.

Many parents tell us that they recognized that something was wrong but not that things were so bad. Researchers in the field of adolescent suicide are working on measures that will be better able to predict attempts, but although the use of these measures is promising, it is still experimental. Unless your child declares his or her intention, the following signs are not specific enough. They won't tell you whether or when your child will make an attempt. They are useful in that they should compel a parent to be very serious about getting professional help or alert the therapist that these behaviors are active.

· Depression
· Statements that show a preoccupation with dying
· Drastic behavior changes
· Mood swings
· Lack of interest in future plans
· Making final plans, including researching suicide methods online
· Previous suicide attempts
· Sudden improvement after a period of depression
· Self-destructive behavior, including drug use and self-injury

Anxiety, isolation, depression, drug abuse, delinquency, and family breakdown are also risk factors. Because no specific symptom will tell parents whether their children will make an attempt, any of the above symptoms should be enough to seek expert help.

## CHAPTER EIGHT

# How Dialectical Behavior Therapy Can Help

I N RECENT YEARS, research into suicide has increased as it has become a significant concern among many groups, including adolescents. There is still a surprisingly small amount of research focusing on BPD and suicide, despite the high suicide rate associated with it. BPD researcher and psychiatrist John Oldham, MD, points out that personality disorders are estimated to be present in more than 30 percent of individuals who die by suicide, 40 percent of individuals who make suicide attempts, and 50 percent of psychiatric outpatients who die by suicide.

In clinical populations (that is, people who seek out and are in treatment) of people with BPD, the rate of suicide is estimated to be between 8 and 10 percent—1,000 times greater than that of the general population (where suicide occurs in 0.01 percent of the population). Up to 90 percent of patients with BPD make suicide attempts. This means that unsuccessful suicide attempts are far more common than completed suicides. Yet unsuccessful suicides take their toll on the individual, their family, and the clinical services that provide care for them.

As studies increasingly show that BPD is far more treatable than previously thought, keeping teens alive to the point of recovery means getting them through suicidality. Treatment must initially gear itself to suicidality so that the prospect of a life of quality can be considered. Dealing with other problems before tackling the issue of suicide risks not addressing the very problem that will permanently prevent recovery.

This chapter will focus solely on dialectical behavior therapy (DBT). I am convinced of its effectiveness not only by its positive clinical outcomes but also by the increasing body of research that shows its efficacy. DBT cannot prevent suicide, but it is an effective treatment for suicidal patients in that it provides them with specific skills to reduce the emotional and interpersonal issues that make them vulnerable to suicide.

*"Dialectical behavior therapy has not answered all my questions, but it has stopped me from killing myself. Now I can get on with the work of finding out what the hell is going on."*

—JEN, SIXTEEN-YEAR-OLD WITH BPD

## DBT: A THERAPY WITH PROMISE

Marsha Linehan, PhD, director of the Behavioral Research and Therapy Clinics at the University of Washington in Seattle, developed DBT and described the research and treatment in her 1993 book *Skills Training Manual for Treating Borderline Personality Disorder.*

DBT is a form of behavioral therapy that focuses on teaching people skills that help them react more normally to overwhelming emotions. The idea is that if adolescents had the skills in the first place, they would use them. For whatever reason, they have not developed adaptive skills to deal with difficult situations, and so at times resort to self-destructive behaviors.

These days, many therapists say that they use DBT; however, some of the teens referred to us who say they have been in DBT have not necessarily been in a DBT therapy program run by a person who has been formally trained in the practice. Therapists may have read books on DBT or been to a lecture and then used it. Formal training, however, requires the therapist to participate in a minimum five-day training session run by a recognized trainer. Proper, or "adherent," DBT encompasses individual therapy, skills groups, skills coaching, a consultation team, and family groups, all of which I will review in this chapter.

Linehan's original work demonstrated the efficacy of DBT in reducing suicidal and self-injurious behaviors among women with BPD. Later, psychologist Alec Miller, PhD, and his colleagues modified DBT to address the needs of adolescents with multiple problems. Research has shown that use of this approach with adolescents reduces suicidal behavior, dropout from treatment, psychiatric hospitalizations, substance abuse, anger, and interpersonal difficulties.

DBT is the acronym for dialectical behavior therapy. But what does that mean? The term *dialectical* is derived from classical philosophy. It refers to a form of argument in which an assertion is first made about a particular issue. This assertion is termed the "thesis." The opposing position is then stated, and this is known as the "antithesis." DBT says that there is wisdom in both positions even if they are completely opposed. In DBT, a "synthesis" of extreme positions is reached by incorporating the valuable features of each position and resolving any contradictions between the two. It is not necessarily a compromise, however.

For example, parents will see cutting as a problem in their child, and it is true that it is a problem. Yet the teen will see cutting as a solution to the problem of how she feels in the moment, and this is also true. Both positions—that it is a problem and that it is a solution—are true. Once this is recognized, rather than fighting about who is right and who is wrong, the "wisdom" in each position is recognized, and both can move on to a new way of thinking. The parents can see that their child is struggling and the teen can develop new skills to deal with intense emotions.

Whereas many therapies focus on the past and the so-called underlying problem, DBT focuses on present behavior. Teens are living with their present problems and cannot change the past. All they can do is be more skillful in living the life they have. Although DBT does not focus on the past, it does not discount it, either, recognizing that it is an important factor in bringing the teen to the present.

For instance, if you were driving to work and got a flat tire, all the reasons in the world as to why you got the flat tire will not get you to work. You have to change the tire. Later, you may consider whether there is something about the road, how often you change your tires, or other reasons behind the cause, but in that moment the reason why the tire is flat is of little consequence in getting you to work. In DBT, the historical reasons why the teen has been cutting for the past three years, for instance, are less the focus than the need for the teen to develop other skills in the moment to deal with the current problem.

## THE **DBT** REVOLUTION

DBT has revolutionized the treatment of BPD for three major reasons. First, scientific research has shown it to be effective, something that few other treatment approaches can claim. Second, it has increased the public awareness of BPD in part because of its effectiveness. Third, not only has DBT proven itself to be a good therapy for patients, but it has also given therapists who treat patients with BPD a way to deal with their own potential burnout, which in turn allows them to continue working with patients who have historically been seen as very difficult to treat.

In the previous version of this book, I highlighted the few studies that had been done showing DBT's efficacy. Since then, there have been so many studies showing its effectiveness that it would take an entire chapter to review all of them. DBT is not a panacea, but it has been put to the test, and both clinical and research outcomes support its utility.

## DBT: PART 1—THE ROLE OF EMOTIONAL VULNERABILITY

DBT is based on a biosocial theory of BPD that says the disorder is a consequence of an emotionally vulnerable child growing up in an invalidating environment. DBT considers three components to emotional vulnerability:

**Emotional sensitivity.** Teens with BPD tend to have emotional reactions that seem to come out of nowhere. Often they have no idea why they reacted the way they did. They often have no idea what the actual emotion they're feeling is, only that it is intense. One analogy is that for many people, eating peanuts is not a problem, but to those who are allergic, exposure to the nut will lead to an extreme reaction. This is not intentional; it is their biology. In the same way, people with BPD react intensely to difficult situations.

**Emotional reactivity.** Adolescents with BPD are not only sensitive but their emotions also tend to be reactive, meaning that they are triggered by events, typically interpersonal situations. Their reactions and subsequent behaviors tend to appear extreme and not consistent with the situation. For instance, a young woman I had in therapy destroyed her cell phone when her boyfriend was five minutes late in calling her. It is important for families to know that emotional reactivity, like in this example, isn't manipulative but rather based on brain biology. Further, secondary feelings of shame and guilt over their behavior can make the person feel even worse. For the teen with emotional sensitivity, it is a horrible way to live.

**Slow to calm down.** Adolescents with BPD also have a hard time calming down and stay upset longer over seemingly trivial matters than teens without the disorder. They have a hard time letting things go. I have seen teens and young adults who have held on to a past conflict for months and years.

## DBT: PART 2—THE ROLE OF ENVIRONMENT

An "invalidating environment" refers to a situation in which a child's experiences are disqualified or "invalidated" by the significant others in his or her life. The word *environment* in this context means the physical and interpersonal surroundings that can affect the mood and behaviors in any person.

Here's what happens in an invalidating experience: A child has an experience or a thought. The parent or caregiver indicates that this experience or thought is not accurate, or will tell the child to get over it or that the problem he or she is struggling with is easy to solve.

For example, seventeen-year-old Bruce is an emotionally intense adolescent who was first admitted to McLean's DBT partial hospitalization program after having been hospitalized for an overdose during a suicide attempt. He completed the DBT program and was discharged back home. Nearly three months after discharge, Bruce's parents called looking for readmission to the unit because he was expressing intense thoughts of suicide. On admission, Bruce told me that he could no longer live at home because he was fighting every day with his parents and they just did not understand him. During a meeting involving Bruce, his parents, and the treatment team, Bruce wanted to talk about the fighting at home. He told us that fighting generally involved loud arguments, yelling, and the occasional throwing of "stuff," as well as a lot of anger.

Bruce's mother acknowledged the fighting—"that's why we are here"—but she repeatedly blamed it on Bruce's girlfriend, who was the "real problem." His mother's assertion that it was Bruce's girlfriend, and the problems that she was causing, invalidated his perspective. His perspective was that it was the fighting at home that had led to his suicidality, not his girlfriend. Bruce's history of emotional intensity, together with his invalidating environment and the high level of chaos at home, produced intolerable feelings that, in turn, led to his wanting to commit suicide.

Even very well-intentioned parents can invalidate their children's experiences, so that statements such as "you're not ugly" or "you're not stupid" are invalidating to a child who sees him- or herself as ugly or stupid.

Obviously, situations such as incest or other forms of abuse are more clearly understood examples of invalidation. Patients with BPD frequently describe a history of childhood sexual abuse. This is regarded within the DBT model as a particularly extreme form of invalidation.

Another aspect of the invalidating environment is that it places a high value on children being self-motivated and able to control themselves. In these situations, the failure of teens to control their behavior is blamed on them. As the adolescents are blamed for their behavior, they are seen as bad people; their inability to control themselves is seen as a negative aspect of their character, rather than as a failure of both the teen and her parents to understand one another and recognize that there is a collective problem.

Whether the invalidating environment is caused by well-intentioned support or destructive abuse, ongoing invalidation over time in an emotionally vulnerable individual is recognized by the biosocial theory as a powerful cocktail for the development of BPD.

The final component of the invalidating environment is one that tells the child that things are easier to solve than they actually are. Just because a parent gets over anger or sadness easily does not mean that their child with BPD can. If the child could, he would. It would be as if a French person yelled at an English speaker for not speaking French. The fact that you can control your emotions does not mean that your child can.

## WHEN PARENTS INVALIDATE THEIR CHILDREN

When some parents first hear of the biosocial theory, they don't like the idea of seeing themselves as "invalidating," in other words, feeling blamed for the troubles of their children. They may think there is an emotional mismatch between them and their children, and in the ways that each sees the world. This explanation particularly resonates with adoptive parents.

Linehan describes the way that the child's emotional vulnerability interplays with the invalidating environment to create a borderline personality as follows: "Children won't have the opportunity to accurately label and understand their feelings nor learn to trust their own responses to events." In such an environment, the children don't receive help to cope with situations that they find difficult or stressful, because many such problems are not acknowledged by their invalidating environment.

An extreme example is that of Jacqui, a very bright, attractive fifteen-year-old from California. She was referred to McLean for self-injury, self-loathing, and suicidality. Her mother, too, was attractive, enhanced by multiple plastic surgeries. The daughter, however, was far more concerned with her own mental health than with the outward appearance of her body. But she struggled to please her mother, who said that she wanted her daughter to be happy and believed that if Jacqui "just lost a few pounds, she would be happy."

Jacqui's mother had found her own happiness in her outward appearance (although Jacqui was not sure just how happy her mother was). Jacqui was trying to find happiness in academic pursuits, which her mother felt was reasonable, but that Jacqui would find true happiness if she focused more on her appearance than her learning. Jacqui's older sister saw life much more the way their mother did. The problem was that Jacqui did not. The issue was far less about who was right or wrong than the recognition of the possibility of another perspective.

We had a family meeting to help Jacqui's mother recognize that her daughter experienced the world in a different way than she herself did. Her mother had a hard time accepting this—"She's a girl, isn't she?"

Jacqui said: "You see, I have been backed into a corner from which I can find no escape. Mom, you have literally told me you don't respect me, don't have to respect me, and will not respect me, yet I have to respect you. I do. I just think that right now I have bigger problems than my weight. Here I am in a hospital and because of that, you blame me for an inability to have a life. My dad has no idea what to do. He cries at night about me, and fights with you. Mentally, I am just above rock bottom; however, in the last few days, the plunge has become a death spiral."

In response, her mother said, "I know that your body image issues play a huge role in your self-esteem and the possibility in your mind that as your parents we might not accept you if you do not appear healthy. Obviously, your fear of abandonment is still a concern. Your grandparents are going to visit next week. I think that you are worried about how you will look to them."

As adolescents look to others for indications as to how they should feel or for help in solving their problems, they discover that they are expected to find the solutions themselves and control their behavior in a "socially acceptable" manner. Jacqui was expected to relieve her stress through losing weight and going to the gym. Instead, she did so by slashing herself up.

Her behavior suddenly exploded and changed from blocking her emotions as she tried to get the approval of her mother to emotional volatility as she tried to get her mother to acknowledge her feelings. Her mother responded erratically to her behavior, and Jacqui sometimes felt supported and at other times not. It was this inconsistency that created an enduring pattern of self-destructive behavior.

## BPD PATIENT CHARACTERISTICS AS TARGETS FOR DBT

Linehan in 1993 described BPD patients as showing the following six typical patterns of behavior that the patient and therapist would target:

**Emotional vulnerability.** Patients with BPD are generally aware of their difficulty in coping with stress. Yet they may blame other people for having unrealistic expectations and making unreasonable demands. Patients with BPD work on improving their ability to regulate their emotions.

**Self-invalidation.** People with BPD invalidate their own responses and have unrealistic goals and expectations. This is a characteristic learned from their invalidating environment. To make matters worse, they then feel ashamed and angry with themselves when they experience difficulty or fail to achieve their goals. Here the goal is to teach the adolescent to self-validate or recognize that his or her perspective can be as valid as anybody else's.

**Unrelenting crises.** Teens with BPD tend to exhibit a pattern of unrelenting crises, where one crisis follows another, often before the previous one has been resolved. In therapy, teens learn to use realistic judgment in evaluating whether a specific situation requires a response that takes it to a crisis level.

**Inhibited grieving.** Because of their difficulty with emotion regulation, people with BPD are unable to face negative feelings, particularly feelings associated with loss or grief. In therapy, adolescents are taught how to recognize and then label feeling states and experience their emotions without labeling them as good or bad.

**Active passivity.** Teens with BPD can be *active* in finding other people who will solve their problems for them, but they are *passive* in solving their own problems. The goal is to teach them to become active in solving their own problems.

**Apparent competence.** BPD patients have learned to give the impression of being competent in response to an invalidating environment. In some situations, they may indeed be competent, but their skills do not generalize across different situations and are dependent on their mood at the moment. For this behavior, the target is for adolescents with BPD to be able to be competent in a way that is *not* dependent on their moods.

These patterns of behavior can lead to powerful and frequently painful emotions. Sometimes, a pattern of self-mutilation tends to develop as a means of coping with these emotions. At times the feelings are so painful and persistent that suicide is seen as the only solution to the misery.

## DBT IN ACTION

This email from the mother of fourteen-year-old Sally shows DBT in action. (The DBT practices are in brackets.) Sally was cutting herself and had tremendous black-and-white, all-or-nothing thinking. Her mother had wanted to know what was "wrong" with her daughter. Instead, we looked at their relationship with the goal of understanding each other's perspective. Her mother wrote:

> "After years of anger at my daughter, I see how I withdrew from her when my husband left us. Therapy is changing this. I'm not my dependable, flawed self. I'm still taking care of everyone's nuts and bolts needs, but I am trying to alter some long-standing patterns [problem solving], forcing a little distance between us, and I think this is what Sally feels in subtle ways. The intensity of our relationship is exhausting, especially now that this therapy shines a beacon on my bad behavior.

> "Sally, too, is changing as she sees me change. She and I have had some real moments of lighthearted affection in the past weeks (and it's interesting how easy it is to forgive your own child). This is wonderful and new and often initiated by Sally [use of newly acquired interpersonal skills]—who does rise above her preoccupation and pain [distress tolerance skills] as she learns to trust that I am making an effort. I look at my behavior for her, and she trusts me for me. We both take risks, but ultimately we have this beautiful new relationship. I'm proud of her and I'm sorry I'm not more reaffirming, and Sally wonders why I'm not, I'm sure."

## Components of DBT Treatment

The dialectical approach to understanding people and the treatment of human problems is not dogmatic, but instead is open and free-flowing between therapist and patient. The most fundamental principles in DBT are the need for change and the need for acceptance. Ultimately, if an adolescent's behavior is going to be different, change will have to occur. Change can only happen when you see your child's point of view. Accepting that things are the way they are because of all that has happened to your child is the starting point for change to occur. DBT has specific techniques of validation designed to counter the self-invalidation of the patient.

For a complete and comprehensive look at DBT for adolescents, *Dialectical Behavior Therapy with Suicidal Adolescents* by Alec Miller, PhD, and Marsha Linehan, PhD, is essential reading, but for the purpose of this chapter, I'll give a simple overview of the skills that form the basis of DBT therapy.

### Weekly Individual Psychotherapy

In individual therapy, once or twice each week, the teen meets one on one with her therapist to look at issues that have come up during the week following what's called a "treatment target hierarchy." Treatment hierarchy means dealing with the most concerning behaviors first and then moving on to less concerning behaviors. Therefore, self-injurious and suicidal behaviors take first priority. Once these have been addressed, therapy then deals with behaviors that are getting in the way of doing therapy, referred to as "therapy-interfering behaviors," and include missing or coming late to sessions, phoning at unreasonable hours, and not returning phone calls. Once these have been addressed, therapy deals with quality of life issues, such as depression, substance abuse, and chronic truancy. Finally, therapy focuses on working toward improving the quality of one's life.

## Group Skills Training

Each week, the teen meets in a group of other teens struggling with BPD. The group is run by a therapist and co-therapist who teach DBT skills. In individual therapy, the patient and therapist discuss how the teen can specifically apply these skills to her life. Under circumstances in which a group is not available, DBT skills may be taught by another member of the team, perhaps another therapist separate from the individual therapist. I have found that group therapy is sometimes more palatable to the teens in that they are in an environment where other kids have similar experiences and these common struggles make them feel more connected and less alienated.

In group skills training, adolescents learn to use specific skills that are broken down into the following four components:

**Mindfulness.** Mindfulness, the key component to DBT, is the capacity to be present in the moment and to do so in a way that is nonjudgmental. This is so important for teens with BPD because many of them tend to live in the suffering of past sorrows or the anxiety and fear of future failure. Because the future has not come to be and the past is gone, grounding teens in the present moment, and teaching them to do so without judging themselves, allows them to quietly examine their thoughts and feelings rather than be thrown around by the tempest of powerful emotions. Mindfulness allows them to balance strong emotions and excessive rationality to achieve a "wise mind," which is the synthesis of emotion and reason. An example of mindfulness in action is noticing that you are angry without judging it as good or bad, and then not doing anything (such as acting aggressively or avoiding the anger) other than noticing.

**Interpersonal effectiveness.** Interpersonal skills training includes teaching teens with BPD effective strategies for getting what they need, learning to say no effectively, and coping with interpersonal conflict. The skills taught are intended to maximize the chances that their goals in a specific situation will be met, while damaging neither the relationship nor their self-respect. An example of this is learning to say no when necessary. Teens with BPD often violate their own values because they won't say no to situations that will end up leaving them with shame and guilt. Learning to say no with confidence and self-respect is a skill that can be taught.

**Distress tolerance.** DBT emphasizes and recognizes that teens with BPD experience profound pain but that it is necessary to learn to bear this pain skillfully. Distress tolerance skills build on mindfulness skills in the sense that adolescents learn to accept, in a nonjudgmental fashion, both who they are and their current situation without making things worse than they already are. Distress tolerance skills are also concerned with tolerating and surviving the many crises that occur in the life of a child with BPD and with accepting life as it is in the moment. So when teens learn to tolerate the breakup of a relationship without making the situation worse, they are using their distress tolerance skills.

**Emotion regulation.** Adolescents with BPD are frequently emotionally intense and labile. They can be angry, afraid, sad, jealous, depressed, or anxious. The DBT skills for emotion regulation teach teens how to manage emotions rather than being managed by them. The teens learn to recognize and reduce their vulnerability to negative emotions while at the same time building positive emotional experiences. Here we teach skills such as opposite action, so when depressed teens want to isolate and crawl into bed, a behavior that may have become habitual, they need to do the opposite, which is to stay out of their room and call a friend, behaviors that will likely change the intensity of the sadness they are feeling.

## Phone Consultation

This as-needed consultation allows teens to contact either their therapist or an on-call therapist. In the context of after-hour calls, these therapists are known as "skills coaches." The point of skills coaching is to provide help during real-life moments when problems appear and adolescents need help in remembering and applying their newly learned skills.

Telephone contact with the skills coach between sessions is important because it helps the teen in the moment. It is often difficult to remember exactly what happened weeks ago and dealing with the crisis as it occurs allows for effective application of skills and handling the situation differently. These are not therapy sessions, but rather brief (ten- to fifteen-minute) calls. The teen agrees that if he is going to do skills coaching he will use the skills the coach is suggesting. Eventually, the adolescent integrates these skills, and the need for coaching begins to diminish.

Specifically, teens are instructed to call before acting on suicidal or self-injury urges. If the teen has already injured him- or herself, he or she cannot have supportive (skills coaching) phone contact with the therapist for twenty-four hours after self-injury, except for basic medical management (such as telling the person to go to an emergency room). This rule provides reinforcement for adaptive coping and negative consequences for maladaptive behavior.

Phone calls are also sometimes used to resolve misunderstandings and conflicts that arise during therapy sessions, instead of waiting until the next session to deal with the emotions.

Generally, the therapist is available to take the patient's calls around the clock, but in a team practice, there might be an on-call schedule. Patients know the skills coach if he or she is not their primary therapist.

When the concept of phone consultation was initially proposed, many clinicians felt that they would be inundated with phone calls, but generally speaking, this has not been the case at McLean Hospital. We have not found that patients abuse the system. In fact, because many patients are so concerned with bothering the therapist after hours they won't call. I have on occasion told patients that if they do not practice skills coaching with me, even for trivial matters, that I will withhold the next session. The idea is to get them to practice calling for help for when they really need it.

## Therapist Support

Therapists who treat patients with BPD attend weekly therapist consultation team meetings with other DBT-trained colleagues. The purpose of these meetings is to support the therapist and prevent the burnout that is so frequently found in therapists who treat BPD patients. These therapists differ from non-DBT trained therapists because they must accept the following assumptions about the teens, and these assumptions establish the therapist's attitude to the treatment:

1. Teens are doing the best they can.
2. Teens want to have lives worth living.
3. Teens need to do better and gain motivation to change.
4. Teens must learn new behaviors in all relevant contexts.
5. Teens cannot fail in DBT.
6. Teens may not have caused all their own problems but they have to solve them anyway.
7. The lives of teens living with BPD are often unbearable as they are currently being lived.

## DBT FOR THE FAMILY

We have looked at DBT for an individual teen, but BPD affects not only the individual but also family and friends. Family interventions in DBT support the adolescent patient and target the improvement of family relationships.

Individual DBT addresses the problems of the person's emotional vulnerability, which we defined earlier as a high sensitivity (a quick reaction to a stimulus), high reactivity (a more intense reaction to a stimulus), and a slow return to baseline mood state.

But in adolescents especially, it is critical to tackle the invalidating environment as well. That's why the family should participate in treatment for the best possible prognosis. Often, and despite the best of intentions, families have reinforced maladaptive behaviors in the patient (for instance, only acknowledging the patient when she cuts herself). The aim of DBT for the family is to teach them to reinforce an adolescent's effective functioning in a consistent manner, which can, in turn, be a potent change intervention. Further, DBT teaches the adolescent to reinforce effective parental interactions. One important way in which the whole family can be involved is during the initial assessment. This is the point at which the patient and family first appear for treatment. The clinical team meets with and coordinates the family's ongoing participation in the treatment program, identifying all the issues that the family as a whole will be addressing.

An interesting aspect of doing an intake interview with parents present is that when we describe the behaviors that define BPD, parents sometimes recognize some of the very same difficulties they share with the adolescent. At times parents acknowledge that they have some of the borderline traits. This is not uncommon, and research shows that about 60 percent of BPD is due to family genetics. When parents recognize their own struggles, they often request their own individual treatment.

Another important way in which the whole family can be involved in treatment is by attending family group therapy sessions, which require a strong commitment from family members. There are two different models for family group therapy:

**Parents' DBT support group.** These group therapy sessions support the parents of adolescents in DBT treatment and provide parents with an overview of the principles of DBT treatment. This group is only for parents and a DBT therapist; it does not include other family members or the BPD teen.

The purpose of this group is to extend and sustain the DBT treatment structures in the home lives of adolescents and their families and clarify how parents can participate in and reinforce the treatment process. Parents are encouraged to communicate with each other and share successes, frustrations, and the challenges of helping their children modify problematic or dangerous behaviors. Most parents' DBT support groups in the outpatient setting generally meet for an hour and a half each week for six months with a group of six to nine couples.

**Multifamily DBT group.** This group is similar to the parents' DBT support group except that it includes other family members and the adolescent with BPD. The group also shares in all aspects of treatment and research and is run in participation with a DBT clinician. One particularly appealing aspect of this group is that newer group members are able to witness more "experienced" families communicate, problem solve, and demonstrate skill application. Most multifamily groups for outpatients meet for an hour and a half each week for six months with a group of six to nine families.

The sessions are generally divided into two parts. DBT skills are usually taught in the first half, with a particular emphasis on family relationships. The second half of every meeting is a multiple family skills application group. In a consultative manner, family members bring up a family issue on which they would like to focus, and group members apply DBT skills to the problem.

In addition to these group sessions, whenever possible, parents should participate in scheduled treatment reviews with the clinical team. It is essential that the parents know what the adolescent with BPD is being taught so they can implement the strategies.

## BRAIN CHANGES AND DBT

We have recently initiated an extensive research project into brain and behavioral changes in adolescents doing DBT, but our results will not be available for some years. However, there is other early research that DBT changes the brain. In a 2006 study, Knut Schnell, MD, and Sabine Herpertz, MD, wanted to see whether improved emotional regulation following DBT led to changes in the brain. They applied five MRI scans each to six female patients with BPD while the patients attended a twelve-week inpatient treatment program. Then the researchers compared the results to the MRIs of six female patients without BPD. They found that patients who got better using DBT showed less activity in the parts of their brains associated with high levels of arousal (such as the amygdala and the hippocampus). This study appears to show that patients with BPD who use DBT have brain changes leading to less activity in the part of their brains that overreact to stress. This implies that the problem-solving parts of their brains are more active.

At this point in time, DBT provides the best hope for the treatment of adolescents with BPD, especially when provided by a trained, skilled, adherent, compassionate, and flexible treatment team.

## CHAPTER NINE

# Other Effective Approaches

NOT ALL ADOLESCENTS WILL COMMIT TO DBT as a primary psychotherapy, and not all clinics or individual practices offer it. So this chapter examines other types of psychotherapy for BPD.

Helping adolescents with BPD make behavioral changes is difficult for at least two reasons. The first is that teens often feel that simply being told to change their behavior is invalidating. They feel that the therapist is missing the problem and does not understand just how hard their life is. (As a rule, adolescents with BPD frequently feel misunderstood and don't have the experience of adults trying to understand them.) Until the diagnosis of BPD is clear, clinicians often diagnose the teen with depression, oppositional defiant disorder, ADHD, or something else. In these situations where other therapies have not helped, patients have told me that they feel like, "Okay, here we go again. Nothing is ever going to change." This belief can precipitate behavior ranging from withdrawal, noncompliance, and early dropout from treatment to anger, aggression, and self-injury.

The second reason that it can be difficult to work with BPD adolescents is that ignoring the need for the teen to change and not working hard at encouraging such change can have serious consequences. Neglecting the need for change can lead to clinicians missing ongoing despair and hopelessness, and worse, suicide.

## THE DIFFICULTY IN TREATING BPD

People who work with adolescents with BPD face many challenges. These challenges are even more difficult when a therapist works alone in private practice, with no peer support or supervision. The following are a few of these challenges:

- Probably the most frightening behaviors, especially for the new therapist, are the self-destruction and suicidal tendencies, both of which are common in teens with BPD. Many of these behaviors are often not intended as suicidal gestures, but more as a relief from the terrible psychic pain that an adolescent is feeling. In my experience, most suicide attempts in adolescents tend to be below the level of lethality and take place in a situation in which they are likely to be found. However, we have treated many teens whose suicide was prevented by the heroic efforts of families and paramedics who reached them just in time. Many of the adolescents I work with tell me that they reported their suicide attempts to friends via phone calls, instant messages, online, or text messages. Despite this, every attempt must be taken seriously, and any attempt can prove fatal.

- Another issue is that of abandonment. Often when adolescents feel understood by their therapists, they cannot tolerate the fear that the therapist will leave them. The adolescents can become suicidal when the therapist goes on vacation, for example. This fear often puts tremendous stress on therapists, sometimes leading them to refer the patients to someone else, in effect abandoning the adolescents and making their worst fears come true.

- As adolescents get closer to their therapist and begin to open up and reveal themselves, they can become desperate for the closeness, cling to the therapist, and make great demands on the therapist's time.

    On the other hand, the adolescents' experience of closeness has frequently not been a fulfilling one because of previous abandonment, perceived abandonment, or abuse. This fear of closeness and the threat of abandonment can then cause adolescents to start distancing themselves from the therapist as the closeness begins to feel intolerable. Therapists often find it overwhelming to deal with both the clinging and the distancing behavior, which can include tantrums, hostility, and terrible devaluation of the therapist.

• Another difficult issue is that the depression that comes with BPD does not respond all that readily to medication. The depression of adolescents with BPD appears to be more existential in nature. Adolescents with BPD tend to struggle with questions about the meaning of life, but when they find no meaning, they become despondent and hopeless. The depression of adolescents with BPD is not a classical depression characterized by sleep, appetite, and energy disturbances, although a more classical depression can co-occur. Therapists have to be able to tolerate the profound depression that the adolescents feel—sometimes for many years—while continuing the therapeutic work with them.

## TREATMENTS OTHER THAN DBT

Defining both treatment and recovery are important. Recently a friend who has recovered from BPD and is a tremendous advocate for people with BPD and for peer-to-peer support sent me this email:

"Call me a dreamer, but I envision the day when people who have been treated for BPD can be involved in defining whether a treatment is effective or not. A clinician's definition of my 'remission' is not necessarily a life worth living.

"If any therapy is going to claim it brings about 'recovery,' it would be helpful to have the BPD community, including those with the disorder and their families, articulate the standards. If we had agreed-upon standards of recovery, treatment outcomes and goals of treatment would be more concrete. The consumer recovery movement has designed assessment tools to measure levels of hope, resilience, and community integration . . . I find these aspects of recovery to be just as important as developing behavioral control."

How true! Just because a person with BPD no longer cuts and rages does not mean that he or she is "cured." The issues of wholeness, completeness, and hope are essential components of health, and this is no less true in BPD.

Researchers are testing to see whether some of the new treatment approaches work better than existing standards of care. For instance, they compare new treatments (such as DBT) to treatment as usual (TAU). TAU is whatever form of treatment would happen under normal conditions in a typical practice or clinic. New forms of treatment for BPD include the following.

## THE STEPPS PROGRAM

STEPPS stands for Systems Training for Emotional Predictability and Problem Solving. It is a cognitive-behavioral skills training approach, by which BPD is characterized as a disorder of emotion and behavior regulation.

STEPPS was created in the Netherlands in 1998 and rapidly gained use as a treatment for BPD there. Researchers in a 2006 report stated that the reasons for its rapid dissemination included its user-friendly manual, twenty-week duration, ability to maintain the patient's current treatment team, and ease of therapist training. It soon became modified for use in other settings, such as programs for adolescents.

Nancy Blum, MSW, Don St. John, PA, Bruce Pfohl, MD, and Don Bartels, MA, at the University of Iowa Hospitals and Clinics adapted and revised the STEPPS program from its original incarnation. The goal is to provide the patient, closely allied friends, family members, and treating clinicians with a common language to communicate clearly about the disorder and the skills used to manage it. Clients learn specific emotion and behavior management skills. Key professionals, friends, and family members whom clients identify as part of their "reinforcement team" learn to reinforce and support the newly learned skills.

The STEPPS program includes two phases—a twenty-week basic skills group and a one-year, twice-monthly advanced group program.

## COGNITIVE-BEHAVIOR THERAPY

Also known as cognitive-behavioral therapy or CBT, this approach is a form of psychotherapy that emphasizes the role of thinking in how we feel and what we do. It is aimed at pointing out and recognizing unhelpful or destructive patterns of thinking and reacting, and then helping the patient change or replace these patterns with more practical or useful responses. CBT is considered to be the "fastest" of the psychotherapies, with therapists often recommending an average of sixteen total sessions. CBT therapists often point to the fact that psychoanalysis, which is another form of psychotherapy, can take years.

Here's an example of how CBT works. Sheila is an eighteen-year-old who feels depressed and abandoned because her drug-abusing boyfriend left her. A CBT therapist would recognize the triggering event to be that Sheila's boyfriend left her, that this caused her to believe that she is not worth loving, which in turn led her to be depressed.

The therapy would aim to identify irrational beliefs, and the therapist would work with Sheila in challenging the negative thoughts on the basis of evidence from Sheila's experience by reframing it, or reinterpreting it in a more realistic light. This helps Sheila develop more rational beliefs and healthy coping strategies.

From the example above, a CBT therapist would help Sheila realize that there is no evidence that she must have this boyfriend to be lovable. It would be important to recognize that she desires a boyfriend but that not having one at the present time does not make her worthless.

If Sheila realizes that her boyfriend leaving her is disappointing, but not catastrophic, and that it means that she and her boyfriend failed as a couple but that she is not a failure as a person, she will feel sad or disappointed, but not depressed. The sadness and disappointment are likely healthy negative emotions that may lead Sheila to consider her choice in boyfriends next time.

### Psychodynamic Therapy

Psychodynamic therapy is a general term for therapies that try to get patients to bring their unconscious thoughts into conscious awareness. It uses the basic assumption that everyone has an unconscious mind and that feelings, memories, and associations held in the unconscious mind are often too painful to explore. Thus, psychological defenses are formed to protect the person against having to deal with the pain. An example of a defense would be denial, which is when a person refuses to acknowledge what is readily apparent to others. The classic example is an alcoholic who denies that he or she is dependent on the use of alcohol. If these defenses overwhelm the person, psychological problems such as depression can occur. Psychodynamic therapists delve into a person's past, searching for the pain from the past to unlock it and allow it to be expressed in a safe environment.

One issue that many non-psychodynamic therapists have had with this approach is that it might take years of intense therapy to find such pain, which means that patients will be "stuck" in therapy until they can work it out. Because the idea behind this kind of therapy is theoretical, it is difficult to research psychodynamic therapies. It is difficult to measure the unconscious. Also, it is not clear that all psychodynamic therapists practice the therapy in the same way, which makes it further difficult to gauge.

Nevertheless, there is increasing research into the effectiveness of psychodynamic therapies, much of it done by professors Peter Fonagy, MD, and Anthony Bateman, PhD. Bateman recommends modifying psychodynamic therapy for it to be successful. He feels that it is less important to find the ways in which patients defend against painful feelings and more important to use a treatment approach that is collaborative, structured, and organized, which he says "takes into account the behavioral and emotional crises that are inevitable during treatment of BPD."

A psychodynamic therapy approach to BPD can be useful. Many adolescents with BPD are hungry for a deeper understanding of their troubles and relationships, and they engage readily in such therapy. Further, once adolescents have the skills to better regulate their emotions and reactions, they appear better able to look at the nature of their past relationships. Psychodynamic therapy is also useful for adolescents who refuse to do DBT and will engage only in what they call "talk therapy."

## MENTALIZATION-BASED TREATMENT (MBT)

Mentalization is the process by which we make sense of each other and ourselves. It is the way in which we interpret interactions with other people. People with BPD tend to have great difficulty in interpreting the behaviors and intentions of others.

The idea is that we each see ourselves as stable in our minds and in the minds of others, but that because people with BPD had great difficulty in trusting early relationships, they are not certain that what they feel is real. So if a child hurt herself, and her caretaker's response to the child being hurt changed all the time, the child would never have a sense of what to expect and over time would question what she should feel. Imagine that a child was sad and that in some circumstances the parents soothed the child, in other instances they yelled at the child to get over it, and yet in others they simply neglected the child. How does the child know whether his inner experience is real? How does the child ever learn what to expect?

From an MBT perspective, the focus in treatment is to help teens stabilize their sense of self. In therapy this is done by getting the teen emotionally aroused. This approach needs to be balanced—that is, done in not too intense and yet not too detached a manner. Because teens with BPD are exquisitely sensitive to all interpersonal interactions, the MBT therapist needs to be aware that therapy will inevitably provoke anxiety, and thereby trigger uncertainties from the patient's childhood. This will in turn lead to escalating and intense emotions and an inability to accurately understand the therapist's motives. Exploring what happens during these moments in therapy is core to the therapy and teaches teens to regulate themselves in similar situations.

## FAMILY THERAPY

Family therapy is the treatment of more than one member of a family in the same therapy session. It has been a critical component of adolescent therapy for many years. The core theory is that the behavior of individuals is influenced and maintained by the way other family members interact with them.

Family therapy has two main goals: It should both educate the family on BPD and treat the family. Both of these goals in turn help the adolescent feel understood. Education, communication, reinforcing adaptive behavior, and collaborative problem solving should be at the core of family therapy.

When we at McLean Hospital begin to explore the features of BPD in family therapy, a parent sometimes identifies with the BPD symptoms and looks for therapy for him- or herself. This in turn has motivated some teens to continue in therapy because they see their parents getting help, and for those parents who get help it has led to improvements in themselves and better relationships with their families.

During family therapy, the therapist should be aware of the nonverbal communication between the patient and the parents. The therapist should point these out during the session to make the family aware of any maladaptive interactions.

A particular type of family therapy is parent skills training groups, which aim to provide support and education for families who often struggle with their children's extreme behaviors. Such groups can also target the sometimes dysfunctional environment to which the adolescent plans to return as well as teach the family members how to model and reinforce adaptive behaviors.

## Interpersonal Psychotherapy

Interpersonal psychotherapy (IPT) is a short-term, highly structured type of psychotherapy that focuses on one area of interpersonal problems. It can be used when a major problem is poor interpersonal relationships, in terms of both number and quality of the relationships. It generally lasts for twelve to sixteen weeks.

In IPT, the patient and therapist generally focus on existing relationships as well as the relationship with the therapist. Together they try to identify common maladaptive patterns to relationships. In using the therapeutic relationship, the therapist aims to identify problematic interactions and patterns of behavior that occur during the therapy, with the idea that this understanding will serve as a template for further relationships. Because IPT helps build social skills, some clinicians believe that it can benefit patients with BPD whose major problem is interpersonal deficits.

## Supportive Psychotherapy

Supportive psychotherapy is the most widely practiced form of individual psychotherapy today. It emphasizes the therapeutic relationship, environmental interventions, education, advice and suggestions, encouragement and praise, limit setting and prohibitions, and undermining maladaptive defenses while enhancing the patient's adaptive defenses, strengths, and talents.

A therapist practicing supportive therapy uses active listening and helps patients see alternatives to their hopelessness. The therapist helps patients move toward creating a meaningful set of plans and goals. Because of this, patients need a sense that the supportive psychotherapist can cope with the despair and hold on to hope for the patient's recovery. The belief is that as patients establish trust in their therapists, they learn to generalize that experience to significant others in their lives. The goal is that they eventually learn healthy self-advocacy to get their needs met rather than what is often seen as "manipulative" behavior.

Robert Friedel, MD, author of *Borderline Personality Disorder Demystified*, is a strong advocate of this approach, but as with any form of therapy, supervision is essential, especially for the inexperienced therapist.

## COGNITIVE-ANALYTIC THERAPY

This therapy uses a collaborative approach between the patient and the therapist to identify self-states, which are the various ways that a person behaves under different circumstances. Generally, we all have self-states that we pull together into one sense of who we are. People with BPD, however, cannot easily do this. Adolescents with BPD often describe being very different (or having different personas) with different people or in different situations.

Cognitive-analytic therapy (CAT) operates on the belief that inadequate parenting leads to an inability to integrate these self-states, leading to rapid shifts between these states and further overall behavioral instability in interpersonal situations. CAT supposes that a person's difficulty is because she developed patterns of unchanging and unhealthy behaviors, and that at times this is simply because the patient had few options in the choices she could have made. This is best illustrated in the following case example.

Kathy was an eighteen-year-old with BPD who spent her entire life in state custody and for the past six years, in a residential home. She was admitted to our unit saying that she felt intense loneliness much of the time, a feeling that was temporarily relieved by sex with boys or girls, many of them strangers. However, even this relief was short-lived and often left her feeling even lonelier. CAT would recognize that the interpersonal behavioral patterns that had served Kathy well in the residential home, where staff and other kids often came and went, favored both rapid and relatively nondiscriminating attachment and equally rapid detachment. In that situation, Kathy was actively discouraged from making close friendships with staff members. Now in a "normal" life, she continued to use the pattern of quick and shallow attachments and detachment. This approach now led to her form superficial relationships with similarly uncaring others and feel lonely as a result. The CAT therapist would work with Kathy to recognize her maladaptive patterns and to change these patterns by, for instance, practicing change in therapy.

## SCHEMA THERAPY

Schema therapy is a relatively new treatment for BPD developed by Jeffrey Young, PhD, a faculty member at Columbia University. Young defines schemas as "broad pervasive themes regarding oneself and one's relationship with others, developed during childhood and elaborated throughout one's lifetime, and dysfunctional to a significant degree." In other words, these are self-defeating life patterns.

Schema theory holds that early patterns have their origins in negative childhood experiences and are particularly resistant to change. For instance, a patient whose parents were cold and distant might have a pattern of getting involved in intimate relationships that don't meet her needs. Then when her needs aren't met, she becomes angry. In part this anger is justified, but in another part it is an overreaction and a response to her experience from childhood of never having had her needs met. Schema therapy consists initially of identifying and recognizing the early patterns of behavior, which the therapist and patient discuss. These patterns are then altered using cognitive reconstruction, behavioral and experiential techniques, and discussion of issues that arise in the therapist-patient relationship.

Schema therapists view patients with BPD compassionately and as needy. The therapist serves as the "good parent" to the patient's vulnerable side. Through the therapist's "limited reparenting," patients with BPD develop a strong, healthy side to calm, soothe, and care for their emotionally intense, changeable temperament.

## ELECTROCONVULSIVE THERAPY

Electroconvulsive therapy, also known as electroshock or ECT, involves the induction of an artificial seizure by passing electricity through a patient's brain, and it is commonly used in depression and other mood disorders. ECT is sometimes used as a treatment for people with BPD who also have depression, although research has shown that it is not very effective in relieving their symptoms.

In a 2004 study, researchers noted that 30 to 80 percent of patients with major depression would be diagnosed with a co-occurring personality disorder during their lifetime and that as many as 50 percent of patients with BPD will experience major depression at some point. Further, the researchers noted that depressed patients with personality disorders often fail to respond to common medications for depression and that they suffer frequent relapses back into depression.

ECT is often considered as a treatment option in patients for whom different antidepressants have failed to lift the depression. In the 2004 study, the researchers found that people with depression who had BPD did not respond as well to ECT as depressed people without BPD and further, the worse the BPD, the less likely the patients were to improve. As is true of many treatments for depression, having co-occurring BPD makes the treatment of the depression far more difficult. Therefore, although ECT *is* used in these cases, a dramatic improvement should not be expected. Having said that, I do refer patients for ECT and in some cases have seen remarkable improvement in symptoms. More research is needed in the use of ECT in BPD patients.

## PARTIAL HOSPITALIZATION

In partial hospitalization, the teen continues to live at home, but goes to the treatment center three to seven days a week for one to three weeks. In a 1999 study, Fonagy and Bateman studied the effect of a partial hospitalization group that offered psychoanalytic therapy compared to a standard psychiatric care group (a group of patients receiving whatever type of therapy they were receiving in their partial hospitalization) in patients with BPD. Treatment was up to eighteen months. The researchers measured the frequency of suicide attempts and acts of self-harm; the number and duration of inpatient admissions; the use of psychiatric medication; and self-reported depression, anxiety, distress, interpersonal function, and social adjustment.

The researchers found that patients who were partially hospitalized showed better outcomes on all measures, including an improvement in depressive symptoms, a decrease in suicidal thinking and suicide attempts, less self-injury, reduced inpatient days, and better social and interpersonal function. These improvements began at six months and continued until the end of treatment at eighteen months. In contrast, the standard psychiatric care group showed limited change or deterioration over the same period. The researchers concluded that psychoanalytically oriented partial hospitalization is superior to standard psychiatric care for patients with BPD.

## RESIDENTIAL TREATMENT

Some adolescents with BPD need a structured out-of-home placement for their behavioral or emotional problems. Residential treatment facilities provide twenty-four-hour care with counseling, therapy, and trained staff (which can include psychiatrists, psychologists, nurses, social workers, and mental health counselors). Adolescents are usually placed in residential treatment only after their families have unsuccessfully tried other ways to help the child. If residential treatment is required for an extended period of time (four months or more), it is known as a long-term residential setting. If the length of time is shorter than that, it is known as a short-term, or acute, residential setting. As with most therapies, residential treatment works best when the family is involved through family counseling.

Our residential treatment unit at McLean Hospital has been working with borderline adolescents since 2007. Sometimes, despite having completed our program, some teens continue to struggle with impulsivity and the urge to self-injure. This is particularly true of our younger teens and may be a reflection of an immature brain that needs more time to develop. In such cases we sometimes refer these young people to a residential treatment center (RTC), which is a residential level of care that can last for a year or more and that includes a school curriculum. Such RTCs are not developed for the treatment of BPD specifically, but instead cater to a broad range of mental health issues.

There are many benefits to residential treatment. For one, a highly trained and experienced staff is less vulnerable to getting caught in polarized positions such as when a staff person is seen as all good or all bad, and what are known as boundary violations, which is when a staff person crosses the physical bounds of the patient–therapist relationship.

## HOSPITALIZATION

Although admitting people with BPD to the hospital is an option, long-term inpatient treatment is neither generally available nor advisable. There is increasing research that hospitalization for BPD should be minimized.

Canadian psychiatrist Joel Paris, MD, has been consistent and clear in pointing out that hospitalizations are not generally necessary—or even useful—for the majority of patients with BPD. In a 2004 article that examined the value of hospitalization for chronically suicidal patients with BPD, Paris recognized that although one in ten of those patients might eventually complete suicide, the outcome of suicide is not readily predictable. He noted that hospitalization is of unproven value for suicide prevention and that it can often produce negative effects, such as teens learning that all they have to say is that they are suicidal and want to get out of their house in order to avoid the repercussions of some consequence for inappropriate behavior.

Another problem is that adolescents sometimes learn more about self-destructive behavior from other self-destructive kids *in* the hospital than out of it! Paris further argued that studies show day treatment to be more effective than hospital admission, and that chronic suicidality could best be managed in an outpatient setting.

Even though hospitalization might not prevent suicide, hospitalization must be considered when a patient's suicidal thinking becomes a suicidal plan with intent to carry out the plan or when there has been significant self-injurious behavior requiring medical attention (such as laceration of tendons, deep cutting with blood loss, or a combination of self-injurious behavior and overdosing with an intent to commit suicide). This is especially true when patients with BPD have a clear episode of major depression or worsening substance abuse.

Hospitalization has not been shown to prevent suicide in teens with BPD. However, once hospitalized, if a teen with BPD who has been suicidal is to be discharged, a careful assessment of all the biosocial factors in the patient's life needs be taken into account prior to discharge.

Marsha Linehan, PhD, once quipped that the best hospital for a borderline patient was a "dirty, dark place with hard beds and bad food where no one will ever talk to them or ever visit!" The purpose of this was to avoid reinforcing hospitalization, because many patients with BPD can be highly charming and become staff favorites. Some patients with BPD learn to get hospitalized to have the staff give them the attention they so desperately crave.

Although the data for the teen with BPD who is self-injurious and suicidal strongly favors a DBT approach, it is by no means the only therapy available, and the flexible therapist should always favor what works over a specific therapy. The goal is to help the teen, not to stick to a specific therapy, particularly if that specific therapy is not working.

## CHAPTER TEN

# The Effect of Medication on Adolescents with BPD

THERE IS NO SIMPLE ANSWER or quick fix to BPD. Although medications are frequently prescribed, often in large quantities, none of them cures this disorder. This is not only evident from the research literature but also from clinical practice and, in many cases, parents note that medications have only marginally, if at all, helped their children. The following email could represent the frustrations and feelings of many parents of adolescents with BPD.

"My daughter is a fourteen-and-a-half-year-old freshman at a local public high school here in Connecticut, but she is currently an inpatient in the adolescent psych unit under the direction of a child and adolescent psychiatrist. This is her eighth hospitalization, and for over three years she has been treated for depression, bipolar, anxiety, ADHD, you name it. Since her first hospitalization, she has been treated with Depakote, Lexapro, Seroquel, Prozac, Zoloft, Abilify, Clonidine, Ritalin, Benadryl, Trazadone, and others I can't remember. She is on five different drugs at the moment. Now she is diagnosed with bipolar II with borderline personality.

"I'm feeling after three years of medications that little progress has been made.

"Her psychiatrist has struggled with her diagnosis. I think that he has shifted to the borderline diagnosis because none of the meds seem to help and she seems to meet the profile.

"Her uncle had bipolar disorder, but he has done well on lithium for many years. I myself was hospitalized for depression ten years ago and after a year on medications I was taken off and am doing well except for the troubles with my daughter.

"Basically my question is: Are there other medications we can use?"

The answer is that medication can only be a part of a more comprehensive solution for adolescents with BPD, and if prescribed, there has to be a clear rationale rather than the sometimes desperate attempt by a prescribing clinician to do something.

## WHY PRESCRIBE?

Clinicians prescribe medications for BPD for several reasons. The first is that BPD has mood symptoms and impulsivity that, if part of a mood disorder, will sometimes respond to medication. One important principle in the treatment of BPD is to slow teens down enough to allow them to learn and then use problem-solving skills. If medication can reduce impulsivity, improve attention, and lift the weight of depression, it might be useful in getting the teen interested and focused enough to attend to therapy.

The second reason why clinicians prescribe medications for BPD is that BPD frequently co-occurs with other disorders—such as anxiety, depression, and bipolar disorder—which can respond to medication.

In an attempt to more specifically address the role of medication in BPD, the American Psychiatric Association (APA) issued a *Practice Guide-*

*line for the Treatment of Patients with Borderline Personality Disorder* in 2001. It recognized that psychotherapy is the primary form of treatment for BPD, but it also recommended the use of medication to target specific symptoms. The APA states:

> "Pharmacotherapy [medication] is used to treat symptoms during periods of acute decompensation [i.e., unstable behavior] as well as trait vulnerabilities. Symptoms exhibited by patients with borderline personality disorder often fall within three behavioral dimensions— affective dysregulation [i.e., mood symptoms], impulsive-behavioral dyscontrol [i.e., impulsivity], and cognitive-perceptual difficulties [i.e., paranoia]—for which specific [medical] treatment strategies can be used."

For mood-related symptoms and impulsivity, the APA suggested antidepressants, anti-anxiety drugs, mood stabilizers, and, as a last resort, electroconvulsive therapy (ECT). For paranoia, hallucinations, and dissociations, the APA recommended low doses of antipsychotic drugs.

However, the APA made these recommendations with adults with BPD in mind. When it comes to children and adolescents, the use of psychiatric medications has become increasingly scrutinized and debated. Controversy has arisen over the rampant use of stimulants to treat ADHD, the increase in suicidal thinking caused by certain antidepressants, and the use of unapproved medications for certain psychiatric conditions. Further, concern has focused on the effect that high doses—and frequently, multiple medications—have on the developing adolescent brain.

Many adolescents arrive on our unit already using, and having been tried on, multiple medications. We often see few positive effects to all the medication, but many of the side effects, such as weight gain, acne, mental slowing, and overall sedation. It is, however, sometimes true that the medications simply need to be adjusted to optimize treatment. The lowest dose possible that treats the symptoms is ideal.

Patients may need to be weaned off one medication before starting others, depending on the medication. The symptoms of too-rapid withdrawal from psychiatric drugs can include extreme nausea, anxiety, insomnia, restlessness, muscular reactions, and even odd behavior.

In the case of minor tranquilizers and sedatives, the reactions to sudden withdrawal can be life-threatening, such as the sudden onset of seizures. Sudden discontinuation of a selective serotonin reuptake inhibitor (SSRI), such as Prozac, can lead to severe flu-like symptoms, such as headache, diarrhea, nausea, vomiting, chills, dizziness, fatigue, and insomnia. Agitation, impaired concentration, vivid dreams, depersonalization, irritability, and suicidal thoughts sometimes occur. These symptoms last anywhere from one to seven weeks and vary in intensity. Patients and families should consult a physician before making the decision to come off any prescribed medication.

## GETTING YOUR ADOLESCENT TO TAKE MEDICATION

Teens who are prescribed medication need to take it consistently and as prescribed. Making sudden changes can lead to severe withdrawal side effects.

Yet it can be difficult to convince adolescents to take medication. I have noted six main reasons as to why they don't want to take the pills: anger, side effects, impulsivity, rule-breaking behavior, negative attitudes toward treatment, and substance abuse. They might be angry that they have the mental illness or angry at their parents and so refuse the medications in protest. Side effects such as acne, weight gain, mental dulling, and sedation can be intolerable. They might impulsively decide that they are no longer going to take the medications, or simply want to defy their parents' wishes. Many teens have had unsuccessful pervious therapies and may simply be negative about any form of treatment. Finally, in some circumstances, alcohol and other drug abuse, whether intentional or not, takes precedence over medication use.

Compliance with any treatment including medications tends to be greatest when parents and adolescents agree on four things: the purpose of the medication, who is responsible for medication administration, their understanding of medication instructions, and the effectiveness of the medication. Better compliance occurs with adolescents understanding their psychiatric illness. An open, honest, and thorough level of communication between adolescents and their families is essential.

An interesting component to compliance is that both parents and adolescents have tremendous access to information because of the Internet. Some websites discuss each and every possible side effect, even if these side effects are not typically seen in clinical practice. Because parents and adolescents might ask about a specific issue, the prescribing clinician must be aware of the possibility of "too much knowledge" being a deterrent to compliance.

## MEDICATIONS USED TO TREAT BPD

No medication has received approval from the Federal Drug Administration (FDA) for the treatment of adolescent BPD. In this section we will discuss medications that have been studied in treating BPD, although these studies have solely focused on adults with BPD.

### ANTIPSYCHOTIC MEDICATIONS

Several antipsychotic medications (which are also called neuroleptic medications) have been used to treat BPD. These drugs were originally developed to treat schizophrenia.

**Olanzapine (Zyprexa).** This atypical antipsychotic was approved by the FDA for the treatment of schizophrenia, acute mania in bipolar disorder, agitation associated with schizophrenia and bipolar disorder, and as maintenance treatment for both bipolar disorder and psychotic depression.

Research has shown that olanzapine can reduce anxiety, paranoia, anger/hostility, and interpersonal sensitivity in BPD. (Interpersonal sensitivity is the accuracy and appropriateness of perceptions, judgments, and responses that we have with respect to one another. People with BPD are sometimes too interpersonally sensitive, and they overjudge situations, such as feeling that no one loves them or that people are talking about them.) However, one concern about the use of olanzapine, especially in adolescents, is the tremendous amount of weight gain it can cause, even more than other atypical antipsychotic medications. (Atypical antipsychotic agents differ from "typical" medications in that they cause fewer side effects at doses that produce comparable control of symptoms.) Adolescents with BPD frequently have poor self-images, and little could make it worse than weight gain. That's why I have not prescribed olanzapine in a dolescent BPD.

**Quetiapine (Seroquel).** Another atypical antipsychotic medication, quetiapine has received FDA approval for the treatment of schizophrenia, acute mania in bipolar disorder, and depressive episodes associated with bipolar disorder. Although it hasn't been approved by the FDA for other uses, doctors prescribe quetiapine to treat post-traumatic stress disorder (PTSD), alcoholism, obsessive–compulsive disorder (OCD), and anxiety disorders, and as a sedative for sleep difficulties. (When doctors prescribe a medication for a condition other than one for which it has been approved by the FDA, it's called an off-label use. This practice is common not only in psychiatry but also across medicine.)

Research has shown that quetiapine is effective in patients with BPD for treating low mood, anxiety, and aggression. I have found quetiapine to be effective in reducing anxiety in some adolescents with BPD. Anxiety frequently plagues adolescents, but anti-anxiety medications—such as the benzodiazepines clonazepam (Klonopin) and lorazepam (Ativan)—have their own problems. These medications are potentially addictive, and drug addiction can be a problem for adolescents with BPD.

**Aripiprazole (Abilify).** This is another atypical antipsychotic medication that the FDA approved to treat schizophrenia and acute manic and mixed episodes associated with bipolar disorder. Studies have shown that aripiprazole reduces depression and anger in patients with BPD.

**Risperidone (Risperdal).** This atypical antipsychotic medication is most often used to treat schizophrenia and other psychotic states, but it is also prescribed for acute manic episodes of bipolar disorder. The FDA has approved it for the treatment of irritability associated with autistic disorder, including symptoms of aggression toward others, deliberate self-injuriousness, temper tantrums, and quickly changing moods in children and adolescents ages five to sixteen. Research in BPD has found that at an average dose of between 3 and 4 milligrams of risperidone per day, there is a significant reduction in aggression and an overall reduction in depressive symptoms.

As with all medications, antipsychotics come with side effects. The FDA requires the manufacturers of all atypical antipsychotics to include a warning about the risk of increased blood sugar and diabetes with these drugs. In addition, increased fat levels in the blood may be an issue with this medication. Some atypical antipsychotics cause tremendous weight gain.

This set of side effects is particularly worrisome because two of them (impaired glucose metabolism and obesity), combined with high triglycerides in the blood, make up what is known as metabolic syndrome, a condition that may increase the risk of cardiovascular disease. Data suggest that olanzapine may be more likely to cause adverse metabolic effects than some of the other atypical antipsychotic medications.

## Antidepressant Medications

Media coverage in the past few years has focused on the use of antidepressants in children. Here is a typical warning the FDA has asked manufacturers of antidepressant medication to include in their prescribing information:

> "Antidepressant medications are used to treat a variety of conditions, including depression and other mental/mood disorders. These medications can help prevent suicidal thoughts/attempts and provide other important benefits. However, studies have shown that a small number of people (especially children and teenagers) who take antidepressants for any condition may experience worsening depression, other mental/mood symptoms, or suicidal thoughts/attempts. Therefore, it is very important to talk with the doctor about the risks and benefits of antidepressant medication (especially for children and teenagers), even if treatment is not for a mental/mood condition."

Trials of SSRIs, such as Prozac, and other antidepressant medications in children and adolescents with major depressive disorder, OCD, and other psychiatric disorders show that the average risk of suicidal thinking was 4 percent, which was twice as high as that in people who took a placebo (sugar pill) in the studies. No suicides occurred in these trials.

The FDA required that the following black-box warning be included for all types of antidepressants:

> "Antidepressants increase the risk of suicidal thinking and behavior (suicidality) in children and adolescents with MDD [major depressive disorder, another term for major depression] and other psychiatric disorders. Anyone considering the use of an antidepressant in a child or adolescent for any clinical use must balance the risk of increased suicidality with the clinical need. Patients who are started on therapy should be observed closely for clinical worsening, suicidality, or un-

usual changes in behavior. Families and caregivers should be advised to closely observe the patient and to communicate with the prescriber."

The FDA requires manufacturers to include a statement with the medication regarding whether the particular drug is approved for any pediatric indication(s) and, if so, which one(s).

I have found increasing suicidal ideation with the use of antidepressants; however, I have also found that starting these medications at much lower doses than suggested by the manufacturer appears to lead to less rapid changes in brain chemistry, which may lessen the irritability and suicidality. It is true that starting at a lower dose may mean that it takes longer for the treatment to take effect, but this is certainly better than the intolerability of suicidal thoughts.

**Selective serotonin reuptake inhibitors (SSRIs).** In the past, because of the potentially lethal side effects of older classes of antidepressants, researchers looked for drugs that maintained the benefits but shed the more troublesome side effects. The SSRIs were developed and are now the most commonly prescribed class of antidepressants. They work by blocking the reuptake of serotonin from the synapse back into the nerve, thereby increasing the amount of serotonin that is available in the synapse. The SSRIs include fluoxetine (Prozac), sertraline (Zoloft), paroxetine (Paxil), fluvoxamine (Luvox), citalopram (Celexa), and escitalopram (Lexapro).

Two of these SSRIs in particular have some research support for being prescribed for BPD: fluoxetine and fluvoxamine. Fluoxetine is used in the treatment of depression, body dysmorphic disorder, OCD, bulimia nervosa, premenstrual dysphoric disorder, and panic disorder. Compared to other SSRIs, fluoxetine can have a strong energizing effect, which sometimes leads the adolescents we treat to complain of feeling more irritable. Fluoxetine has been shown to reduce the chronic dysphoria (depression) and impulsive aggression common among borderline patients.

Fluvoxamine is used to treat OCD by decreasing persistent and unwanted thoughts (obsessions) and urges to perform repeated tasks (compulsions such as hand-washing, counting, and checking) that interfere with daily living. Although not approved for depression or bulimia, it is sometimes used for both of these conditions. Research has shown that it can produce a long-lasting reduction in rapid mood shifts, but not in impulsivity or aggression when compared to a placebo (sugar pill). In an earlier chapter we looked at the hypothalamic pituitary adrenal (HPA) axis, the group of nerves and hormones that deal with human stress and that is very active in people who have been abused or experienced trauma. Research has shown that fluvoxamine reduces the overactivity of the HPA axis in BPD patients with a history of sustained childhood abuse.

**Tricyclic antidepressants.** Tricyclic antidepressants are drugs that work by preventing the reuptake or repackaging of the neurotransmitters norepinephrine, dopamine, or serotonin by nerve cells. The neurotransmitter theory of depression is that these "chemicals" are low in the brain. Generally, after a neurotransmitter has been released by a nerve cell, it is either broken down or taken back into the nerve cell. The purpose of taking the neurotransmitter back into the cell so that it can be repackaged and then used again. This process is known as reuptake. By preventing or blocking the reuptake, more of the chemical is available in the brain, and thus available to counter depression caused by low levels of the chemical. The tricyclic antidepressants include amitriptyline, nortriptyline, desipramine, and imipramine. (I haven't included brand names for these drugs because many of them are old and no longer branded.)

Although this class of medications works very well for depression, it is seldom used today as a first choice because of potential side effects. These drugs can cause bladder problems, constipation, dry mouth, sexual problems, blurred vision, dizziness, drowsiness, and unwanted weight changes. Far more serious, they can cause the heart to have abnormal beats and rhythms. When taken in an overdose or a suicide attempt, they can quickly lead to death from cardiac arrest.

Imipramine is an old antidepressant that has also been used to treat attention deficit disorder (ADD) and bedwetting in children. Because of its side effects, it is rarely used in child psychiatry today. However, imipramine has been studied in children with BPD. In a 1981 study, the authors looked at three case histories of children with BPD. Each child failed to benefit from intensive hospital treatment until imipramine was added to the treatment. Then there was substantial improvement in peer interactions, treatment compliance, and bizarre behaviors.

## MOOD-STABILIZING/ANTISEIZURE DRUGS

This class of drugs has been approved to even out moods and decrease seizures in conditions such as epilepsy. However, sometimes doctors prescribe these drugs for BPD.

**Divalproex or ivalproex sodium (Depakote).** This drug has been approved to treat manic episodes associated with bipolar disorder. A manic episode is a distinct period of abnormally and persistently elevated, expansive, or irritable mood, with symptoms such as talking too fast, motor hyperactivity, reduced need for sleep, racing thoughts, and poor judgment. This medication also treats epilepsy and migraines.

A 2002 study found that divalproex sodium was a safe and effective agent in the treatment of women with BPD and comorbid bipolar II disorder, significantly decreasing irritability and anger, the tempestuousness of relationships, and impulsive aggressiveness.

Common side effects of this drug are tiredness, dizziness, upset stomach, vomiting, tremors, hair loss, and irritability. Weight gain affects 30 to 50 percent of people who take Depakote. Exercise and a reduced-calorie diet can help, but nevertheless weight gain is a problem.

Most of the aforementioned side effects are "nuisance" side effects and disappear after stopping the medication or as the adolescent gets used to the medication. However, there are rare side effects that require medical attention, such as weakness, sluggishness, swelling of the face, loss of appetite, vomiting, and yellowish eyes or skin, which may indicate a serious liver problem. Other serious concerns are pain in the abdomen, upset stomach, vomiting, or loss of appetite, which may indicate a serious pancreas problem. Finally, easy bruising, nosebleed, and other abnormal bleeding can occur, which may indicate a serious blood system problem.

**Topiramate (Topamax).** This antiseizure drug is only approved for the treatment of seizures or epilepsy. In psychiatry, it has been used—though not approved—for rapid cycling (a form of bipolar with rapid mood changes when a person has four or more episodes of mania and or depression per year), mixed bipolar states, and PTSD. It has also been successfully used to decrease binge eating and overeating caused by other psychiatric medications. Unlike other mood stabilizers, topiramate does not appear to cause weight gain, and in fact it may actually cause weight loss.

Topiramate has been shown to be safe and effective in the treatment of anger in women with BPD, and it may also cause significantly greater weight loss in patients with BPD compared with a placebo. Again, this is important to consider because many of the medications used in psychiatry cause significant weight gain.

The major side effects of topiramate are psychomotor slowing, memory problems (which are of special concern with adolescents in school and are particularly common when a high starting dose is used or the medication dose is increased suddenly), fatigue, confusion, sleepiness, and kidney stones, which affect only about 1 percent of people who take the drug.

**Lamotrigine (Lamictal).** This is an anticonvulsant that the FDA approved in 2003 to treat bipolar disorder. Psychiatry increasingly uses it because of its relatively benign side effects. It has also been used in certain people with major depression and PTSD, although it is not approved for these conditions. Research has shown that both BPD and bipolar symptoms improved in bipolar patients with BPD taking lamotrigine.

About one in ten people taking lamotrigine develops a mild rash (like a sunburn) and about one in a thousand develops a severe rash (like a bad case of poison ivy) that requires treatment. The more severe the rash, the less likely it is that a patient will be able to continue the medication. In any case, all rashes should receive immediate medical attention. A few deaths have occurred in people who have developed a severe, lamotrigine-induced rash known as Stevens–Johnson syndrome.

In clinical practice, and as with the use of many drugs in adolescent psychiatry, side effects are dose-dependent. For lamotrigine, the rash is more likely to develop when the initial dose is high or started too rapidly or when someone is also taking divalproex. Other side effects tend to be nuisance-like in nature; however, patients should be aware of the following rare side effects: agitation, anxiety, irritability, difficulty concentrating, confusion, depression, and emotional instability.

**Oxcarbazepine (Trileptal).** An anticonvulsant and mood-stabilizing drug, oxcarbazepine is used primarily in the treatment of epilepsy and bipolar disorder. A 2006 study of seventeen patients with BPD by Silvio Bellino, MD, and colleagues from the University of Turin in Italy found oxcarbazepine to be effective and well tolerated. Side effects can include fatigue, nausea, vomiting, headache, dizziness, drowsiness, and blurred or double vision. It can cause hyponatremia (low blood sodium), so blood sodium levels should be tested if the patient complains of severe fatigue.

### BENZODIAZEPINE ANTI-ANXIETY DRUGS

It has been my clinical experience that the benzodiazepines are not effective in patients with personality disorders because they are easily addictive and can cause excitement and other paradoxical reactions in patients with BPD. These drugs include the following.

**Alprazolam (Xanax).** This drug is indicated for the treatment of generalized anxiety disorder (GAD) and the management of panic disorder with or without agoraphobia.

**Clonidine (Catapres).** This medication is better known for its use in treating high blood pressure. However, it is frequently used in psychiatry because it appears to block the effects of adrenaline, which can lead to anxiety, so although not approved by the FDA for these purposes, it has also been used to relieve anxiety, alleviate sleeping difficulties, aid in alcohol withdrawal, and help smoking cessation and other conditions. Research has shown that clonidine significantly reduces the aversive inner tension (a very unpleasant mood or inner, emotional state), dissociative symptoms, urge to commit self-injury, and suicidal ideations commonly found in BPD. The strongest effects are seen between thirty and sixty minutes after taking the drug. Common side effects can include chest pain, low blood pressure, weakness, and sedation.

## NATURAL REMEDIES USED TO TREAT BPD

Many people remember a time when mothers and grandmothers made children swallow spoonfuls of fish oil every day. They claimed that it was good for everything that ailed or could possibly ail the young ones. It looks like research is proving that this old wisdom may have merit. The big issue is the intake of what are known as the essential fatty acids (EFAs).

Fatty acids are components of fats. EFAs are those that you need to get from your diet because your body cannot produce them. Two fatty acids vital to our survival are EPA (eicosapentaenoic acid) and DHA (doco-sahexaenoic acid). Some researchers consider EPA to be the single most vital nutrient in brain function and nerve stimulation. DHA is thought to constitute a major building block of the brain, forming about 8 percent of the brain by weight.

An important fact is that EFAs make up 45 percent of the fatty acids in the membranes of the nerve cells in our brains and are critical to nerve cell function. EFAs make cell membranes more fluid, and omega-3 fatty acids in particular improve communication between the brain cells.

Many studies support the intake of omega-3 fatty acids for good health, most significantly mental well-being and cardiac health. As a na-tion, we have reduced our consumption of fish and markedly increased the amount of refined foods in our diets. Because of this, it is estimated that the amount of omega-3 fatty acids in our diet has reduced somewhere between 50 and 80 percent.

There has been much research on the importance of EFAs as they re-late to psychiatric disorders. One study found that fifty-three children with ADHD had significantly lower blood levels of EFAs, compared with forty-three children who were not diagnosed with ADHD. A 2004 study looked at the relationship between dietary intake of EFAs and hostility in young people. Researchers found that consumption of any fish rich in EFAs, com-pared with no consumption, was associated with lower odds of hostility in young people. Depression has been directly related to fish consumption. A 2001 study reported a strong relationship between fish consumption and lower rates of depression in countries such as Japan, Korea, and Taiwan. Between these three studies, we have evidence that low EFAs are associated with depression, anger, and impulsivity, which are three major symptoms of BPD.

In 2003, Mary Zanarini of McLean Hospital and colleagues con-ducted an eight-week study of the omega-3 fatty acids in twenty female patients with BPD and compared their results to ten women with BPD who did not take omega-3 fatty acids. They found that omega-3 fatty acids were superior to a placebo in diminishing aggression as well as the severity of depressive symptoms in BPD. The researchers concluded that omega-3 fatty acids are a potentially useful form of medication therapy in BPD.

On a personal note, I am not a big advocate of multivitamins or other supplements. However, it is increasingly clear that we have significantly reduced the amount of omega-3 fatty acids in our diets. Because of this, it is the one supplement that I take and that I encourage my own kids to take. It is not a cure for BPD, but in people not getting enough fish in their diets, a supplement may be necessary for healthy brain function.

## TREATMENT OF BPD CO-OCCURRING WITH ANOTHER PSYCHIATRIC ILLNESS

Having BPD occur with any other condition forces the clinician to consider that an already challenging treatment is going to require even more thought and energy. For example, consider BPD occurring with bipolar disorder.

In a 2005 study, researchers noted that patients who suffered from both BPD and bipolar I disorder posed unique treatment challenges. They found that patients who had both disorders took more than twice as long for their symptoms to stabilize than those with bipolar disorder alone. The bipolar–BPD group received significantly more atypical mood-stabilizing medications per year than the bipolar-only group. The rate of patients dropping out of therapy was also higher in the BPD–bipolar group.

Now that you are versed in BPD's treatment approaches, the next chapter will look at specific strategies for parents and caregivers to use when dealing with their BPD adolescent.

## CHAPTER ELEVEN

# Tips and Strategies for Parents of BPD Adolescents

THE MOST COMMON QUESTION that parents ask when dealing with their child with BPD is: "Can you tell me what to do?" All of the parenting techniques that may have worked with their other kids don't always seem to work with their child with BPD. As a parent, you know that you are doing the very best that you can. However, children with BPD can often feel that it is their parents' intention to make them feel worse. They can lash out often and, eventually, most parents get worn down in a feeling of helpless despair. And yet there is a lot that parents can do in raising a child with BPD, which is what this chapter is all about.

## DBT SKILLS

Dialectical behavior therapy (DBT) uses acronyms as devices to remember skills. In the DBT tradition, I will use the acronym VALIDATE, which stands for: Validate, Accept, Let Go, be Interested, Describe, Tell the truth, be Effective. The acronym helps parents remember the techniques on the following pages.

## VALIDATE

From a BPD perspective, to validate means to confirm that you have heard what the other person is saying, recognize that he may have a perspective different from yours, and communicate that you understand what he is saying. It does not mean that you agree with his point of view, that his is a correct point of view, or that you condone his behavior.

Invalidation is the opposite, meaning that you discount, delegitimize, or explicitly state that what the other person is thinking, feeling, or doing makes no sense. Saying things such as "you're overreacting," "you are wrong," "you shouldn't feel that way," or "get over it," are examples of invalidating statements.

The problem with making such invalidating statements is that they have the effect of punishing teens for their emotional displays. Imagine telling a child with asthma to "get over it" or to "start breathing and quit wheezing." The person with asthma has difficulty breathing in certain circumstances and similarly the child with BPD has difficulty in controlling his emotions in certain situations. It is important to recognize this and know that it is just not that easy for him to simply "get over" things.

Worse than the feeling of being punished is that sometimes the invalidating comments have the effect of reinforcing the very behavior that you want your child to stop doing. This is because telling people not to react in a certain way can lead to them feeling misunderstood and becoming even angrier. Ultimately, teens with BPD learn that what they are feeling is not "correct," and they learn not to trust their own experience. Not knowing whether to feel a certain way can lead to tremendous confusion. Because the teen does not know how or what to feel, he has a hard time learning how to control his emotions. Over time not only does the child feel increasingly invalidated but he also learns to self-invalidate, or deny his very own experiences.

When Steven, a seventeen-year-old boy with BPD, was distraught at having failed his driving test, one that he had been practicing for months, his parents told him: "It's your fault. If you had practiced more instead of hanging out with your weed buddies, you would have passed." His grandparents, on the other hand, told him: "Stop worrying, it's not a big deal; it's only one test. Driving is easy. You'll get it right next time." Both of these responses are typical examples of invalidating statements. This is because neither takes into account how Steven feels about having failed. His parents blame him for his failure and conclude that he therefor has no right to feel the way he does. His grandparents appear more sympathetic but are simply telling him to stop feeling the way he does about the driving test.

For an adolescent—or anyone, for that matter—to tell himself repeatedly to not feel or think the way he does can be miserable and lead to depression and hopelessness. A hundred different people failing the driving test would have a hundred different responses. Each response is unique to that person. A more sensitive child will respond differently than a less sensitive child, and recognizing that is what validation is all about.

Another typical type of invalidation is one that makes the problem seem easier to solve than it is for the person. Our seventeen-year-old Steve is also a smoker. He smokes a pack a day and his parents hate the behavior. "Just quit," they tell him. It might be easy for the parent who has quit, or never started in the first place, to not smoke, but to the addicted teen who might also use smoking as a way to calm down, it is not that easy. A parent's exasperation at a seemingly easy-to-solve problematic behavior is also a classic example of invalidation. If you were sitting with a group of Harvard mathematicians discussing quadratic equations, and as you don't have the skill set to solve quadratic equations—assuming you are not a mathematician—their telling you that the equations are easy or that you should simply solve the problem is the equivalent of you telling your child with BPD that an emotional problem is easy to solve.

This idea of validation seems simple enough but it can be very hard to put into actual practice. When we ask parents why it is difficult to validate their child we hear the following concerns.

- I am afraid that I am agreeing with their behavior.
- I am afraid that I will make them even more upset.
- They win and I lose.
- It means that I accept the facts as they see it.
- They won't learn to do things differently if I don't point out what they are doing wrong.
- As a parent I have to hold on to my values.

Practice validation by listening to a friend or partner who might have a different point of view than yours. As you practice, bring the idea of validation increasingly into your relationship with your BPD teen. The point is that validation simply is a stance of nonjudgmental, effective curiosity. Once you get where your child is coming from, you have a fighting chance of being more effective in dealing with adversarial situations that might have otherwise ended up going unresolved in an escalation of emotions.

## ACCEPTANCE

Denying the reality that you have a child with BPD, wishing it were otherwise, or fighting it leads to suffering and misery. Nonacceptance won't change the situation. Acceptance is the only way to challenge the denial of reality.

Accepting that your child has BPD means accepting that he or she will have moments of feeling suicidal, have intense emotions, act impulsively, and may self-injure. Denying this reality does not help you, and the more you fight it the more you will suffer. Acceptance does not mean resignation, however. It does not mean lying down and letting life roll over you. Accepting reality as it is means that you might be able to do something about it. Imagine that you have a flat tire as you are driving on the highway. Saying that you should not have had one or that it just isn't so is going to make your situation much worse if you keep driving on the flat tire. Be willing to accept the reality. The process of acceptance does not necessarily come easily, and you will catch yourself in nonacceptance many times Be willing to accept that the situation has occurred, notice when you get to nonacceptance, and turn your mind to acceptance again and again.

## Let Go

We all have dreams for our children. Some are grand, filled with academic achievement, financial success, and the perfect spouse. Others simply want their child to be happy. The problem comes when our children don't attain the dreams we have for them.

I recall a family from a big-name school; the parents had met at that school and their first three children went to the same school. The parents were in finance and their children had all studied economics at the school. The pressure on their youngest daughter was immense, and there was no discussion about whether she would go to the school.

However, she had no interest in the school, was more artistically inclined, and had little passion for finance. She suffered from the pressure and quietly accepted when she was admitted on the basis of her good grades and her family's connections. Soon she started to self-injure and isolate herself from her peers. She became involved in dangerous relationships and attempted suicide.

For her parents, the attempt came as a total shock, and yet the young woman said she had been suffering for a long time. Her parents imagined that her getting into the school would make her feel better, but it was never where she had wanted to go. Her parents had to accept this, then let go of their dreams for her and allow her room to breathe and find her place in the world. Letting go is particularly difficult if you see the world in rigid, rule-bound ways. But not letting go can lead to far more serious consequences in such cases. So how do you let go?

The first thing is letting go of that attachment to certainty, which will produce an emotion when you imagine letting go. Observe the emotion as it arises. Acknowledge that it exists. Then try to stand back from it as if it were a painting in a gallery that you wanted to examine from a distance. Experience the emotion as a wave, coming and going. Label it. Is it anger? Disappointment? Sadness? You may find it helpful to concentrate on some part of the emotion as it passes through your body. "Is my body tense? Is my heart beating fast?"

As you notice it, imagine it as a small wave lapping at your feet on the beach, coming and going, not knocking you down. Don't push it away or deny it is there. Simply notice it. Pushing emotions away tends to make them bigger in the long run, and they will return like a flood that will be more difficult to manage. Don't judge the emotion. Don't play it over and over in your head. You are not the emotion. You are not angry. You *feel* angry. These two ways of thinking about this are very different. You do not have to act on your emotion. Simply notice it. When you can do this, it validates your experience and, though painful, it will free you from the fight against reality. Letting go will get you there.

## BE INTERESTED

The art of parenting children with BPD is to be genuinely interested in their life, school, and life goals. All too often parents feel too worried to be openly curious, too determined to get their own points across, and too persistent in making sure that their teen knows what is expected. Listening with interest and curiosity is key.

In DBT, we practice the skill of fully participating in the moment, and the first skill to being a good listener is to fully participate in listening. Because we practice tuning out much of what life throws at us, the risk is that we do the same with our teen, who feels unknown and unheard. Be aware of your body language, turning toward your child with a calm, kind, uncritical, and curious expression. If you don't have the time to talk, you will appear tense and disinterested.

The next skill is not to be distracted. Put away the cell phone, newspaper, or book. Nothing is more interesting at that moment than your child. Show your interest by reducing distractions. Then, if your child talks to you, the occasional nod of the head will indicate that you are following what he or she is saying. It is a subtle move but it will have its effect. Don't say that you understand if you don't. This often leads to the teen feeling even more misunderstood or even angrier.

Finally, concentrating on what your child is saying is essential to being interested. Think about times when you have experienced not being listened to. If your teen is open to a discussion, ask clarifying questions, and if you don't understand, say something such as, "I really want to understand but am missing something. Can you explain it in a different way?" This will encourage your child to move away from scripted answers and get her thinking mind moving.

## DESCRIBE

In establishing better communication with your BPD teen, it is important to simply describe the situation involving your teen without passing judgment because often the facts are indisputable. For example, "You were home at 11:30 last night, and I am curious as to why," is different than "You were home at 11:30 last night and you did so to push my buttons." In this situation, if the teen's curfew was 11, you might say, "You were home late last night." This is the factual description of what happened, but does not imply intention or cause. On the other hand, if you said, "You were home late last night. Were you with your druggie friends?" you might be making not only assumptions but also inserting judgment as to the quality and character of all of your child's friends. This may or may not have been the case, but in the absence of data, such editorializing gets parents into trouble with their teen because the teen experiences it as persistent criticism.

Staying curious means simply describing what you know. There are a multitude of reasons that could explain why the teen was late. Coming to the worst possible conclusion helps neither of you. Describing is saying what you see. If you are washing dirty dishes, you would say: "The water is soapy and warm. The dishes have tomato sauce on them." Saying, "It's not fair that I have to wash the dishes" is not describing.

Describing is also stating how you feel. For instance, saying, "I feel disappointed that you were home late" would be describing. "I feel disappointed that you were doing drugs and were home late" would not be describing unless you had evidence that your teen was doing drugs. Describing also diminishes intensifying emotional responses because it stays away from assumptions that might be wrong and hurtful as a consequence.

Practice describing by taking events around you and noting specific facts and feelings you have about the event. For instance, "My daughter is going on a date tonight. Her new boyfriend got his license three weeks ago. I feel anxious that he is not a good driver. I have the thought that he will crash the car." Not describing would be, "My daughter is going out with a new boy and given her choice in boyfriends he is probably bad news and the fact that he is a new driver he is likely to drink and drive and crash the car." Describing would include noticing body sensations, such as, "I notice that my neck muscles are tense thinking about her getting into the car with the boy." Then notice your thoughts: "I have the thought that he is going to be just as bad news as all her past boyfriends."

Another way to practice describing is to pick an activity such as cooking a meal or walking the dog and simply state what you notice. What do you see? What do you smell? If you are cooking, what do you taste? Don't judge these experiences, simply put words to them. In dealing with your BPD teen, describing what is gets you out of the struggle of interpretation that might have nothing to do with the actual situation.

## Tell the Truth

All too often, being honest with your BPD teen can be difficult because it can mean having to say no to a request. This in turn can lead to your child becoming angry and explosive, and can make it aversive for you to confront your child over some behavior. Don't lie or blame someone else. Lying or blaming others over time erodes your self-respect. The problem with not being truthful is that you become helpless over time. Ultimately, avoiding telling the truth will come back to haunt you because invariably the truth comes out. Furthermore, your child can't trust you and often trust is the very quality that you are trying to build in the relationship.

## Be Effective

Being effective means doing what the situation calls for. This means letting go of feeling right so strongly that it overrides your ability to make decisions that may correct a situation. The idea of being right and not budging from your position because it is a matter of principle might feel good to you while you are standing up for what you believe in, but might be ultimately destructive in the relationship.

An example of effectiveness is when you are stuck in the right-hand lane of an off-ramp and have been waiting for quite a while and then someone comes whizzing in from your left and cuts in front of you. Certainly you have been waiting and deserve your turn, but crashing into the car or getting into a fight because you are right is not the effective thing to do. In another example, say your child came home at 11:05 p.m., five minutes late. Did your teen break the curfew of 11? Yes. Are you right? Yes. Is grounding your teen for a month the effective thing to do? No! You are trying to shape your teen's behavior, and being five minutes late is far better than being hours late.

## PSYCHOEDUCATION IS ESSENTIAL

Even when there is no crisis, it is important that families learn as much about BPD as they can. This is a dynamic process because information about BPD continues to evolve. Yesterday's understandings of BPD may not be relevant today. You might feel alienated by your child's condition, even by your own extended family, and including other family members in the therapeutic process will help. You can learn more by:

- Developing a broad understanding of BPD. Understanding that BPD is a health condition like any other illness and sharing this information and research about the condition with others helps avoid the guilt, blame, shame, and stigma that parents often feel.
- Developing effective interactions with your BPD teen. This book is dedicated to this idea. Showing nonjudgmental empathy and a willingness to understand the experience of your teen will lead to less conflict in the family and more peace of mind for you.
- Developing new ways of communicating. Continuing to communicate in a way that perpetuates the problem makes no sense. Allowing teens to express themselves as a way to understand them and listening to them with open and genuine curiosity will give you a deeper understanding of their struggle.
- Developing a collaborative treatment team. Building an open and collaborative relationship with the team will allow for more effective treatment. The team will potentially include a psychiatrist or other prescriber, therapist, school counselor, pediatrician, and family therapist. Discussions with these professionals should be honest, frank, and direct. There should be explicit agreements as to how and when communication will be shared.

# New Hope
# for Living
# with BPD

## CHAPTER TWELVE

# Voices of BPD

O NE OF THE MOST SOBERING ASPECTS OF BPD is that it kills
up to 10 percent of its victims. If we are to have any hope of changing this statistic, it is essential that we recognize how profoundly
painful the emotional turmoil of BPD can be.

BPD can ravage a person's self-esteem. After a difficult phone call
with her mother, a seventeen-year-old girl told me: "I've never had lower
self-esteem in my entire life. In my entire life! Do you know how low my
self-esteem has been during the course of my life? It's been low. It's been so
low that I've made myself throw up for hours just because I had a bagel.
And it's lower now. I feel like shit."

It is a feeling like this, compounded by aloneness and hopelessness over
many years, that makes patients with BPD seriously contemplate suicide.
Even if we cannot contemplate such utter self-loathing, accepting that
people who suffer from BPD experience self-hatred and worse is important
if we are to understand this condition.

It is critical to recognize that BPD occurs, and has its roots, in childhood and adolescence. The scientific data to date support this, the clinical
work validates it, but more compelling, the personal stories demand it.
Without an accurate diagnosis, patients are often destined for lives of

misery as they struggle to be understood and at times are treated with therapies that are not effective.

Because BPD affects not only those who struggle with it but also the people who work with them in therapy and the families who love them, it is important to get a wide panorama of perspectives that shows the transactional nature of the disorder and its impact from various perspectives.

*"You know that feelings can't kill you, but you're sure this is the one exception."*

—LAUREN, AGE EIGHTEEN, ON HAVING BPD

## VOICES OF PATIENTS

The following words by eighteen-year-old Lauren—who felt that her experience of living with BPD might best explain the suffering, hoping, and coping with the condition—are compelling:

"What do you do when your feelings are so overwhelming that it's uncomfortable to just sit with yourself? You squirm around in your chair, or your bed, or the couch trying to get rid of this thing that's causing so much discomfort but you can't because it's inside of you. And you just want it out.

"You're smothered in these absolutely horrible feelings and you can't breathe and there's just no way to get away from it. You know that feelings can't kill you, but you're sure this is the one exception. Nothing can even distract you from these feelings because they're so prominent. They've taken over everything. You try to walk around and hope that maybe these feelings will disappear on their own. But the more you try to ignore them, the worse they get. They're determined to make you miserable. You just want to shake yourself, or bang your head against a wall. Tear up a pillow or smash a mirror. All because you're so angry with yourself for letting these feelings consume you like they have.

"And then you want to self-destruct somehow—cause pain in some other place so you can get away from the pain that's gnawing at your insides. Focus on something else. Pain that is self-inflicted and controlled is tolerable. Pain that you can't stop or get rid of is even more reason to be mad at yourself.

"Why can't I control my feelings? Why can't I stop this? Why can't I just be numb? Why can't I get away from the awfulness that is following me?

"The magnitude of these feelings increases by the second. You think you've had all you can take, and then the feelings consume you even more. You try to act normal because you don't want to give in to these feelings. Don't want to let them win. But in reality, they've already won. They've taken over every aspect of your life.

"So tell me. What do you do with these horrific feelings that are buried so deep within you that you wouldn't even know where to start looking to dig them out? They're like cancer—they just spread and spread and spread.

"What do you do?

"Anger and sweetness can be turned on and off like the flick of a switch, and all the emotions in between can take over in one second, and wash away in the next. Self-hatred and self-loathing run far deeper than anybody can imagine, to the point of being able to *physically* feel them. BPD is a disorder that's hard to escape from, hard to change, and even harder to live with.

"I battle myself every day to maintain some sort of control over these symptoms. There are days when I feel like I've gotten a grip on myself and that I've finally begun to overcome my battle.

Other days, I feel like I *am* my disorder, and it's all I ever will be: a shell of person, who is halfway between being alive and dead.

"I describe myself as having two conflicting personalities—one being the 'good' me, the other being the 'bad' me. They are continuously at war with each other, each begging to have a permanent place in the spotlight.

"The 'good' me is the healthy me. I'm confidant, energetic, sweet, witty, and open. I'm in control, I want to get better, and I'm motivated to accomplish life's daily tasks. The 'bad' me comes out when I feel vulnerable, attacked, or abandoned. I'm absolutely horrific to be around when I'm in this state because I say terrible things to the person my anger is directed toward. My all-or-nothing thinking takes over, and nobody can say anything to retrieve me from the funk I fall into. I'm always completely aware that I'm doing it, and I don't *want* to be doing it. Yet I feel powerless to stop it. Once the anger washes over me, I'm a completely different, awful person. I'm someone I don't know, and someone I don't want to be.

"When the anger subsides and I have time to reflect on my actions, the guilt comes in full force. Why did I get so mad in the first place? Why couldn't I stop myself? How could I say that? I bet that person hates me. I hate me. I should just die. No matter how guilty I feel afterward, it'll happen again, and eventually the relationship will end. I lashed out because I felt abandoned, and I got abandoned in the process. And then the self-hatred intensifies.

"Every emotion and every feeling that I feel is intense. I don't feel sad, I feel painfully miserable. The misery seems to filter through my veins, cycling through my body with the blood, hardly ever being released. I don't get mad, I get furious. My rage always feels justified, never inappropriate. And all the guilt funnels into self-hatred. I suppose this goes hand in hand with the all-or-nothing thinking that is so classic of BPD. If I feel, I feel as strongly as possible. Otherwise, I don't feel at all. This has always been the case for me, and only recently did I find out that most people with BPD share in this. I don't think anybody could ever fully register the magnitude and intensity in which we feel.

"The self-hatred, guilt, and intensity of my emotions take their toll. I crave for a way to end the pain, to somehow let that filtering misery out of my veins. Cutting almost always provides that relief. When I hate myself, I want to self-destruct in any way imaginable. I want to inflict physical pain on my body to match the emotional turmoil going on inside me. I want to punish myself for being such a dreadful person. As soon as the razor crosses over my skin, I feel the release of all the pent-up anger, hatred, and sorrow that the skin seems to be holding in. The deeper the cut, the more satisfaction I find. I want the ugliness that's on the inside to be seen on the outside. The benefits are always temporary, and shame sets in rather quickly. Yet in the midst of such misery, even a second of relief is worth it.

"I wouldn't necessarily say that I feel sorry for myself, but I do feel a great deal of sadness for the person I've become. I know who I am underneath this mess, and I know the potential I have to do great things in life. The real me shines through every once in a while, and that is the person I know I want to revive. I'm sad for the way I treat the people I love and care about. I absolutely despise BPD, and I hate that I've let it consume me the way that it has. At times, I don't feel like I have enough fight or drive to overcome my disease, especially when I feel it has overcome me. I've been suicidal more days than not, and prior to my last bout of treatment, had no idea how I was still alive.

"I've found that hope is one of the hardest things to maintain with BPD. It can be lost so easily in the poor prognosis, horrible stigma, and self-loathing. Hope is lost in the guilt, the despair, the pain, the loneliness, and the constant fight. At my worst, I lost all hope, and was living to die. I was stashing pills and alcohol, waiting for the exact right moment when I could take them all and leave everything behind.

"But my hope was restored due to the extraordinary care I received at McLean Hospital. Hope came to me through sharing a room with two other amazing girls also diagnosed with BPD, and through feeling less alone because of it. It came from dialectical behavior therapy and a magnificent support team. It especially came to me through a wonderful doctor, who had the patience to deal with me at the toughest times and saw me at my worst, yet still continued to tell me I could beat this. The support given to me brought back the will to conquer my illness. I was continuously told I could do it. That recovery was indeed possible. That I wasn't a lost cause. I was an empty person when I walked in the doors of that hospital, and a whole one when I walked back out.

"There isn't a day that goes by when I'm unaware of my disorder. It's always on my mind, and I continuously question the validity of my feelings and actions. I struggle to tell the difference between borderline thoughts and normal ones, and I'm nowhere near perfecting this art. I constantly worry that I'm going to lash out at someone, or get angry for something ridiculous. I fear the loss of my relationships with others due to the horrible track record I have so far. And my black-and-white thinking is far more frequent than I even realize. I still struggle with suicidal thoughts and urges to hurt myself, and sometimes I'm positive I won't be victorious in the war with myself.

"I've realized the battle with BPD will never really end, but I've also realized that help is available, and I don't have to feel the wretched misery that comes along with the disease. I have hopes and dreams, and the strength to go on. I do know that some day, somehow, I will be okay."

One of the major problems I hear about from many of the adolescents we work with is their difficulty in romantic (and other) relationships. There is often a tremendous fear that the other person will discover just how "bad" or "awful" they are. Another fear is that they will "poison" the other person with their "badness." But even after years of therapy and increasing confidence, and even when the BPD symptoms are no longer present, the fear that their past will be discovered can make many shy away from intimate relationships.

Eric, twenty, now living a life worth living, but with a past full of self-doubt, self-injury, and substance abuse, put it this way:

"It is difficult for me to initiate talking to a girl, especially if I am interested in her, because I fear that she will ask me about my past. I don't want my past to taint her view of me now, or for her to think that I am crazy. Eventually, I have to become more comfortable talking about myself to new people, but I think that the kind of relationship that would work for me is someone who is more understanding, and more focused on the present."

I was working with Julie, a bright fifteen-year-old, who felt strongly that she wanted to give up. She sent me an email containing the elements of her struggle:

"I've always asserted that I just simply feel too much. When I feel anger, I perceive every little action as a grievous injury, and desire to passive-aggressively exact revenge, or sever ties completely with a person whom I normally truly care about. In contrast, when I feel love, it is equally as overpowering, as I feel overwhelming compassion and liking for those I care about. When my emotions oscillate, my mood state can change as rapidly as every few minutes, or be as persistent as to last for days.

"An emotion that tends to linger is sadness, which provokes thoughts that I am worthless, toxic to others, and deserve to be sequestered away from the rest of humanity. Crippling guilt and shame drive me to slash and burn my skin in an effort to punish myself. Evidently, I feel too much. If I had to rate the aspects of BPD that bother me the most, my emotional sensitivity and reactivity would be at the top. Another pattern is that I frequently believe that others are angry at me or hate me. The slightest cue can incite these thoughts, such as a period of silence, a tone of voice, or a glance. Even when I know this is irrational, the thought that the person is furious with me feels like reality in the moment. A small part of me hopes that someday I will be free of these symptoms, and live a happy, fulfilling life, but I struggle holding on to hope."

*"Our charming, handsome, artistic, athletic son became an unrecognizable stranger. Attempts to reach him were met with silence or explosive anger. Therapists were unable to develop any kind of relationship with him."*

—THE MOTHER OF A SEVENTEEN-YEAR-OLD WITH BPD

## THE VOICE OF A PARENT

In as much as adolescents with BPD suffer with their condition, parents, too, suffer profoundly. Parents often have to deal with the rage of adolescents with BPD, the guilt of feeling they might have done something to cause the problem, the accusations of bad parenting by other members of the family, the feeling that they have not given their other children enough attention, and the stigma of having children who are "known" as having troubles. The mother of a seventeen-year-old with BPD shared the following thoughts:

> "There were signs, but we didn't see them. As people who approach life with confident optimism, we embarked on the adventure of creating a family with naive, enthusiastic energy.

> "Nature versus nurture? As adoptive parents we were convinced that the loving environment we'd create for our first child would guide his development and form a personality as open and gregarious as ours.

> "Mother Nature is a powerful force. She equipped Sean with a temperament that rebuffed our relentlessly misguided efforts to shape our son in our image. Convinced that he would eventually emerge from his wary, reluctant ways, we unwittingly practiced invalidation early and often. Failing to appreciate how fragile his makeup truly was, we forged ahead, exposing him to new experiences without realizing the layers of trauma they provoked.

> "When Sean was three, a neighbor trained in early childhood education asked with concern if we had noticed that he was unusually solemn and guarded. 'He's just shy,' we replied. A dozen years later, a forensic psychologist described hypervigilance.

> "When he was four, we took him to the performance of his favorite musician, a performer of silly animal-themed songs. As

children around him enthusiastically clapped, sang, and laughed, Sean sat through the show without expression. After the concert we gently sought to understand what about the experience had so frightened him. On the contrary, he described the afternoon as the best ever. Our inability to read any emotion in his flat affect continued for years.

"When he was ten, Sean's pitching helped his Little League team make the playoffs. During the final game the opposing coach bellowed jeers and catcalls at every throw. The crowd watched the league's leading pitcher wither under the assault. The game was lost on walks. Sean left the field in stoic silence. Our attempts to encourage him to express his feelings, to process the defeat, met with resolute resistance. He never picked up a baseball glove again. A pattern of dissociating when faced with traumas large and small was emerging.

"When he was in middle school Sean took up lacrosse. Wielding the stick with ferocious intensity, he left his understated personality on the sidelines. He played attack with a vigor that caused spectators to gasp. Deep-seated anger had found an outlet. We were perplexed that even though he wore heavily padded gloves during these contests, his knuckles were constantly bloodied and scabbed. Eventually we discovered that he was punching holes in the walls of his room to further express anger and pain.

"When he was fourteen, his first girlfriend chose his best friend as her graduation dance date. Unbeknownst to us, he began chugging a couple of beers on the way to school to dull the pain of seeing the newly formed couple together. A pattern of self-soothing through substance abuse had begun.

"When he was a freshman in high school, he quarterbacked the junior varsity football team. A series of concussions undermined his short-term memory, but he never revealed that he was suddenly unable to retain geometry formulae, history dates, or Spanish verb forms. A month after telling us that he looked forward to making the honor roll at his new school he was failing every class and sitting on the bench at every practice and game. He withdrew to the point that the school psychologist mused that Sean lacked a core identity.

"Neuropsychological testing indicated mild ADHD. First Adderall and then Concerta became part of Sean's daily regimen. As his school performance continued to fail to meet expectations, he self-medicated with dextromethorphan and marijuana. Eventually he dabbled in cocaine and mushrooms. His depression deepened to the point that he wouldn't leave his bed. At the beginning of the spring term he was sent home from boarding school on a medical leave. Chronic feelings of emptiness pervaded his being.

"Former teachers who loved and supported our winsome, mysterious son answered the call when we sought tutors to help him complete the school year. Unable to generalize the success that their cheerleading helped him achieve, Sean sought solace in liquor, secretly drinking himself to sleep every night.

"Engagement in family life declined into total avoidance. Our charming, handsome, artistic, athletic son became an unrecognizable stranger. Attempts to reach him were met with silence or explosive anger. Therapists were unable to develop any kind of relationship with him.

"As a new school year approached, we sought the advice of educational consultants, realizing that Sean was unable to successfully navigate public high school. The plan for a comprehensive intervention was laid; therapeutic boarding school was the next stop on his journey. His perception of abandonment manifested itself in extraordinary cutting behaviors. He was placed on twenty-four-hour watch, accompanied everywhere to ensure his safety. When it became clear that he was finding ways to self-injure while alone in the toilet stall, the school declared him too risky a resident. The first of eight psychiatric hospitalizations, ranging from three days to three months, ensued.

"So there you have it. This piece is a series of examples demonstrating the underlying borderline clues, some of which began to manifest themselves earlier than adolescence: fear of abandonment, chronic feelings of emptiness, dissociation, anger, and impulsivity in the form of substance abuse. There were early signals of the disorder unobserved/ignored, thereby unwittingly deepening the sense of invalidation. We continue to look for answers to the source of his suffering. Are they unresolved loss issues stemming from his adoption? Was it due to a lack of resilience to sustain the dislocation of our multiple geographical moves? We have not ruled out sexual abuse at the hands of a day care provider or camp counselor. Was there neurological damage from his football concussions? Finally, the BPD diagnosis makes sense of the symptomatology. Once that is understood, a case can be made for the efficacy of a commitment to DBT, family therapy, a structured environment, the family connections model (see page 234), and hope."

Such thoughtful and careful consideration in trying to answer the BPD puzzle takes time and reflection, and it is such unwavering dedication to understanding and hope that gives kids with BPD and their families a chance, and makes working with such families a blessing.

## THE VOICE OF A MENTAL HEALTH COUNSELOR

In reading historical accounts of how mental health staff saw patients with BPD, I noticed that their perspectives at that time were frequently pessimistic and often pejorative. When people with BPD have frequent hospitalizations, they often suffer significant revictimization by mental health counselors, who often consider them persona non grata because of the sometimes difficult-to-manage behaviors associated with BPD.

By the time the adolescents with BPD are admitted to our unit, many of them have had multiple hospitalizations or been institutionalized in some setting. Early identification and intervention for children and adolescents who exhibit BPD symptoms is essential if we want to significantly change these "difficult behaviors" later on in life and not have them exposed to the persistently negative attitudes that can follow them.

Paul Jay, LICSW, is a senior social worker who has worked with adolescents for many years and has been the director of an adolescent residential unit at McLean Hospital. He oversees and supervises the mental health staff on the unit. Paul has often pointed out that the residential staff or mental health counselors spend more time with the patients than the clinicians do, and as such have a more comprehensive and authentic perspective on the day-to-day interactions that our kids have with their parents and peers. His staff provides invaluable daily feedback to the clinicians. These are his thoughts:

> "Medication was used readily to control the behavior of adolescents with BPD. The problem was that in too many cases the medication did not work. Symptoms were muted, but only delayed until the age of consent to treatment was reached and medication was no longer a parental prerogative. By that time too many adolescents had grown weary of the required and enforced counseling sessions, which seemed to focus on changing behavior because of guilt and shame. Their failure in therapy to

conform to the behavioral expectations of the therapist, parents, and others in authority further degraded their sense of competence and self-esteem. Yes, many felt guilt and shame for the way they behaved, but few could translate those feelings into why they behaved the way they did. They felt hopeless and helpless.

"I remember attending a clinical conference in the late 1970s on the diagnosis and treatment of personality disorders. The instructor saved the discussion on BPD until the very end. As with celebrity, there was excitement and anticipation in the audience as the topic neared. When the instructor finally mentioned BPD, there was a collective buzz. We all knew that we were about to discuss the Cadillac of all the personality disorders and the bane of every clinician. The instructor labeled it as such. After going through the diagnostic criteria for BPD, the instructor said, in effect, that there was little understanding as to how BPD developed and even less understanding as to how to treat it. The instructor continued to say that the weekly crises, poor application of learning, and low motivation for change in people with BPD burned out clinicians. Further, people with BPD were manipulative, attention seeking, chronically suicidal, and treatment rejecting. He ended by saying that those who did in fact choose to work with BPD clients needed to limit their sessions to a maximum of five for their own well-being. It's a wonder how we all survived!

"Today there is growing support for the idea that the clusters of symptoms associated with BPD is seen in adolescents. The talk among clinicians now is, while still hesitant, that adolescents have 'features' and 'emerging' characteristics of BPD. This is progress mostly because the advances in the clinical understanding and treatment of adult BPD can now be applied to adolescents. In adults, the stigma associated with BPD has been reduced by recognition that the stereotype is not true. Adults are not manipulative, but rather attempting in their behavior to lessen the overwhelming feelings of inadequacy and pain. Adults with BPD act in maladaptive ways to relieve pain, suffering, and emptiness when no other way seems possible.

"The hallmark for treating adolescents with BPD is an environment that is safe, structured, and consistent. In the acute residential treatment (ART) at McLean, our staff is trained in DBT and the biosocial theory [behind the causes of BPD]. Our staff applies the behavioral, cognitive, and learning principles that continue to prove effective in working with adolescents who present with BPD symptoms. Understanding the biosocial theory of BPD helps staff provide firm, but caring and nurturing, intervention with residents that promotes motivation for change while helping them accept who they are.

"Without such training, staff can rapidly burn out in dealing with what appears to be manipulative behavior. Also, BPD adolescents can at times see people as either all-good or all-bad, and staff can often feel targeted and personalize the attacks. A strong and supportive consultation team is an essential asset for the residential team working with this population group.

"For the adolescents, change capability is developed through skills training in mindfulness, interpersonal effectiveness, emotional regulation, self-soothing, and contingency planning. Once the skills are learned, staff also apply the behavioral interventions of rewards and punishment to modify persistently disordered behavior.

"During the residential component of the day (after the 'clinical' and school day parts are over) the kids return to a less scripted environment where they interact with each other and participate in cooking, journaling, watching TV, and other activities of daily living. These interactions can at times lead to the problematic behaviors that had the adolescent admitted in the first place as they argue over cliques being formed, etc.

"Residents are then required to analyze problematic behavior through the completion of a chain analysis, which is a detailed look at the antecedents (what happened before) and the consequences (what happened after) the behavior. The chain analysis helps the staff and adolescents understand which skills are needed to stop the problem behavior and which reinforcers contribute to the motivation to continue the behavior.

"Work of this nature must be done in an environment that validates the emotional pain experienced by residents and provides the safety necessary to explore reasons to change. Adolescents in the ART find plenty of reassurance from peers with similar problems and patterns of behavior [and learn] they are not alone in their feelings and that help is possible. Many find relief in just learning that others experience similar emotional discomfort and have relied on similar maladaptive means to feel better. In particular, adolescents with a trauma history, especially sexual abuse, benefit from finally being able to express their sense of self-loathing and despair to a peer group that can relate to many of their feelings. They often feel as if a burden has been lifted and that they are allowed to move on in their lives to a healthier sense of well-being.

"One major difficulty in treating adolescents with BPD on a residential unit is the generalizing of learning back to the home environment. Often, adolescents perceive their home environment to be invalidating and unsupportive. Patterns of destructive interactions have developed over time and become intractable.

"Adolescents feel that the balance of power in their family is heavily shifted toward the parents and that, regardless of how much they change, things simply will not improve. It is not uncommon to hear adolescents say during their course of treatment, 'I think that my parents should be admitted here.'

"It is imperative that parents learn to understand and make changes along with their adolescents in treatment. Staff know the skills that each adolescent is working on, which allows them to reinforce these skills and encourage parents to continue this work [when their adolescents return home].

"While working with adolescents with BPD symptoms can be difficult, it is also tremendously rewarding in many ways. Witnessing these adolescents learn and develop new ways to navigate the world and overcome hopelessness and despair is impressive and inspiring. Adolescents finding hope where there previously was none creates an appreciation for life that is untarnished by years of suffering. Watching while parents of adolescents come to realize that their children can be better, and seeing their sense of relief, is gratifying. Hearing the adolescent and parents communicate with each other without contempt is its own reward, and knowing that you have helped someone to live a life worth living is what all clinicians strive to accomplish."

The author of a 2000 study reported the impact of being a community mental health center case manager for someone with BPD. The case managers spent more time with BPD patients than with other patients, monitoring their own thoughts and feelings, expressing concerns about the potential for patient suicide, and setting boundaries with the BPD patients.

In a 2006 study, the authors noted that caring for patients with a diagnosis of BPD was a problem area for mental health professionals and that a diagnosis of BPD at times influenced the level and quality of interaction that staff had with BPD patients. The authors stated that it is inherent to psychiatric nursing that nurses be able to establish rapport, develop trust, and demonstrate empathy with psychiatric patients.

In their study, they found that a proportion of psychiatric nurses experienced negative emotional reactions and attitudes toward people with BPD. Further, the majority of nurses perceived people with BPD as manipulative and almost one-third of nurses reported that patients with BPD made them angry. More than one-third felt that they did not know how to care for people with BPD.

What we see is that as a general rule, counselors, nurses, case managers, and clinicians of all types find it difficult to work with patients with BPD. This compounds an already bad situation for patients. They suffer with their pain and then feel uncared for. Education is an important part of addressing this issue, as is providing clinicians with the necessary skills and a support team to help deal with the potential burnout.

## THE VOICE OF A CASE MANAGER

Jennifer Mehrtens, LICSW, is a former case manager on the adolescent treatment unit at McLean Hospital. She is extensively trained in DBT and has worked with clients with BPD across a wide range of settings—not only on our unit but with prison populations and in outpatient clinics as well. Here she talks about the challenges of working with adolescents with BPD, their families, and the health care system:

> "The greatest struggle is a patient's pattern of idealizing (you are wonderful!) and devaluing (you are terrible and you aren't helping!) of the therapist. The task is to maintain a balance so as to not reinforce this pattern while acknowledging the equally unhelpful nature of trying to be the all-good therapist (constantly trying to rescue the patient) or all-bad therapist (constantly trying to get rid of the patient).

> "Another major challenge is sitting calmly with the patient's anger, particularly when the anger is directed at you, which it often is as the borderline patient is exquisitely sensitive and can react to minor or perceived slights. Staying calm and not [being] defensive is an important skill to develop.

> "Adolescents are rarely in treatment alone. You work with a system that can often be as reactive and chaotic as the individual. There are frequently multiple competing agendas, such as insurance companies feeling that they will no longer cover patients' treatment, supervisors feeling that you are trying too hard or not hard enough, parents who are frantic for a faster cure, schools that are not convinced by reassurance that a kid is safe, colleagues who see that treatment should go one way or another, and then ultimately self-doubt that maybe you can't help. Maintaining a clear focus on your role, treatment plan, and formulation can be a major chal-

lenge as the pressure to respond to the intense desperation in the system increases.

"Finally, the risk of a negative outcome with the borderline adolescent is higher than with any other group. It is a challenge to resist acting out of fear and also responding appropriately when the patient is at acute risk. Finding a way to manage your own anxiety in response to the patient's desperate emotions and behavior is critical, and perhaps only possible in the presence of a very supportive team of colleagues."

## VOICES IN CONTEMPORARY CULTURE

In the earlier reflection by Lauren, her writing shows her capacity to express a very personal pain. The clarity of her writing leaves little doubt as to her enduring distress, sprinkled with hints of hope. Not all adolescents with BPD are as articulate, even if their pain is as disabling. Others feel that poetry, music lyrics, and movies capture their experience.

Adolescents often point out that *Girl, Interrupted*, the autobiographical account of author Susanna Kaysen's two-year treatment for BPD, took place at McLean Hospital. In the movie of the same title, Kaysen (portrayed by Winona Ryder) was admitted to McLean after an impulsive suicide attempt in which she downed fifty aspirin with a bottle of vodka. Given her suicide attempts, moodiness, and history of promiscuity, she was diagnosed with BPD. Needless to say, *Girl, Interrupted* (both the book and the movie) is a favorite on our unit.

*"[A] major challenge is sitting calmly with the patient's anger, particularly when the anger is directed at you, which it often is as the borderline patient is exquisitely sensitive and can react to minor or perceived slights."*

—JENNIFER MEHRTENS, FORMER CASE MANAGER, MCLEAN HOSPITAL, BELMONT, MASSACHUSETTS

## VOICES IN HISTORICAL CHARACTERS

Many psychiatric units have posters on their walls with lists of famous people who have suffered from mental illnesses. The kids know that Abraham Lincoln suffered from depression, that Virginia Woolf had mood swings and committed suicide, and that Vincent van Gogh had bipolar disorder and cut off his ear. Some adolescents want to know whether anyone famous has suffered from BPD, especially given that 2 percent of the population has the condition.

Perhaps the most famous person to have suffered from BPD may have been the late Princess Diana. Although many authors have made the claim, in her excellent and meticulously researched book *Diana in Search of Herself: Portrait of a Troubled Princess*, author Sally Bedell Smith writes:

> "While one cannot say with certainty that Diana had a borderline personality disorder, the evidence is compelling. The most important factor setting the borderline personality apart from those with other disorders is early parental loss—in Diana's case the departure of her mother and the emotional withdrawal of her father for several years following the Spencer divorce."

Here is an excerpt from a November 1995 interview that the BBC conducted with Princess Diana. Note the classic BPD themes in her answers:

**Q:** Were you overwhelmed by the pressure from people initially?

**A:** Yes, I was very daunted because as far as I was concerned I was a fat, chubby, twenty-year-old, twenty-one-year-old, and I couldn't understand the level of interest.

**Q:** What effect did the depression have on your marriage?

**A:** Well, it gave everybody a wonderful new label—Diana's unstable and Diana's mentally unbalanced. And unfortunately that seems to have stuck on and off over the years.

**Q:** According to press reports, it was suggested that it was around this time things became so difficult that you actually tried to injure yourself.

**A:** Mmm. When no one listens to you or you feel no one's listening to you, all sorts of things start to happen. For instance, you have so much pain inside yourself that you try and hurt yourself on the outside because you want help, but it's the wrong help you're asking for. People see it as crying wolf or attention seeking, and they think because you're in the media all the time you've got enough attention . . . But I was actually crying out because I wanted to get better in order to go forward and continue my duty and my role as wife, mother, Princess of Wales. So yes, I did inflict upon myself. I didn't like myself, I was ashamed because I couldn't cope with the pressures.

**Q:** What did you actually do?

**A:** Well, I just hurt my arms and my legs, and I work in environments now where I see women doing similar things and I'm able to understand completely where they're coming from.

**Q:** The depression was resolved, as you say, but it was subsequently reported that you suffered bulimia. Is that true?

**A:** Yes, I did. I had bulimia for a number of years. And that's like a secret disease. You inflict it upon yourself because your self-esteem is at a low ebb, and you don't think you're worthy or valuable. You fill your stomach up four or five times a day—some do it more—and it gives you a feeling of comfort. It's like having a pair of arms around you, but it's temporarily, temporary. Then you're disgusted at the bloatedness of your stomach, and then you bring it all up again. And it's a repetitive pattern, which is very destructive to yourself.

**Q:** Did you seek help from any other members of the Royal Family?

**A:** No. You, you have to know that when you have bulimia you're very ashamed of yourself and you hate yourself, so—and people think you're wasting food—so you don't discuss it with people. And the thing about bulimia is your weight always stays the same, whereas with anorexia you visibly shrink. So you can pretend the whole way through. There's no proof.

As is true of many patients with BPD, both the early loss of an important attachment figure and the effects of Diana's parents' divorce were traumatic and in her case led to lifelong problems, including abandonment fears, anxiety, mood swings, bulimia, self-mutilation, lying, and medication abuse. Diana was prescribed Prozac and psychotherapy, but none of it seemed to help, and during an official visit to a women's mental health clinic she said that the women "were unlikely to find much help from some psychotherapist."

Although Princess Diana was thought to have BPD, some well-known media figures not diagnosed with BPD have shared their own histories of despair and self-injury in media interviews. A seventeen-year-old patient showed me the following piece on musician Courtney Love from his favorite magazine *Spin*. He felt that it mirrored his experience of what he did when he was feeling out of control. Love had been asked about Kurt Cobain's overdoses and she said the following:

"Some people OD. I've never OD'ed, ever. I've gotten really f***ing blasto, but instead of OD'ing, I chatter and start talking too much, screaming and running around naked and getting hysterical, cutting my arms, you know, crazy shit. Breaking windows. But I never have fallen on the floor blue."

Fiona Apple, a singer and songwriter, has been very open about being raped when she was twelve. She described the consequences of this trauma in a *Rolling Stone* magazine interview:

> "I definitely had an eating disorder. What was really frustrating for me was that everyone thought I was anorexic, and I wasn't. I was really depressed and self-loathing. For me, it wasn't about being thin; it was about getting rid of the bait attached to my body. A lot of it came from the self-loathing that came from being raped at the point of developing my voluptuousness. I just thought that if you had a body and if you had anything on you that would be grabbed, it would be grabbed. So I did purposely get rid of it."

Soon she started to self-injure and would bite her lip until it bled. She continues in the interview:

> "I have a little bit of a problem with that. It's a common thing. It just makes you feel. And it'll be bleeding, and I can't stop, because it almost feels so good when I bite my lip. I'm just saying, 'This happened to me, this happened to a lot of people.' Why should I hide sh*t? Why does that give people a bad opinion of me? It's a reality. A lot of people do it. Courtney Love pulled me aside at a party and showed me her marks."

BPD in adolescence presents as an emotional roller coaster, with numbing, loneliness, hopelessness, self-injury, suicidality, drug use, and promiscuity. Many of the songs that these adolescents listen to, the artists they identify with, and the celebrities they attempt to emulate personify many of the symptoms of BPD. It is important that parents recognize the darker side of adolescent culture as they attempt to understand their adolescents with BPD.

## CHAPTER THIRTEEN

# BPD and Adoption

I WROTE THIS CHAPTER AFTER LONG CONSIDERATION. This is because I strongly believe in adoption and all the promise and hope it has given to countless children and families.

On our unit we have seen many families with adopted children, and the vast majority of families care tremendously for their adolescent with BPD. Many of these parents feel terrible that they might have "caused" BPD in their children. Parents should not blame themselves, but I have found that it is sometimes hard to convince them not to do so. The reason is that even if they played some role in the environmental component of their child's BPD, it was rarely if ever intentional and the past can't be undone. Parents can change only what they do now and in the future, not what they did in the past. But mostly, simply looking for blame neither helps the child nor results in peace for parent or child.

Some of the things we do as parents cause our children to suffer, but these actions are rarely done intentionally. Living in the past of regrets and "should haves" only leads to more suffering because there is no changing what happened. Accepting that none of us is perfect and living life more effectively and mindfully should be the task at hand.

Research shows that adopted children are more likely than biological children to have special health care needs, moderate or severe health problems, learning disabilities, developmental delays, and other mental health difficulties.

During any given week, 10 to 30 percent of the adolescents on our unit diagnosed with BPD are adopted. Although the data on BPD and adoption are scant, one anecdotal report of a family support group for parents with adolescents with BPD showed that 40 percent of the adolescents had been adopted. Parents often ask whether the adoption had anything to do with their child having BPD.

"I have a seventeen-year-old daughter with BPD, and I need more information regarding adoption and borderline personality disorder," one parent recently asked me. "I have read that there is a larger than normal percentage of adopted people with attention deficit disorder, learning disabilities, depression, and other psychological problems. My questions are: Are adopted kids more prone to BPD? Is there any research? Can reuniting my daughter with her birth mother change the course of her BPD?" Unfortunately, I am not aware of any comprehensive studies. My hope is that research will eventually shed some light on the matter.

There are many reasons why parents give up their children for adoption. These include the age of the mother, ability to care for the child, emotional and physical disability of the parent or child, personal circumstances, and many others. Sometimes the parent does not voluntarily give up the child. Some children are taken away from their parents by courts and state agencies because of the chaotic and abusive nature of their households, which are factors associated with the development of BPD. Sometimes parents with their own psychiatric problems recognize that they cannot parent a child, and a genetic predisposition to emotional problems may have been passed on to their children.

Another theory about the development of BPD is that early attachment is disrupted. For example, perhaps the baby is difficult to soothe, the adoptive parent may have difficulty bonding, or an interaction between the two makes it difficult to develop a stable attachment.

The most important thing to know, however, is that it is important to deal with what is rather than what might have been. Research shows that attempted suicide is twice as common among adolescents who live with adoptive parents than among adolescents who live with biological parents. Adoption and BPD are both risk factors for attempted suicide, and so getting the kids to develop and practice the skills necessary to deal with strong emotions and interpersonal difficulties should be the task at hand.

Further, adopted adolescents are more than twice as likely as their non-adopted counterparts to receive mental health services. Although these findings don't tell us why this is true, it should alert parents and clinicians to the possibility of the need for earlier mental health assessment in adopted children who begin to have behavioral problems.

## FAMILY CONNECTEDNESS

One attribute that appears to diminish the risk of suicidal behavior in adopted adolescents is family connectedness. Family connectedness is a combination of family engagement in shared interests, curiosity about each other's lives, and a nonjudgmental approach when considering each other's perspectives. All of these are consistent with the tenets of dialectical behavior therapy (DBT).

The types of fears that adopted adolescents with BPD have expressed in therapy include a sense that they were taken away from their biological parents because they were bad people and that because of this they can never measure up or they cannot be loved. Other kids have said that they felt they were simply being "given" to someone else. A most haunting fear that some kids express is the concern that, as one teen put it, "How could I possibly trust that anyone could love me if my own biological parents couldn't?"

Although there is no guarantee that adoptive parents can prevent these fears in their adopted children, focusing on the connection is essential. Parents have shared a variety of strategies for connecting, including establishing family rituals that bond and celebrate the family and involving the child in establishing such rituals. One family said that they had a karaoke night once a month. The father admitted that he was a terrible singer while his adopted daughter had a wonderful voice. His willingness to initially feel humiliated allowed for great mirth within the family, and later his own ability to laugh at himself and tolerate distress improved!

Another family went on a camping trip twice a year armed with cameras to try and capture each other on film doing "interesting" things, such as wallowing in mud or building a bonfire. Other families have said that connecting their own past (like a dad fishing with his dad) with their present (dad now fishing with his adopted son) helped maintain a sense of family history.

Sometimes, though, despite trying these bonding activities, adopted kids feel an ongoing disconnect. It is essential to recognize this and consider that the child might simply not see interactions and events the way that parents see them. Becoming curious and listening nonjudgmentally is critical in both developing a deeper understanding of the child and establishing that, despite seeing things differently, children can trust that their parents will listen. This process can at times take months and years, even in a safe and nurturing environment.

Further, when parents see the rumblings of difficult behavior in their adopted children, they need to have a clear idea of how they will respond to such issues. Waiting to respond only when a situation has erupted is too late and can lead to unhealthy and ineffective responses. Parents should recognize and avoid habitually showing irritation and annoyance in response to misbehavior, as this often leads to an escalation of the problem behavior by the adolescent. In some adopted children and adolescents, behavior is a direct consequence of pre-adoption trauma, and anger and frustration by the adoptive parent can simply reinforce a pattern of familiar consequences for the child. Responding with empathy to the anger or sadness the child is expressing can be profoundly validating and healing.

A mother who was looking for treatment for her sixteen-year-old daughter with BPD, whom she had adopted at fourteen months from Columbia, told me the following:

> "While it is difficult to discern what is what, I could in one sense say that I noticed things the minute I met Julia at ten months old. She was very distressed when the adoption worker left us together and just seemed anxious to me, but she was an adorable child. At that time I spent one week with her because that was all the Columbian adoption authorities would allow until the paperwork was complete. I then had to leave her in Colombia, return home, and did not see her again for four months, when, again, more behaviors appeared that I now realize were probably significant.

> "Her behavior during her initial introduction to her sister, Jamie, whom we had also adopted, was very interesting to me. It took place at fourteen months on the kitchen floor, and Julia's reaction was strikingly similar to the 'goodbye' behavior when the two parted last September, at fourteen years, as Julia was off to the residential program. At fourteen months old, she appeared distant and not interested in Jamie (they were born eight days apart). At fourteen years old, she was far more concerned with her fingernails and new hairdo than the enormity of the moment. In both cases, Jamie, who was looking for connection, meaning, etc., in the moment, was figuratively slapped in the face and visibly hurt. What was a temperamental difference between the girls versus the early symptoms of a disorder is impossible to say.

"Anyway, she is at a therapeutic residential school now and she called me last night. For the first time in sixteen years (!) she asked me about some scarring on her back and shoulders. It has taken her all this time to be ready for that question. I had been ready for years, but it was still difficult. I explained that it had occurred in Colombia sometime between my first visit and when I eventually picked her up at fourteen months and that beyond that, I had no explanation. She went very 'dark' and into what her new therapist describes as 'full borderline behavior.' I think I mentioned that she was adorable, that's what got me hooked, but when I saw the scars, I had to get her out of the country. The authorities told me that she had fallen, but it looks as if someone had taken a stick to her, at least that's what our pediatrician says."

"Full borderline behavior" was hopeless emptiness, which alternated with reactive rage and then rapidly back to isolation, and then finally behaving as if nothing had happened. What the therapist was describing was what Julia's mother had struggled with for years before finding help.

## POSSIBLE RISK FACTORS FOR BPD IN ADOPTED CHILDREN

Why should an adopted child be at greater risk for developing BPD? For one thing, if the biological family's mental health history is not known it is possible that a child inherited genes for psychiatric illness.

Also, it is possible that if the child has a markedly different temperament than his or her parents, then an environment for being misunderstood and ultimately "invalidated" has been created. A common experience on our unit is that of the emotionally intense or dysregulated kid and the reserved parents with far less emotional range. If temperament is genetically determined (as it appears to be), then it is possible that the child inherited an emotionally intense nature that, when exposed to a less reactive or uncertain response from his or her adopted parents, would make attachment, and therefore the capacity to form a stable image of the self, more difficult. Another way to think about this is to consider the friends you have. We tend to connect to people who are emotionally similar to us. "Birds of a feather flock together," the old saying goes. Children with BPD are birds of a different emotional feather and so may have difficulty flocking together.

Another question that arises is whether adopted children sense the initial rejection by their biological parents as abandonment and therefore have to answer the question, "If my own parents abandoned me, why won't everyone else?" If this fear is present, it can contribute to the fear of abandonment in patients with BPD. The loss of the birth parents as a result of adoption sets the stage for the feelings of loss and abandonment that some adopted adolescents experience. Another element that can compound such feelings of rejection and abandonment are other losses, such as the loss through separation of a brother or sister, grandparents, and others in the extended family because of the adoption. In many of the adolescents we see, there is also a loss of cultural connection or language, especially when the kids are adopted from abroad.

It is obviously impossible to know whether these children would have developed BPD had they remained with their birth parents or been adopted by temperamentally closer parents. However, a case could be made for considering temperament in the adoption match, although this would be difficult with very young infants.

Another important issue to consider is that adopted people often begin to have questions about their identities during adolescence. The task of identity development during adolescence is often more difficult for the adopted teenager because of the additional adoption issues. Adopted adolescents' identity development includes questions about their biological families and what became of them, why they were placed for adoption, whether they resemble their birth parents, and where the adolescents "belong" in terms of education, social class, and culture. Children with BPD have a difficult enough time with the issue of identity and an adopted child with BPD is likely to be all the more confused.

In one case, for instance, a wealthy WASP family had adopted a young girl from the Philippines. They recognized that their daughter began to have problems when she turned fourteen. What they missed, however, was that the family had hired a cleaning crew that would come twice a week to the house, and that the crew consisted of young women from the Philippines. The girl told us that she recognized that (in her words) "these cleaning people" looked more like her, and acted more like how she felt, than her adopted family did. Also, she suddenly felt very uncomfortable with her wealth in the context of the relative poverty of the cleaning crew. Her sense of who she was became confused and precipitated a crisis that led to cutting behaviors and suicidal thinking. It took months of therapy, and the family recognizing the need for their daughter to have a connection with her strong sense of culture, for her to get better.

## SIBLING COMPETITION

Another complicated issue that appears in adolescents with BPD is that of the relationship with the biological children of the adoptive parents.

Carlos was referred to us from New Mexico. He had become increasingly depressed over many years and no amount of therapy or medication seemed to change the course of his depression. His parents told us that Carlos had been adopted soon after birth, given up by his teenage mother who was the daughter of a seasonal agricultural worker from Mexico. The parents considered themselves particularly blessed because the adoptive mother had experienced fertility problems and was unable to have children of her own. For them, Carlos was the wonder child.

As is sometimes the case, a few years after the adoption, the mother became pregnant. The pregnancy was complicated, which required her to spend less time with Carlos. Her son was born four weeks premature, causing her to spend much of the next four months with him, in and out of hospital.

Carlos became sullen and distant, although he did not otherwise appear to have behavioral problems. He never truly bonded with his younger brother. He was not mean, but not close, and his mother acknowledged that she spent a lot of time with her biological child because he had been sickly.

Carlos's withdrawal became a depression, and his parents started to look for therapy soon after his eleventh birthday. Eventually, Carlos started cutting himself, and he appeared at our unit with multiple scars all over his body. After months of therapy, he was able to talk about his sense that his mother loved his brother more than she loved him, and that he had been angry that his brother had ever been born, but because his brother had been sick, he couldn't express his anger.

The theme appears again and again of whether a child feels that he or she can be loved enough—in Carlos's case, that his first mother had given him up, that his adoptive mother had bought a substitute child, but that now that she had her own, he once again had been abandoned.

For highly sensitive children, these early attachments problems can have profound and enduring consequences in the ongoing development of the child.

## WELL-INTENTIONED LOVE

The following thoughts are worth repeating from an earlier chapter. They accurately capture the experience of parents raising their adoptive children with BPD, and they will also resonate as true with parents raising their biological children with BPD.

"There were signs, but we didn't see them. As people who approach life with confident optimism, we embarked on the adventure of creating a family with naive, enthusiastic energy. Nature versus nurture? As adoptive parents we were convinced that the loving environment we'd create for our first child would guide his development and form a personality as open and gregarious as ours.

"Mother Nature is a powerful force. She equipped Sean with a temperament that rebuffed our relentlessly misguided efforts to shape our son in our image. Convinced that he would eventually emerge from his wary, reluctant ways, we unwittingly practiced invalidation early and often. Failing to appreciate how fragile his makeup truly was, we forged ahead, exposing him to new experiences without realizing the layers of trauma they provoked."

A capacity for insight such as this, which acknowledges that a child's experience may have been different from what the parents perceived, goes a long way toward reversing the effects of any invalidation. With such acknowledgement, therapists need to work with parents and adolescents in a nonblaming, nonjudgmental approach that recognizes that things are the way they are, and the focus is on a future worth living for the entire family. This is true whether the child is adopted or not.

In the next and final chapter I will review what research shows about the long-term outcome of BPD.

## CHAPTER FOURTEEN

# BPD:
# The Good Prognosis Diagnosis

A S WITH MANY OTHER CHRONIC and initially misunderstood conditions, such as HIV/AIDS and cancer, BPD was considered a disorder that clinicians did not want to treat and that if so diagnosed, a person with BPD was destined to a life of judgment, emotional suffering, and rejection. Hospital staff believed that people with BPD were manipulative and likely to cause havoc on their units. As with other chronic conditions, research has made BPD far more understood than before, and new therapies targeting BPD are leading to faster recovery rates and better outcomes.

Before digging deeper into this topic, here is the latest, and promising, research on BPD. Investigators in Canada in 2013 wanted to determine the long-term outcome of adolescents who were diagnosed with BPD before age eighteen. They followed a group of forty-seven adolescent girls over a ten-year period. Of those girls, thirty-one had been diagnosed with BPD while sixteen had not. After 4.3 years, only eleven of the thirty-one girls still met the criteria for BPD and no new cases had developed. Those who still met the criteria, however, were significantly more likely to suffer from major depression, to abuse substances, and to have a history of childhood sexual abuse. The important point is that most adolescents who meet the criteria for BPD can be expected to no longer be symptomatic for the disorder within four years.

## YESTERDAY

The early studies of BPD outcomes were not optimistic at all. BPD was more than a diagnosis; it was a label that, once earned, was not removed. When I first became interested in BPD in the early 1990s, I read the scant literature available at the time, and I found one study particularly interesting. It was the first study that held some promise of change in those with BPD. Thomas McGlashan, MD, reported on the outcome of patients with BPD who had spent years in a long-term psychiatric facility. He noted that the typical course was that people with BPD generally showed poor work and social functioning through their twenties and early thirties and that functioning improved and stabilized during their forties. He also noted that a subgroup of patients deteriorated during their late forties and early fifties, usually in response to a divorce, death of a spouse, or breakup of a significant relationship.

These findings were important because they were the first to show some improvement in functioning or that patients could get better. I remember thinking, "Okay, if my adolescents can hang on for another fifteen to twenty years, they can get better!" But I also thought that fifteen to twenty years was a long time for someone to suffer.

McGlashan found that the older a person was, the less likely he or she was to continue to suffer from BPD. It was as if the rage of BPD simply burned itself out. The idea was that if patients who suffered from BPD could be kept alive long enough, then things would get better for them.

## TODAY

The following is from a therapy session with a seventeen-year-old patient:

> "You may not be 100 percent sure of anything, but I sure as hell am.
> This may be the only thing I'm sure of. I am genuinely convinced that
> I do not belong in this world. Some people have bad days. I've had
> a bad life. I don't think anything surprises me anymore. I used to be
> surprised that, after thinking I had hit rock bottom, I found an even
> lower place. But I know now that things will get worse and worse. I
> honestly don't think most people could spend a day inside my head
> without wanting to jump out a window themselves."

How could I possibly tell this young woman that all she had to do was stay
alive for the next fifteen or twenty years and then she would be better, unless she got divorced, had a breakup, or experienced the death of a spouse?
With the offer of such unrelenting misery, who wouldn't consider suicide as
a possible solution?

Today, however, there is tremendous hope. Apart from the Canadian
study, an Australian study found that only 40 percent of BPD teens between the ages of fifteen and eighteen met the criteria for the disorder after
a two-year follow-up. Although this may seem like a rather large number,
it is much smaller than those of other major mental illnesses. For instance,
those who have schizophrenia in their adolescence have an 80 to 90 percent
chance of having it in their adulthood.

Another ten-year study in adolescent twins also found a decrease in
rates of diagnosis from fourteen to twenty-four years of age, with a significant reduction in symptoms every two to three years. These findings are
similar to adult studies that show that the majority of adult BPD patients
no longer meet the criteria for the diagnosis.

What we don't know is which factors predict which outcomes in adolescents with BPD. However, the preliminary review of studies on our unit
suggests that childhood sexual abuse and substance abuse worsen outcomes.

These findings again are consistent with studies that show that these factors worsen the outcomes in adults. In adults with BPD, having poor executive function, which means more impulsivity and less planning of responses and behavior, translates into poorer outcomes.

A large adult study based at McLean, the Collaborative Longitudinal Personality Disorders Study (CLPS), showed that 85 percent of people with BPD went into remission remitted during ten years of follow-up. This means that after ten years, they no longer met the criteria for BPD. In addition, only 11 percent relapsed. This means that only a fraction of people with BPD who no longer have it will relapse. The point is that once the disorder goes into remission, it usually remains that way.

Another large study, the McLean Hospital Study of Adult Development, found that nearly 75 percent of patients had no active symptoms after six years, and after this period of time, only 6 percent relapsed back into BPD. This research, which I will describe more completely later in this chapter, focused on adults with BPD. Our thinking is that if we can get to the BPD symptoms earlier in the course of the disorder, we might shorten this time period even more.

## TOMORROW

Mary Zanarini, EdD, arguably one of the world's foremost researchers in BPD, has spearheaded our research on adolescents with BPD. In the next few years, we will be reporting on the data we have gathered. For now her long-term research focuses on adults with BPD, a group she has been following for more than twenty years. Here are some key findings from her research:

- The absence of active BPD symptoms after six years of treatment was much more common than had previously been thought. For many years, clinicians thought that this group of patients was a lost cause. However, one McLean study showed that 74 percent of patients were without active symptoms after six years.

- These remissions were generally stable, and the recurrence of BPD once in remission was rare, only about 6 percent. What this means is that once a person gets better, the chance of the symptoms returning is low, which is great news.
- Completed suicides were far rarer than anticipated—about 4 percent as compared to the 10 percent in previous outcome studies. It is likely that for people with BPD who require inpatient treatment, the rate of suicide is higher than for outpatients with BPD who never need hospitalization.
- Based on the research, BPD is best described as having two sets of conditions—those that subside quickly and those that take longer to abate. The symptoms that tend to improve relatively quickly include suicidality, self-injury, and impulsivity. These symptoms are often the immediate reason for needing costly forms of treatment, such as psychiatric hospitalizations. The symptoms that are closely associated with ongoing psychosocial impairment—such as chronic feelings of intense anger, emptiness, and profound abandonment—are much more difficult to treat.
- People with BPD overall continuously improved their life functioning over time. The various researchers felt that people with BPD were somewhat belatedly achieving the developmental milestones of young adulthood. This is significant because we found that some imaging and EEG studies have suggested that brains of people with BPD appear to mature more slowly than those without BPD pathology.

The researchers' final and heartening conclusion was that all these findings, taken together, suggest that the prognosis for BPD is better than previously recognized.

Despite this optimism, it is worth repeating what Kiera van Gelder, author of *The Buddha and the Borderline* and a leader in the BPD peer-to-peer recovery movement, in which former patients help current patients, has had to say about measures of recovery: "Call me a dreamer, but I envision the day when people who have been treated for BPD can be involved in defining whether a treatment is effective or not. A clinician's definition of my 'remission' is not necessarily a life worth living."

With this in mind, I want to look at specific research that warrants highlighting.

## BPD AND POST-TRAUMATIC STRESS DISORDER (PTSD)

A 2006 study noted that there was limited research on the impact of PTSD co-occurring in people with BPD. Researchers found that patients with PTSD and BPD reported significantly higher levels of general distress, physical illness, anxiety, and depression than those with BPD alone. People who suffer from both BPD and PTSD are likely to require more intensive clinical services to reduce distress and improve their functioning. Perhaps not surprisingly, it is our clinical experience that BPD patients who suffer not only from PTSD but also any other psychiatric condition, such as bipolar disorder or substance abuse, tend to be significantly more impaired than those who do not have co-occurring conditions.

In a 2014 preliminary study presented by my colleague Cynthia Kaplan, PhD, adolescents with BPD who also had PTSD had more symptoms of BPD, were "sicker" than their counterparts with BPD alone on admission to the hospital, and although they improved, still remained symptomatic upon discharge. The exciting part is that through Kaplan's efforts we have implemented the protocol of prolonged exposure treatment, spearheaded by researcher Melanie Harned, PhD, at the University of Washington, for adolescents who have BPD and PTSD. In essence, prolonged exposure treatment requires the teen with BPD to repeatedly revisit the traumatic experience by describing the event aloud in great detail. The narrative is recorded and the teens listen to the recording between sessions to maximize therapeutic value. Revisiting the event in this way promotes processing and helps the adolescent realize that he or she can cope with the distress associated with the memory. We are finding a great reduction in both BPD and PTSD symptoms once patients have completed this treatment.

## DBT Outcomes in Adolescents

A 2006 study from Germany found that suicide ranked as the second leading cause of death in adolescents in that country. Study researchers further noted that impulsivity, self-injurious behavior, depression, and conduct disorder put these adolescents at high risk for suicide and suicidal behavior (which, incidentally though not unexpectedly, are similar to the risk factors for adolescent suicide in the United States).

Because DBT directly addresses suicidality, the researchers wanted to test whether DBT was an effective method of treatment for adolescents. They studied adolescents who had made repeated suicide attempts and found that patients who were treated with DBT during the research made no suicide attempts. This type of study is beginning to change the perspectives and attitudes of clinicians working with highly suicidal adolescents because finally clinicians have an evidence-based treatment that will reduce the very behaviors that burn them out. This is good news for people with BPD who historically have found it hard to find therapists willing to work with them.

## International Research on BPD Reports Similar Results

BPD outcomes research is being performed everywhere from Germany to Australia, from Canada to Japan. Although there are some (at times significant) societal differences among these cultures, the outcomes of BPD are fairly similar.

In a 2006 study, Japanese researchers reviewed the records of seventy-two patients with BPD who had received treatment at a university hospital between 1973 and 1989. Five of the seventy-two, or 7 percent, had committed suicide. This percentage is similar to the findings of American and

Canadian BPD researchers. A significant difference from American studies was that Japanese patients with BPD were more likely to live with their families than American patients with BPD. The Japanese researchers also found that overinvolvement by family members predicted poor patient outcomes, which is interesting because many families were historically accused by clinicians of not being involved enough, especially in BPD. Overinvolved families are sometimes overprotective of their loved ones with BPD. As a result, the overprotected family member with BPD remains dependent and fails to grow and develop. Overinvolvement can create conflict and resentment among family members who try to break out of the dependency role. In addition, the study found that a higher number of hospitalizations was predictive of poor outcomes.

## PUTTING ALL THE STUDIES TOGETHER

Studies examining the natural course of BPD over the life span have all shown that the rates of BPD decline from youth to adulthood. However, there is evidence that different BPD symptoms have different patterns; so, for instance, impulsivity decreases more quickly as teens age, but mood symptoms and anger tend to persist.

However, almost all of the studies have dealt with people who come into treatment, so we don't exactly know what happens to people who never seek treatment. For instance, does impulsivity decrease *because* of treatment? In an attempt to address this question, a 2013 in Germany followed 2,488 people of various ages from adolescence to late adulthood who had never received treatment. Researchers compared the rates of BPD, impulsivity, and depression, and found that over the course of the study, the rate of BPD dropped sharply as the teens aged and then the rate reached a stable plateau. Impulsivity also dropped as the teens aged. However, rates of depression increased over time as people aged, and having BPD as an adolescent led to an enduring negative mood state.

## THE BOTTOM LINE ON OUTCOMES

As shown here, the research on adolescent BPD is finally taking off. Preliminary studies show that within four years, more than 60 percent of adolescents with BPD will no longer meet the diagnosis. These results support making the diagnosis in adolescents when symptoms are present, as opposed to not doing so, or making an alternative diagnosis that will expose the child to unnecessary medications and prolong suffering. Targeted, effective, and comprehensive early treatment means that maladaptive behavioral patterns won't consolidate and be as established as they would be if tackled later in life. As I have mentioned before, in my clinical experience there are very few adults with BPD who did not have symptoms in adolescence, so not treating adolescents with BPD symptoms risks a bleak future.

I was asked recently: "What if you are wrong and you are teaching skills to people who don't have BPD?" I don't have a problem with this for two reasons: First, the adolescents we see are referred for some problematic behavior generally related to self-injury or suicidal thoughts. These symptoms deserve treatment. Second, the skills we teach, such as conflict resolution and emotion regulation, are applicable to many aspects of adolescent life, including test-taking anxiety, stage fright, interpersonal disputes, and many other situations. Parents sometimes say that while they don't know whether their children learned anything, they sure learned skills that help them in their everyday lives. A DBT skills-based treatment has, in my opinion, little downside.

Anecdotally, we hear back from parents of adolescents who have completed an intensive DBT treatment on our residential unit that the majority of them are doing well. (We will soon undertake more formal research to have a better sense of the actual outcomes.) One such anecdote comes from the parent of a sixteen-year-old female with BPD discharged from McLean Hospital. She had been admitted after a serious suicide attempt, and her family was in a state of crisis. This is what her parent said:

"Apart from a few minor blips, Lindsey is doing very well, and we're all making strides together and apart. I'm learning to take it day to day, and we're both learning to enforce the positive and draw lines in the sand with the negative. We're all learning from each other, and it's all good."

# Resources

In the former edition of this book, I provided a list of resources for parents and clinicians. No sooner was the book published than these started to change. Because of this I am not going to name specific programs because new ones emerge nearly every month. I will, however, point to certain organizations that have remained at the forefront of advocacy and education. I encourage parents to use these resources and the Internet to keep current.

## ONLINE RESOURCES

### Borderline Personality Disorder Resource Center

*www.bpdresourcecenter.org*

The Borderline Personality Disorder Resource Center at New York-Presbyterian Hospital-Weill Cornell Medical College has been set up specifically to help those affected by the disorder find the most current and accurate information on the nature of BPD and sources of available treatment.

### BPD Central

*www.bpdcentral.com*

BPD Central is a list of resources for people who care about someone with BPD. It is one of the oldest and largest sites about BPD on the Web.

## BPD Today

*www.borderlinepersonalitytoday.com*

The aim of this site is "to provide the latest information about mental health disorders to mental health clinicians as well as consumers and families who are now beginning to demand better treatment."

## Dialectical Behavioral Therapy Self Help

*www.dbtselfhelp.com/index.html*

This website is a service for people who are seeking information about dialectal behavior therapy (DBT), provided in a comprehensive, yet easy-to-read format.

## National Alliance on Mental Illness (NAMI)

*www.nami.org*

NAMI is the nation's largest grassroots mental health organization dedicated to improving the lives of persons living with serious mental illness and their families. Founded in 1979, it has become the nation's voice on mental illness. NAMI is a national organization with chapters in every state and in many local communities that raise awareness through education, advocacy, support groups, and access to treatment and services.

## National Education Alliance for Borderline Personality Disorder

*www.borderlinepersonalitydisorder.com*

The mission of the National Education Alliance for Borderline Personality Disorder is to raise public awareness, provide education, promote research on BPD, and enhance the quality of life of those affected by this serious mental illness.

## Personality Disorders Awareness Network (PDAN)

*www.pdan.org/bpd.php*

PDAN is a not-for-profit organization dedicated to projects that help children, families, and individuals understand and cope with various personality disorders. PDAN was established in 2001 to increase public awareness of personality disorders.

## Treatment and Research Advancements (TARA) National Association for Personality Disorder

*www.tara4bpd.org*

TARA's mission is to foster education and research in the field of personality disorder, specifically but not exclusively borderline personality disorder; to support research into the causes, psychobiology, and treatment of personality disorders; to support and encourage educational programs and endeavors targeting mental health professionals, consumers of mental health services, families, and/or the community at large in order to reduce stigma and increase awareness of personality disorder; to disseminate available information on etiology and treatment; and to advocate for the accomplishment of these goals.

## RECOMMENDED BOOKS

*Borderline Personality Disorder Demystified: An Essential Guide for Understanding and Living with BPD* by Robert O. Friedel, MD

*Dialectical Behavior Therapy with Suicidal Adolescents* by Alec L. Miller, PsyD; Jill H. Rathus, PhD; and Marsha M. Linehan, PhD

*Get Me Out of Here: My Recovery from Borderline Personality Disorder* by Rachel Reiland

*Siren's Dance: My Marriage to a Borderline: A Case Study* by Anthony Walker, MD

*Surviving a Borderline Parent: How to Heal Your Childhood Wounds & Build Trust, Boundaries, and Self-Esteem* by Kimberlee Roth and Freda B. Friedman, PhD, LCSW

*Understanding and Treating Borderline Personality Disorder: A Guide for Professionals and Families* edited by John G. Gunderson, MD, and Perry D. Hoffman, PhD

# Bibliography

## JOURNAL ARTICLES

Abbar, M., P. Courtet, F. Bellivier, M. Leboyer, J. P. Boulenger, D. Castelhau, M. Ferreira, C. Lambercy, D. Mouthon, A. Paoloni-Giacobino, M. Vessaz, A. Malafosse, and C. Buresi. "Suicide Attempts and the Tryptophan Hydroxylase Gene," *Nature*, 2001, 6(3):268–73.

Adachi, T., T. Masumura, M. Arai, N. Adachi, S. Akazawa, and H. Arai. "Self-Administered Electroconvulsive Treatment with a Homemade Device," *Journal of ECT*, 2006, 22(3):226–27.

Agrawal, H. R., J. Gunderson, B. M. Holmes, K. Lyons-Ruth. "Attachment Studies with Borderline Patients: A Review," *Harvard Review of Psychiatry*, 2004, 12(2):94–104.

Akiskal, H. S., M. L. Bourgeois, J. Angst, R. Post, H. Moller, and R. Hirschfeld. "Re-evaluating the Prevalence of and Diagnostic Composition within the Broad Clinical Spectrum of Bipolar Disorders," *Journal of Affective Disorders*, 2000, 59(Supplement 1):S5–S30.

Anderson, S. W., A. Bechara, H. Damasio, et al. "Impairment of Social and Moral Behavior Related to Early Damage in Human Prefrontal Cortex," *National Neuroscience*, 1999, 2:1032–37.

Archer, R. P., J. D. Ball, and J. A. Hunter. "MMPI Characteristics of Borderline Psychopathology in Adolescent Inpatients," *Journal of Personality Assessment*, 1985, 49(1):47–55.

Arranz, B., A. Eriksson, E. Mellerup, P. Plenge, and J. Marcusson. "Brain 5-HT1A, 5-HT1D and 5-HT2 Receptors in Suicide Victims," *Biological Psychiatry*, 1994, 35(7):457–63.

Asaad, T., T. Okasha, and A. Okasha. "Sleep EEG Findings in ICD-10 Borderline Personality Disorder in Egypt," *Journal of Affective Disorders*, 2002, 71(1-3):11–18.

Asberg, M. "Neurotransmitters and Suicidal Behavior: The Evidence from Cerebrospinal Fluid Studies," *Annals of the New York Academy of Sciences*, 1997, 836:158–81.

Asnis, G. M., J. Eisenberg, H. M. van Praag, C. Z. Lemus, J. M. Harkvay Friedman, and A. H. Miller. "The Neuroendocrine Response to Fenfluramine in Depressive and Normal Controls," *Biological Psychiatry*, 1988, 24:117–20.

Atmaca, M., M. Kuloglu, E. Tezcan, O. Gecici, and B. Ustundag. "Serum Cholesterol and Leptin Levels in Patients with Borderline Personality Disorder," *Neuropsychobiology*, 2002, 45(4):167–71.

Avdibegovic, E., and O. Sinanovic. "Consequences of Domestic Violence on Women's Mental Health in Bosnia and Herzegovina," *Croatian Medical Journal*, 2006, 47(5):730–41.

Bargh, J. A., and K. Y. McKenna. "The Internet and Social Life," *Annual Review of Psychology*, 2004, 55:573–90.

Barnow, S., C. Spitzer, H. J. Grabe, C. Kessler, and H. J. Freyberger. "Individual Characteristics, Familial Experience, and Psychopathology in Children of Mothers with Borderline Personality Disorder," *Journal of the American Academy of Child and Adolescent Psychiatry*, 2006, 45(8):965–72.

Bateman, A., and P. Fonagy. "Effectiveness of Partial Hospitalization in the Treatment of Borderline Personality Disorder: A Randomized Controlled Trial," *American Journal of Psychiatry*, 1999, 156:1563–69.

Battle, C. L., M. T. Shea, D. M. Johnson, S. Yen, C. Zlotnick, M. C. Zanarini, C. A. Sanislow, A. E. Skodol, J. G. Gunderson, C. M. Grilo, T. H. McGlashan, and L. C. Morey. "Childhood Maltreatment Associated with Adult Personality Disorders: Findings from the Collaborative Longitudinal Personality Disorders Study," *Journal of Personality Disorders*, 2004, 18(2):193–211.

Becker, A. E., R. A. Burwell, S. E. Gilman, D. B. Herzog, and P. Hamburg. "Eating Behaviors and Attitudes Follow Prolonged Exposure to Television among Ethnic Fijian Adolescent Girls," *British Journal of Psychiatry*, 2000, 180:509–14.

Becker, D. F., C. M. Grilo, W. S. Edell, and T. H. McGlashan. "Comorbidity of Borderline Personality Disorder with Other Personality Disorders in Hospitalized Adolescents and Adults," *American Journal of Psychiatry*, 2000, 157(12):2011–16.

Becker, D. F., C. M. Grilo, W. S. Edell, and T. H. McGlashan. "Diagnostic Efficiency of Borderline Personality Disorder Criteria in Hospitalized Adolescents: Comparison with Hospitalized Adults," *American Journal of Psychiatry*, 2002, 159(12):2042–47.

Becker, D. F., T. H. McGlashan, and C. M. Grilo. "Exploratory Factor Analysis of Borderline Personality Disorder Criteria in Hospitalized Adolescents," *Comprehensive Psychiatry*, 2006, 47(2):99–105.

Bellino, S., E. Paradiso, and F. Bogetto. "Oxcarbazepine in the Treatment of Borderline Personality Disorder: A Pilot Study," *Journal of Clinical Psychiatry*, 2005, 66(9):1111–15.

Bellino, S., L. Patria, E. Paradiso, R. Di Lorenzo, C. Zanon, M. Zizza, and F. Bogetto. "Major Depression in Patients with Borderline Personality Disorder: A Clinical Investigation," *Canadian Journal of Psychiatry*, 2005, 50(4):234–38.

Berk, M. S., E. Jeglic, G. K. Brown, G. R. Henriques, and A. T. Beck. "Characteristics of Recent Suicide Attempters with and without Borderline Personality Disorder," *Archives of Suicide Research*, 2007, 11(1):91–104.

Berlin, H. A., E. T. Rolls, and S. D. Iversen. "Borderline Personality Disorder, Impulsivity, and the Orbitofrontal Cortex," *American Journal of Psychiatry*, 2005, 162(12):2360–73.

Bolton, E. E., K. T. Mueser, and S. D. Rosenberg. "Symptom Correlates of Posttraumatic Stress Disorder in Clients with Borderline Personality Disorder," *Comprehensive Psychiatry*, 2006, 47(5):357–61.

Bradley, R., C. Zittel Conklin, and D. Westen. "The Borderline Personality Diagnosis in Adolescents: Gender Differences and Subtypes," *Journal of Child Psychology and Psychiatry*, 2005, 46(9):1006-19.

Brambilla, P., P. H. Soloff, M. Sala, M. A. Nicoletti, M. S. Keshavan, and J. C. Soares. "Anatomical MRI Study of Borderline Personality Disorder Patients," *Psychiatry Research*, 2004, 131(2):125–33.

Brassington, J., and R. Krawitz. "Australasian Dialectical Behaviour Therapy Pilot Outcome Study: Effectiveness, Utility and Feasibility," *Australasian Psychiatry*, 2006, 14(3):313–19.

Brodsky, B. S., K. M. Malone, S. P. Ellis, R. A. Dulit, and J. J. Mann. "Characteristics of Borderline Personality Disorder Associated with Suicidal Behavior," *American Journal of Psychiatry*, 1997, 154(12):1715–19.

Brown, J. D., K. W. Childers, and C. S. Waszak. "Television and Adolescent Sexuality," *Journal of Adolescent Health Care*, 1990, 11(1):62–70.

Chabrol, H., K. Chouicha, A. Montovany, S. Callahan, E. Duconge, and H. Sztulman. "Personality Disorders in a Nonclinical Sample of Adolescents," *L'Encephale*, 2002, 28(6 Pt 1):520–24.

Chanen, A. M., H. J. Jackson, P. D. McGorry, K. A. Allot, V. Clarkson, and H. P. Yuen. "Two-Year Stability of Personality Disorder in Older Adolescent Outpatients," *Journal of Personality Disorders*, 2004, 18(6):526–41.

Chen, E. Y., M. Z. Brown, T. T. Lo, and M. M. Linehan. "Sexually Transmitted Disease Rates and High-Risk Sexual Behaviors in Borderline Personality Disorder versus Borderline Personality Disorder with Substance Use Disorder," *Journal of Nervous and Mental Disease*, 2007, 195(2):125–29.

Chethik, M. "The Borderline Child." In *Basic Handbook of Child Psychiatry*, J. Noshpitz, ed. New York: Basic Books, 1979.

Coccaro, E. F., L. J. Siever, H. M. Klar, G. Mauer, K. Cochrane, T. B. Cooper, et al. "Serotonin Studies in Patients with Affective and Personality Disorders," *Archives of General Psychiatry*, 1989, 46:587–99.

Cohen, P., H. Chen, T. N. Crawford, J. S. Brook, and K. Gordon. "Personality Disorders in Early Adolescence and the Development of Later Substance Use Disorders in the General Population," *Drug and Alcohol Dependence*, 2007, 88S1:S71–S84.

Crandell, L. E., M. P. H. Patrick, and R. P. Hobson, "Still-Face Interactions between Mothers with Borderline Personality Disorder and Their 2-Month-Old Infants," *The British Journal of Psychiatry*, 2003, 183:239–47.

Crawford, T. N., P. Cohen, and J. S. Brook. "Dramatic-Erratic Personality Disorder Symptoms: I. Continuity from Early Adolescence into Adulthood," *Journal of Personality Disorders*, 2001, (4):319–35.

Crick, N. R., D. Murray-Close, and K. Woods. "Borderline Personality Features in Childhood: A Short-Term Longitudinal Study," *Developmental Psychopathology*, 2005, 17:1051–70.

Crowell, S. E., T. P. Beauchaine, E. McCauley, C. J. Smith, A. L. Stevens, and P. Sylvers. "Psychological, Autonomic, and Serotonergic Correlates of Parasuicide among Adolescent Girls," *Developmental Psychopathology*, 2005, 17(4):1105–27.

Crumley, F. E. "Adolescent Suicide Attempts and Borderline Personality Disorder: Clinical Features," *Southern Medical Journal*, 1981, 74(5):546–49.

Davidson, K., J. Norrie, P. Tyrer, A. Gumley, P. Tata, H. Murray, and S. Palmer. "The Effectiveness of Cognitive Behavior Therapy for Borderline Personality Disorder: Results from the Borderline Personality Disorder Study of Cognitive Therapy Trial," *Journal of Personality Disorders*, 2006, 20(5):450–65.

Davidson, M., R. Mohs, and L. J. Siever. "Affective and Impulsive Personality Traits in the Relatives of Patients with Borderline Personality Disorder," *American Journal of Psychiatry*, 1991, 148(10):1378–85.

Deans, C., and E. Meocevic. "Attitudes of Registered Psychiatric Nurses Towards Patients Diagnosed with Borderline Personality Disorder," *Contemporary Nurse*, 2006, 21(1):43–49.

De la Fuente, J. M., P. Tugendhaft, and N. Mavroudakis. "Electroencephalographic Abnormalities in Borderline Personality Disorder," *Psychiatry Research*, 1998, 77(2):131–38.

Deltito, J., L. Martin, J. Riefkohl, B. Austria, A. Kissilenko, C. Corless, and P. Morse. "Do Patients with Borderline Personality Disorder Belong to the Bipolar Spectrum?" *Journal of Affective Disorders*, 2001, 67(1-3):221–28.

Dinn, W. M., C. L. Harris, A. Aycicegi, P. B. Greene, S. M. Kirkley, and C. Reilly. "Neurocognitive Function in Borderline Personality Disorder," *Progress in Neuropsychopharmacology*, 2004, 28(2):329–41.

Donegan, N. H., C. A. Sanislow, H. P. Blumberg, R. K. Fulbright, C. Lacadie, P. Skudlarski, J. C. Gore, I. R. Olson, T. H. McGlashan, and B. E. Wexler. "Amygdala Hyperreactivity in Borderline Personality Disorder: Implications for Emotional Dysregulation," *Biological Psychiatry*, 2003, 54(11):1284–93.

Dubo, E. D., M. C. Zanarini, R. E. Lewis, and A. A. Williams. "Childhood Antecedents of Self-Destructiveness in Borderline Personality Disorder," *Canadian Journal of Psychiatry*, 1997, 42(1):63–69.

Dulit, R. A., M. R. Fyer, A. C. Leon, B. S. Brodsky, and A. J. Frances. "Clinical Correlates of Self-Mutilation in Borderline Personality Disorder," *American Journal of Psychiatry*, 1994, 151:1305–11.

Ebner-Priemer, U. W., S. Badeck, C. Beckmann, A. Wagner, B. Feige, I. Weiss, K. Lieb, and M. Bohus. "Affective Dysregulation and Dissociative Experience in Female Patients with Borderline Personality Disorder: A Startle Response Study," *Journal of Psychiatric Research*, 2005, 39(1):85–92.

Engel, M. "Psychological Testing of Borderline Psychotic Children," *Archives of General Psychiatry*, 1963, 8:426–34.

Fallon, P. "Traveling Through the System: The Lived Experience of People with Borderline Personality Disorder in Contact with Psychiatric Services," *Journal of Psychiatric and Mental Health Nursing*, 2003, 10(4):393–401.

Feske, U., B. Mulsant, P. Pilkonis, P. Soloff, D. Dolata, H. Sackeim, and R. F. Haskett. "Clinical Outcome of ECT in Patients with Major Depression and Comorbid Borderline Personality Disorder," *American Journal of Psychiatry*, 2004, 161:2073–80.

Fleischhaker, C., M. Munz, R. Bohme, B. Sixt, and E. Schulz. "Dialectical Behaviour Therapy for Adolescents (DBT-A)—A Pilot Study on the Therapy of Suicidal, Parasuicidal, and Self-Injurious Behaviour in Female Patients with a Borderline Disorder," *Zeitschrift fur Kinder- und Jugendpsychiatrie und Psychotherapie*, 2006, 34(1):15–25.

Fossati, A., L. Novella, D. Donati, M. Donini, and C. Maffei. "History of Childhood Attention Deficit/Hyperactivity Disorder Symptoms and Borderline Personality Disorder: A Controlled Study," *Comprehensive Psychiatry*, 2002, 43(5):369–77.

Frankenburg, F. R., and M. C. Zanarini. "Divalproex Sodium Treatment of Women with Borderline Personality Disorder and Bipolar II Disorder: A Double-Blind Placebo-Controlled Pilot Study," *Journal of Clinical Psychiatry*, 2002, 63(5):442–46.

Fruzzetti, A. E., P. D Hoffman, and Swenson, C. "Advances in Theory and Practice: Dialectial Behavioral Therapy—Family Skills Training," *Family Process*, 1999, 38:399–414.

Gardner, D. L., and R. W. Cowdry. "Alprazolam-Induced Dyscontrol in Borderline Personality Disorder," *American Journal of Psychiatry*, 1985, 142(1):98–100.

Gest, S. "Behavioral Inhibition: Stability and Associations with Adaptation from Childhood to Early Adulthood," *Journal of Personality and Social Psychology*, 1997, 72:467–75.

Giesen-Bloo, J., R. van Dyck, P. Spinhoven, W. van Tilburg, C. Dirksen, T. van Asselt, I. Kremers, M. Nadort, and A. Arntz. "Outpatient Psychotherapy for Borderline Personality Disorder: A Randomized Trial of Schema Focused Therapy versus Transference Focused Therapy," *Archives of General Psychiatry*, 2006, 63(6):649–58.

Golier, J. A., R. Yehuda, L. M. Bierer, V. Mitropoulou, A. S. New, J. Schmeidler, J. M. Silverman, and L. J. Siever. "The Relationship of Borderline Personality Disorder to Posttraumatic Stress Disorder and Traumatic Events," *American Journal of Psychiatry*, 2003, 160(11):2018–24.

Goodman, M., and A. S. New. "Impulsive Aggression in Borderline Personality Disorder," *Current Psychiatry Reports*, 2000, 2(1):56–61.

Grilo, C. M., D. F. Becker, D. C. Fehon, M. L. Walker, W. S. Edell, and T. H. McGlashan. "Gender Differences in Personality Disorders in Psychiatrically Hospitalized Adolescents," *American Journal of Psychiatry*, 1996, 153(8):1089–91.

Grilo, C. M., C. A. Sanislow, A. E. Skodol, J. G. Gunderson, R. L. Stout, M. T. Shea, M. C. Zanarini, D. S. Bender, L. C. Morey, I. R. Dyck, and T. H. McGlashan. "Do Eating Disorders Co-Occur with Personality Disorders? Comparison Groups Matter," *International Journal of Eating Disorders*, 2003, 33(2):155–64.

Gross, E. F. "Adolescent Internet Use: What We Expect, What Teens Report," *Journal of Applied Developmental Psychology*, 2004, 25:633–49.

Gunderson, J., I. Weinberg, M. Daversa, K. Kueppenbender, M. Zanarini, M. T. Shea, A. E. Skodol, C. A. Sanislow, S. Yen, L. C. Morey, C. M. Grilo, T. H. McGlashan, R. L. Stout, and I. Dyck. "Descriptive and Longitudinal Observations on the Relationship of Borderline Personality Disorder and Bipolar Disorder," *American Journal of Psychiatry*, 2006, 163:1173–78.

Gurvits, I. G., H. W. Koenigsberg, and L. J. Siever. "Neurotransmitter Dysfunction in Patients with Borderline Personality Disorder," *Psychiatric Clinics of North America*, 2000, 23(1):27–40.

Guzder, J., J. Paris, P. Zelkowitz, and R. Feldman. "Psychological Risk Factors for Borderline Pathology in School-Age Children," *Journal of the American Academy of Child and Adolescent Psychiatry*, 1999, 38(2):206–12.

Helgeland, M. I., E. Kjelsberg, and S. Torgersen. "Continuities between Emotional and Disruptive Behavior Disorders in Adolescence and Personality Disorders in Adulthood," *American Journal of Psychiatry*, 2005, 162:1941–47.

Henry, C., V. Mitropoulou, A. S. New, H. W. Koenigsberg, J. Silverman, and L. J. Siever. "Affective Instability and Impulsivity in Borderline Personality and Bipolar II Disorders: Similarities and Differences," *Journal of Psychiatric Research*, 2001, 35(6):307–12.

Hollander, E., A. C. Swann, E. F. Coccaro, P. Jiang, and T. B. Smith. "Impact of Trait Impulsivity and State Aggression on Divalproex versus Placebo Response in Borderline Personality Disorder," *American Journal of Psychiatry*, 2005, 162(3):621–24.

Houston, R. J., N. A. Ceballos, V. M. Hesselbrock, and L. O. Bauer. "Borderline Personality Disorder Features in Adolescent Girls: P300 Evidence of Altered Brain Maturation," *Clinical Neurophysiology*, 2005, 116(6):1424–32.

Ikuta, N., M. C. Zanarini, K. Minakawa, Y. Miyake, N. Moriya, and A. Nishizono-Maher. "Comparison of American and Japanese Outpatients with Borderline Personality Disorder," *Comprehensive Psychiatry*, 1994, 35(5):382–85.

Iribarren, C., J. H. Markovitz, D. R. Jacobs Jr., P. J. Schreiner, M. Daviglus, and J. R. Hibbeln. "Dietary Intake of n-3, n-6 Fatty Acids and Fish: Relationship with Hostility in Young Adults—The CARDIA Study," *European Journal of Clinical Nutrition*, 2004, 58(1):24–31.

Irle, E., C. Lange, and U. Sachsse. "Reduced Size and Abnormal Asymmetry of Parietal Cortex in Women with Borderline Personality Disorder," *Biological Psychiatry*, 2005; 57(2):173–82.

Jacobsen, T., and V. Hofmann. "Children's Attachment Representations: Longitudinal Relations to School Behavior and Academic Competency in Middle Childhood and Adolescence," *Developmental Psychology*, 1997, 33:703–10.

Joyce, P. R., P. C. McHugh, J. M. McKenzie, P. F. Sullivan, R. T. Mulder, S. E. Luty, J. D. Carter, C. M. Frampton, C. Robert Cloninger, A. M. Miller, and M. A. Kennedy. "A Dopamine Transporter Polymorphism Is a Risk Factor for Borderline Personality Disorder in Depressed Patients," *Psychological Medicine*, 2006, 36(6):807–13.

Joyce, P. R., J. M. McKenzie, R. T. Mulder, S. E. Luty, P. F. Sullivan, A. L. Miller, and M. A. Kennedy. "Genetic, Developmental and Personality Correlates of Self-Mutilation in Depressed Patients," *Australian and New Zealand Journal of Psychiatry*, 2006, 40:225–29.

Juengling, F. D., C. Schmahl, B. Hesslinger, D. Ebert, J. D. Bremner, J. Gostomzyk, M. Bohus, and K. Lieb. "Positron Emission Tomography in Female Patients with Borderline Personality Disorder," *Journal of Psychiatric Research*, 2003, 37(2):109–15.

Kagan, J., and N. Snidman. "Temperamental Factors in Human Development," *American Psychologist*, 1991, 46:856–62.

Kasen, S., P. Cohen, A. E. Skodol, J. G. Johnson, and J. S. Brook. "Influence of Child and Adolescent Psychiatric Disorders on Young Adult Personality Disorder," *American Journal of Psychiatry*, 1999, 156(10):1529–35.

Katz, L. Y., S. Gunasekara, and A. L. Miller. "Dialectical Behavior Therapy for Inpatient and Outpatient Parasuicidal Adolescents," *Adolescent Psychiatry*, 2002, 26:161–78.

Kellner, C. H., R. M. Post, F. Putnam, R. Cowdry, D. Gardner, M. A. Kling, M. D. Minichiello, J. R. Trettau, and R. Coppola. "Intravenous Procaine as a Probe of Limbic System Activity in Psychiatric Patients and Normal Controls," *Biological Psychiatry*, 1987, 22(9):1107–26.

Koenigsberg, H. "Integrating Psychotherapy and Pharmacotherapy in the Treatment of Borderline Personality Disorder," *In Session: Psychotherapy in Practice*, 1997, 3(2):39–56.

Kooimana, C. G., S. van Rees Vellingaa, P. Spinhovenb, N. Draijerc, R. W. Trijsburgd, and H. G. M. Rooijmansa "Childhood Adversities as Risk Factors for Alexithymia and Other Aspects of Affect Dysregulation in Adulthood," *Psychotherapy and Psychosomatics*, 2004, 73:107–116.

Kullgren, G. "Factors Associated with Completed Suicide in Borderline Personality Disorder," *The Journal of Nervous and Mental Disorders*, 1998, 76(1):40–44.

Kutcher, S., G. Papatheodorou, S. Reiter, and D. Gardner. "The Successful Pharmacological Treatment of Adolescents and Young Adults with Borderline Personality Disorder: A Preliminary Open Trial of Flupenthixol," *Journal of Psychiatry and Neuroscience*, 1995, 20(2):113–18.

Lange, C., L. Kracht, K. Herholz, U. Sachsse, and E. Irle. "Reduced Glucose Metabolism in Temporo-Parietal Cortices of Women with Borderline Personality Disorder," *Psychiatry Research*, 2005, 30; 139(2):115–26.

Lee, R., T. D. Geracioti, J. W. Kasckow, and E. F. Coccaro. "Childhood Trauma and Personality Disorder: Positive Correlation with Adult CSF Corticotropin-Releasing Factor Concentrations," *American Journal of Psychiatry*, 2005, 162:995–97.

Lewinsohn, P. M., P. Rohde, J. R. Seeley, and D. N. Klein. "Axis II Psychopathology as a Function of Axis I Disorders in Childhood and Adolescence,"

*Journal of the American Academy of Child and Adolescent Psychiatry*, 1997, 36(12):1752–59.

Leyton, M., H. Okazawa, M. Diksic, J. Paris, P. Rosa, S. Mzengeza, S. N. Young, P. Blier, and C. Benkelfat. "Brain Regional-[11C]Methyl-L-Tryptophan Trapping in Impulsive Subjects with Borderline Personality Disorder," *American Journal of Psychiatry*, 2001, 158:775–82.

Linehan, M. *Cognitive Behavioral Treatment of Borderline Personality Disorder.* New York: Guilford Press, 1993.

Linehan, M. *Skills Training Manual for Treating Borderline Personality Disorder.* New York: Guilford Press, 1993.

Linehan, M., H. E. Armstrong, A. Suarez, D. Allmon, and H. L. Heard. "Cognitive-Behavioral Treatment of Chronically Parasuicidal Borderline Patients," *Archives of General Psychiatry*, 1991, 48:1060–64.

Lofgren, D. P., J. Bemporad, J. King, K. Lindem, and G. O'Driscoll. "A Prospective Follow-Up Study of So-Called Borderline Children," *American Journal of Psychiatry*, 1991, 148:1541–47.

Lyons-Ruth, K., B. Repacholi, S. McLeod, and E. Silva. "Disorganized Attachment Behavior in Infancy: Short-Term Stability, Maternal and Infant Correlates, and Risk-Related Subtypes," *Developmental Psychopathology*, 1991, 3:377–96.

Mahler, M. "Clinical Studies in Benign and Malignant Cases of Childhood Psychosis—Schizophrenia-Like," *American Journal of Orthopsychiatry*, 1949, 19:s297, footnote.

Miller, A. L. "Dialectical Behavior Therapy: A New Treatment Approach for Suicidal Adolescents," *American Journal of Psychotherapy*, 1999, 53(3):413–17.

Miller, F. T., T. Abrams, R. Dulit, and M. Fyer. "Substance Abuse in Borderline Personality Disorder," *American Journal of Drug and Alcohol Abuse*, 1993, 19(4):491–97.

Minzenberg, M. J., J. H. Poole, and S. Vinogradov. "Adult Social Attachment Disturbance Is Related to Childhood Maltreatment and Current Symptoms in Borderline Personality Disorder," *The Journal of Nervous and Mental Disorders*, 2006, 194(5):341–48.

Minzenberg, M. J., J. H. Poole, and S. Vinogradov. "Social-Emotion Recognition in Borderline Personality Disorder," *Comprehensive Psychiatry*, 2006, 47(6):468–74.

Moreno, M. A. "Cyberbullying," *JAMA Pediatrics*, 2014, 168(5):500.

Nehls, N. "Being a Case Manager for Persons with Borderline Personality Disorder: Perspectives of Community Mental Health Center Clinicians," *Archives of Psychiatric Nursing*, 2000, 14(1):12–18.

Nehls, N. "Borderline Personality Disorder: The Voice of Patients," *Research in Nurses and Health*, 1999, 22(4):285–93.

New, A. S., R. L. Trestman, and V. Mitropoulou. "Serotonergic Function and Self-Injurious Behavior in Personality Disorder Patients," *Psychiatry Research*, 1997, 69:17–26.

Nickel, C., M. Simek, A. Moleda, M. Muehlbacher, W. Buschmann, R. Fartacek, E. Bachler, C. Egger, W. K. Rother, T. H. Loew, and M. K. Nickel. "Suicide Attempts versus Suicidal Ideation in Bulimic Female Adolescents," *Pediatrics International*, 2006, 48(4):374–81.

Nickel, M. K. "Aripiprazole in the Treatment of Patients with Borderline Personality Disorder: A Double-Blind, Placebo-Controlled Study," *American Journal of Psychiatry*, 2006, 163(5):833–38.

Nickel, M. K. "Topiramate Treatment of Aggression in Female Borderline Personality Disorder Patients: A Double-Blind, Placebo-Controlled Study," *Journal of Clinical Psychiatry*, 2004, 65(11):1515–19.

Nixon, M. K., P. F. Cloutier, and S. Agarwal. "Affect Regulation and Addictive Aspects of Repetitive Self-Injury in Hospitalized Adolescents," *Journal of the American Academy of Child and Adolescent Psychiatry*, 2002, 41:1333–41.

Nock, M. K., T. E. Joiner, K. H. Gordon, E. Lloyd-Richardson, and M. J. Prinstein. "Non-Suicidal Self-Injury among Adolescents: Diagnostic Correlates and Relation to Suicide Attempts," *Psychiatry Research*, 2006, 144(1):65–72.

Norra, C., M. Mrazeka, F. Tuchtenhagena, R. Gobbeléb, H. Buchnerb, H. Saßa, and S. C. Herpertza. "Enhanced Intensity Dependence as a Marker of Low Serotonergic Neurotransmission in Borderline Personality Disorder," *Journal of Psychiatric Research*, 2003, 37(1):23–33.

Oldham, J. M., A. E. Skodol, H. D. Kellman, S. E. Hyler, L. Rosnick, and M. Davies. "Diagnosis of DSM-III-R Personality Disorders by Two Structured Interviews: Patterns of Comorbidity," *American Journal of Psychiatry*, 1992, 149:213–20.

Palmer, S., K. Davidson, P. Tyrer, A. Gumley, P. Tata, J. Norrie, H. Murray, and H. Seivewright. "The Cost Effectiveness of Cognitive Behavior Therapy for Borderline Personality Disorder: Results from the BOSCOT Trial," *Journal of Personality Disorders*, 2006, 20(5):466–81.

Paris, J. "Is Hospitalization Useful for Suicidal Patients with Borderline Personality Disorder?" *Journal of Personality Disorders*, 2004, 18(3):240–47.

Perrella, C., D. Carrus, E. Costa, and F. Schifano. "Quetiapine for the Treatment of Borderline Personality Disorder: An Open-Label Study," *Progress in Neuro-Psychopharmacology & Biological Psychiatry*, 2007, 31(1):158–63.

Philipsen, A., H. Richter, C. Schmahl, J. Peters, N. Rusch, M. Bohus, and K. Lieb. "Clonidine in Acute Aversive Inner Tension and Self-Injurious Behavior in Female Patients with Borderline Personality Disorder," *Journal of Clinical Psychiatry*, 2004, 65(10):1414–19.

Philipsen, A., C. Schmahl, and K. Lieb. "Naloxone in the Treatment of Acute Dissociative States in Female Patients with Borderline Personality Disorder," *Pharmacopsychiatry*, 2004, 37(5):196–99.

Pinto, A., W. L. Grapentine, G. Francis, and C. M. Picariello. "Borderline Personality Disorder in Adolescents: Affective and Cognitive Features," *Journal of the American Academy of Child and Adolescent Psychiatry*, 1996, 35(10):1338–43.

Pooley, E. C., K. Houston, K. Hawton, and P. J. Harrison. "Deliberate Self-Harm Is Associated with Allelic Variation in the Tryptophan Hydroxylase Gene (TPH A779C), but not with Polymorphisms in Five Other Serotonergic Genes," *Psychological Medicine*, 2003, 33(5):775–83.

Prado, C. "Functional Impairments in Patients with Borderline Personality Disorders Demonstrated by NeuroSPECT HMPAO Tc 99 m in Basal Conditions and Under Frontal Activation," *Alasbimn Journal*, 2002, 2(7): Article No. AJ07-1.

Preston, G. A., B. K. Marchant, F. W. Reimherr, R. E. Strong, and D. W. Hedges. "Borderline Personality Disorder in Patients with Bipolar Disorder and Response to Lamotrigine," *Journal of Affective Disorders*, 2004, 79(1-3):297–303.

Raine, A., M. Buchsbaum, and L. LaCasse. "Brain Abnormalities in Murderers Indicated by Positron Emission Tomography," *Biological Psychiatry*, 1997, 42:495–508.

Raine, A., T. Lencz, and S. Bihrle. "Reduced Prefrontal Gray Volume and Autonomic Deficits in Antisocial Personality Disorder," *Archives of General Psychiatry*, 2000, 57(2):119–27.

Raine, A., J. Stoddard, and S. Bihrle. "Prefrontal Glucose Deficits in Murderers Lacking Psychosocial Deprivation," *Neuropsychology and Behavioral Neurology*, 1998, 11:1–7.

Rey, J. M., A. Morris-Yates, M. Singh, G. Andrews, and G. W. Stewart. "Continuities between Psychiatric Disorders in Adolescents and Personality Disorders in Young Adults," *American Journal of Psychiatry*, 1995, 152(6):895–900.

Rey, J. M., M. Singh, A. Morris-Yates, and G. Andrews. "Referred Adolescents as Young Adults: The Relationship between Psychosocial Functioning and Personality Disorder," *Australia and New Zealand Journal of Psychiatry*, 1997, 31(2):219–26.

Rinne, T., W. van den Brink, L. Wouters, and R. van Dyck. "SSRI Treatment of Borderline Personality Disorder: A Randomized, Placebo-Controlled Clinical Trial for Female Patients with Borderline Personality Disorder," *American Journal of Psychiatry*, 2002, 159:2048–54.

Rocca, P., L. Marchiaro, E. Cocuzza, and F. Bogetto. "Treatment of Borderline Personality Disorder with Risperidone," *Journal of Clinical Psychiatry*, 2002, 63:241–44.

Rogosch, F. A., and D. Cicchetti. "Child Maltreatment, Attention Networks, and Potential Precursors to Borderline Personality Disorder," *Developmental Psychopathology*, 2005, 17(4):1071–89.

Russ, M. J., S. D. Roth, A. Lerman, T. Kakuma, K. Harrison, R. D. Shindledecker, J. Hull, and S. Mattis. "Pain Perception in Self-Injurious Patients with Borderline Personality Disorder," *Biological Psychiatry*, 1992, 32(6):501–11.

Sakai, J. T., S. E. Young, M. C. Stallings, D. Timberlake, A. Smolen, G. L. Stetler, and T. J. Crowley. "Case-Control and Within-Family Tests for an Association between Conduct Disorder and 5HTTLPR," *American Journal of Medical Genetics Part B Neuropsychiatric Genetics*, 2006, 141(8):825–32.

Salzman, C., A. N. Wolfson, A. Schatzberg, J. Looper, R. Henke, M. Albanese, J. Schwartz, and E. Miyawaki. "Effect of Fluoxetine on Anger in Symptomatic Volunteers with Borderline Personality Disorder," *Journal of Clinical Psychopharmacology*, 1995, 15:23–29.

Sansone, R. A., J. L. Levitt, and L. A. Sansone. "The Prevalence of Personality Disorders among Those with Eating Disorders," *Eating Disorders*, 2005, 13(1):7–21.

Schafer, M., B. Schnack, and M. Soyka. "Sexual and Physical Abuse During Early Childhood or Adolescence and Later Drug Addiction," *Psychotherapie Psychosomatik Medizinische Psychologie*, 2000, 50(2):38–50.

Schmahl, C., M. Bohus, F. Esposito, R. D. Treede, F. Di Salle, W. Greffrath, P. Ludaescher, A. Jochims, K. Lieb, K. Scheffler, J. Hennig, and E. Seifritz. "Neural Correlates of Antinociception in Borderline Personality Disorder," *Archives of General Psychiatry*, 2006, (6):659–67.

Schmahl, C., and J. D. Bremner. "Neuroimaging in Borderline Personality Disorder," *Journal of Psychiatric Research*, 2006, 40(5):419–27.

Schmahl, C., W. Greffrath, U. Baumgartner, T. Schlereth, W. Magerl, A. Philipsen, K. Lieb, M. Bohus, and R. D. Treede. "Differential Nociceptive Deficits in Patients with Borderline Personality Disorder and Self-Injurious Behavior: Laser-Evoked Potentials, Spatial Discrimination of Noxious Stimuli, and Pain Ratings," *Pain*, 2004, 110(1-2):470–79.

Schmahl, C. G., E. Vermetten, B. M. Elzinga, and J. D. Bremner. "A Positron Emission Tomography Study of Memories of Childhood Abuse in Borderline Personality Disorder," *Biological Psychiatry*, 2004, 55(7):759–65.

Schnell, K., and S. C. Herpertz. "Effects of Dialectic Behavioral Therapy on the Neural Correlates of Affective Hyperarousal in Borderline Personality Disorder," *Journal of Psychiatric Research*, 2006, 8(3):133–142.

Segal-Trivitz, Y., Y. Bloch, Y. Goldburt, D. Sobol-Havia, Y. Levkovitch, and G. Ratzoni. "Comparison of Symptoms and Treatments of Adults and Adolescents with Borderline Personality Disorder," *International Journal of Adolescent Medicine and Health*, 2006, 18(2):215–20.

Sharp, C., C. Ha, J. Michonski, A. Venta, and C. Carbone. "Borderline Personality Disorder [BPD] in Adolescents: Evidence in Support of the Childhood Interview for *DSM-IV* [BPD] in a Sample of Adolescent Inpatients," Comprehensive Psychiatry, 2012, 53 (6): 765-74.

Silverman, J. M., L. Pinkham, T. B. Horvath, E. F. Coccaro, K. Howard, S. Schear, S. Apter, M. Davidson, R. Mohs, and L. J. Siever. "Affective and Impulsive Personality Disorder Traits in the Relatives of Patients with Borderline Personality Disorder," *American Journal of Psychiatry*, 1991, 148(10):1378–85.

Slap, G., E. Goodman, and B. Huang. "Adoption as a Risk Factor for Attempted Suicide During Adolescence," *Pediatrics*, 2001, 108(2):E30.

Smith, D. J., W. J. Muir, and D. H. Blackwood. "Borderline Personality Disorder Characteristics in Young Adults with Recurrent Mood Disorders: A Comparison of Bipolar and Unipolar Depression," *Journal of Affective Disorders*, 2005, 87(1):17–23.

Soloff, P. H., A. Fabio, T. M. Kelly, K. M. Malone, and J. J. Mann. "High-Lethality Status in Patients with Borderline Personality Disorder," *Journal of Personality Disorders*, 2005, 19(4):386–99.

Soloff, P. H., K. G. Lynch, T. M. Kelly, K. M. Malone, and J. J. Mann. "Characteristics of Suicide Attempts of Patients with Major Depressive Episode and Borderline Personality Disorder: A Comparative Study," *American Journal of Psychiatry*, 2000, 157:601–608.

Soloff, P. H., C. C. Meltzer, C. Becker, P. J. Greer, T. M. Kelly, and D. Constantine. "Impulsivity and Prefrontal Hypometabolism in Borderline Personality Disorder," *Psychiatry Research*, 2003, 123(3):153–63.

Steinberg, B. J., R. Trestman, V. Mitropoulou, M. Serby, J. Silverman, E. Coccaro, S. Weston, M. de Vegvar, and L. J. Siever. "Depressive Response to Physostigmine Challenge in Borderline Personality Disorder Patients," *Neuropsychopharmacology*, 1997, 17(4):264–73.

Stone, M. H., S. W. Hurt, and D. K. Stone. "The PI-500: Long-Term Follow-Up of Borderline In-Patients Meeting DSMIII Criteria I: Global Outcome," *Journal of Personality Disorders*, 1987:1291–98.

Stone, M. H., D. K. Stone, and S. W. Hurt. "Natural History of Borderline Patients Treated by Intensive Hospitalization," *Psychiatric Clinics of North America*, 1987, 10:185–206.

Swartz, H. A., P. A. Pilkonis, E. Frank, J. M. Proietti, and J. Scott. "Acute Treatment Outcomes in Patients with Bipolar I Disorder and Co-Morbid Borderline Personality Disorder Receiving Medication and Psychotherapy," *Bipolar Disorders*, 2005, 7(2):192–97.

Tanskanen, A., J. R. Hibbeln, J. Hintikka, K. Haatainen, K. Honkalampi, and H. Viinamaki. "Fish Consumption, Depression, and Suicidality in a General Population," *Archives of General Psychiatry*, 2001, 58(5):512–13.

Tebartz van Elst, L., B. Hesslinger, T. Thiel, E. Geiger, K. Haegele, L. Lemieux, K. Lieb, M. Bohus, J. Hennig, and D. Ebert. "Frontolimbic Brain Abnormalities in Patients with Borderline Personality Disorder: A Volumetric

Magnetic Resonance Imaging Study," *Biological Psychiatry*, 2003, 15; 54(2):163–71.

Thatcher, D. L., J. R. Cornelius, and D. B. Clark. "Adolescent Alcohol Use Disorders Predict Adult Borderline Personality," *Addictive Behaviors*, 2005, 30(9):1709–24.

Thompson, R., E. Briggs, D. J. English, H. Dubowitz, L. C. Lee, K. Brody, M. D. Everson, and W. M. Hunter. "Suicidal Ideation among 8-Year-Olds Who Are Maltreated and at Risk: Findings from the LONGSCAN Studies," *Child Maltreatment*, 2005, 10(1):26–36.

Torgersen, S. "Genetics of Patients with Borderline Personality Disorder," *Psychiatric Clinics of North America*, 2000, 23(1):1–9.

Valkenburg, P. M., J. Peter, and A. P. Schouten. "Friend Networking Sites and Their Relationship to Adolescents' Well-Being and Social Self-Esteem," *Cyberpsychology and Behavior*, 2006, 9(5):584–90.

Van Den Bosch, L. M., M. W. Koeter, T. Stijnen, R. Verheul, and W. Van Den Brink. "Sustained Efficacy of Dialectical Behaviour Therapy for Borderline Personality Disorder," *Behaviour Research and Therapy*, 2005, 43(9):1231–41.

Van Den Bosch, L. M., R. Verheul, W. Langeland, and W. Van Den Brink. "Trauma, Dissociation, and Posttraumatic Stress Disorder in Female Borderline Patients with and without Substance Abuse Problems," *Australia and New Zealand Journal of Psychiatry*, 2003, 37(5):549–55.

Van Wel, B., I. Kockmann, N. Blum, B. Pfohl, D. W. Black, and W. Heesterman. "STEPPS Group Treatment for Borderline Personality Disorder in The Netherlands," *Annals of Clinical Psychiatry*, 2006, 18(1):63–7.

Weiger, W. A., and D. M. Bear. "An Approach to the Neurology of Aggression," *Journal of Psychiatric Research*, 1988, 22:85–98.

Westen, D., J. Shedler, C. Durrett, S. Glass, and A. Martens. "Personality Diagnoses in Adolescence: DSM-IV Axis II Diagnoses and an Empirically Derived Alternative," *American Journal of Psychiatry*, 2003, 160:952–66.

Whitlock, J., J. Muehlkamp, A. Purington, J. Eckenrode, P. Barreira, G. Baral-Abrahms, T. Marchell, V. Kress, K. Girard, C. Chin, and K. Knox. "Non-Suicidal Self-Injury in a College Population: General Trends and Sex Differences," *Journal of American College Health*, 2011, 59(8):691–8.

Whitlock, J. L., J. L. Powers, and J. Eckenrode. "The Virtual Cutting Edge: The Internet and Adolescent Self-Injury," *Developmental Psychology*, 2006, 42(3):407–17.

Wilson, S. T., E. A. Fertuck, A. Kwitel, M. C. Stanley, and B. Stanley. "Impulsivity, Suicidality and Alcohol Use Disorders in Adolescents and Young Adults with Borderline Personality Disorder," *International Journal of Adolescent Medicine and Health*, 2006, 18(1):189–96.

Wingenfeld, K., M. Driessen, B. Adam, and A. Hill. "Overnight Urinary Cortisol Release in Women with Borderline Personality Disorder Depends on Comorbid PTSD and Depressive Psychopathology," *European Psychiatry*, 2006, 194(12):967–970.

Yoshida, K., E. Tonai, H. Nagai, K. Matsushima, M. Matsushita, J. Tsukada, Y. Kiyohara, and R. Nishimura. "Long-Term Follow-Up Study of Borderline Patients in Japan: A Preliminary Study," *Comprehensive Psychiatry*, 2006, 47(5):426–32.

Zanarini, M. C., and F. R. Frankenburg. "Olanzapine Treatment of Female Borderline Personality Disorder Patients: A Double-Blind, Placebo-Controlled Pilot Study," *Journal of Clinical Psychiatry*, 2001, 62(11):849–54.

Zanarini, M. C., and F. R. Frankenburg. "Omega-3 Fatty Acid Treatment of Women with Borderline Personality Disorder: A Double-Blind, Placebo-Controlled Pilot Study," *American Journal of Psychiatry*, 2003, 160(1):167–69.

Zanarini, M. C., F. R. Frankenburg, J. Hennen, D. B. Reich, and K. Silk. "Axis I Comorbidity in Patients with Borderline Personality Disorder: 6-Year Follow-Up and Prediction of Time to Remission," *American Journal of Psychiatry*, 2004, 161:2108–14.

Zanarini, M. C., F. R. Frankenburg, J. Hennen, D. B. Reich, and K. R. Silk. "The McLean Study of Adult Development: Overview and Implications of the First Six Years of Prospective Follow-Up," *Journal of Personality Disorders*, 2005, 19(5):505–23.

Zanarini, M. C., F. R. Frankenburg, and E. A. Parachini. "A Preliminary, Randomized Trial of Fluoxetine, Olanzapine, and the Olanzapine-Fluoxetine Combination in Women with Borderline Personality Disorder," *Journal of Clinical Psychiatry*, 2004, 65(7):903–907.

Zanarini, M. C., F. R. Frankenburg, M. E. Ridolfi, S. Jager-Hyman, J. Hennen, and J. G. Gunderson. "Reported Childhood Onset of Self-Mutilation among Borderline Patients," *Journal of Personality Disorders*, 2006, 20(1):9–15.

Zanarini, M. C., F. R. Frankenburg, L. Yong, G. Raviola, D. B. Reich, J. Hennen, J. I. Hudson, and J. G. Gunderson. "Borderline Psychopathology in the First-Degree Relatives of Borderline and Axis II Comparison Probands," *Journal of Personality Disorders*, 2004, 18(5):439–47.

Zanarini, M. C., A. A. Williams, R. E. Lewis, R. B. Reich, S. C. Vera, M. F. Marino, A. Levin, L. Yong, and F. R. Frankenburg. "Reported Pathological Childhood Experiences Associated with the Development of Borderline Personality Disorder," *American Journal of Psychiatry*, 1997, 154(8):1101–1106.

Zanarini, M. C., L. Yong, F. R. Frankenburg, J. Hennen, D. B. Reich, M. F. Marino, and A. A. Vujanovic. "Severity of Reported Childhood Sexual Abuse and Its Relationship to Severity of Borderline Psychopathology and Psychosocial Impairment among Borderline Inpatients," *The Journal of Nervous and Mental Disorders*, 2002, 190(6):381–87.

Zeanah, C. H. "Beyond Insecurity: A Reconceptualization of Attachment Disorders of Infancy," *Journal of Consulting and Clinical Psychology*, 1996, 64:42–52.

Zeanah, C. H., and N. A. Fox. "Temperament and Attachment Disorders," *Journal of Clinical Child and Adolescent Psychology*, 2004, 33:32–41.

Zeanah, C. H., A. Keyes, and L. Settles. "Attachment Relationship Experiences and Childhood Psychopathology," *Annals of the New York Academy of Science*, 2003, 1008:22–30.

Zeanah, C. H., M. Scheeringa, N. W. Boris, S. S. Heller, A. T. Smyke, and J. Trapani. "Reactive Attachment Disorder in Maltreated Toddlers," *Child Abuse and Neglect*, 2004, 28:877–88.

Zelkowitz, P., J. Paris, J. Guzder, and R. Feldman. "Diatheses and Stressors in Borderline Pathology of Childhood: The Role of Neuropsychological Risk and Trauma," *Journal of the American Academy of Child and Adolescent Psychiatry*, 2001, 40(1):100–105.

Zimmerman, M., and J. I. Mattia. "Axis I Diagnostic Comorbidity and Borderline Personality Disorder," *Comprehensive Psychiatry*, 1999, 40(4):245–52.

Zimmerman, M., L. Rothschild, and I. Chelminski. "The Prevalence of DSM-IV Personality Disorders in Psychiatric Outpatients," *American Journal of Psychiatry*, 2005, 162:1911–18.

Zweig-Frank, H., J. Paris, and J. Guzder. "Psychological Risk Factors for Dissociation and Self-Mutilation in Female Patients with Borderline Personality Disorder," *Canadian Journal of Psychiatry*, 1994, 39(5):259–64.


## BOOKS

Ainsworth, M., M. C. Blehar, E. Waters, and S. Wall. *Patterns of Attachment: A Psychological Study of the Strange Situation*. Hillsdale, NJ: Erlbaum, 1978.

Alderman, T. *The Scarred Soul: Understanding and Ending Self-Inflicted Violence*. Oakland, CA: New Harbinger, 1997.

American Psychiatric Association. *Diagnostic and Statistical Manual of Mental Disorders, Fourth Edition, Text Revision (DSM-IV-TR)*. Washington DC: American Psychiatric Publishing, 2000; and *DSM-5*, Arlington, VA, 2013.


## OTHER REFERENCES

Batty, D. "Transsexual expert 'put patients at risk,'" *Guardian Unlimited*, Friday, November 3, 2006.

BBC interview with Princess Diana, November 1995.

Bohart, A. C., and L. Greenberg, eds. *Empathy Reconsidered: New Directions in Psychotherapy.* Washington DC: American Psychological Association.

Brodzinsky, D. M. "Long-Term Outcomes in Adoption." *Adoption*, 1993, 3(1): 153–66.

Caspi, A. "Personality Development across the Lifespan." In *Handbook of Child Psychology, vol. 3, 6th ed., Social, Emotional, and Personality Development*, edited by W. Damon, 311–88. New York: Wiley, 1998.

Caspi, A., and R. L. Shiner. "Personality Development." In *Handbook of Child Psychology, vol. 3, 6th ed., Social, Emotional, and Personality Development*, edited by W. Damon, 300–65. New York: Wiley, 2006.

Chanen, A. "An MRI Study of the Orbitofrontal Cortex and Medial Temporal Lobe in Adolescent Borderline Personality Disorder." ORYGEN Research

Center, Department of Psychiatry, The University of Melbourne, Australia.

Freud, A. "The Assessment of Borderline Cases." In *The Writings of Anna Freud*, vol. 5. New York: International Universities Press, 1969.

Fruzzetti, A. E. "Couples and Family Dialectical Behavior Therapy: Brief Intervention Outcomes." Paper presented at the 3rd Annual Convention of the International Society for Dialectical Behavior Therapy, Washington DC, 1998.

Fruzzetti, A. E., A. Rubio, and S.R Thorp. "DBT as an Alternative to Anger Management for Male Batterers." Paper presented at the 3rd Annual Convention of the International Society for Dialectical Behavior Therapy, Washington DC, 1998.

The Grove Street Adolescent Residence of The Bridge of Central Massachusetts, Inc. "Using Dialectical Behavior Therapy to Help Troubled Adolescents Return Safely to Their Families and Communities." *Psychiatric Services*, 2004, 55:1168–70.

Lyons-Ruth, K. "Maternal Depressive Symptoms, Disorganized Infant-Mother Attachment Relationships and Hostile-Aggressive Behavior in the Pre-School Classroom." In *Rochester Symposium on Developmental Psychology, vol. 4, A Developmental Approach to Affective Disorders*, edited by D. Cicchetti and S. Roth, 131–71. Hillsdale, NJ: Erlbaum, 1992.

U.S. Food and Drug Administration. *Public Health Advisory: Suicidality in Children and Adolescents Being Treated with Antidepressant Medications.* Washington, DC: FDA, October 15, 2004.

Vela, R. M., E. H. Gottlieb, and H. P. Gottlieb. "Borderline Syndromes in Childhood: A Critical Review." In *The Borderline Child*, edited by K. S. Robson, 32–48. New York: McGraw-Hill, 1983.

# Acknowledgments

I could not have written this book without the support and input of many people, but it would have been pointless were it not for the kids and families who struggle daily with the impact of BPD.

At McLean Hospital, Cynthia Kaplan, Joe Gold, and Phil Levendusky have strongly supported the dedicated treatment of adolescents with BPD and were there when we started 3East. Michael Hollander and Janna Hobbs were balancing guides as we continued to provide services to the ever-growing group of young people who needed them.

Judy Mintz, Gillian Galen, Ben Banister, Peg Polomsky, and Lisa Adams have taken on leadership in providing services throughout our continuum. My colleague psychiatrists Mona Potter, Julie Vanderfeen, Sophia Maurasse, and Ximena Sanchez have added the medical perspective through a DBT lens. Sarah Hunt continues to work tirelessly to interface with the outside world to make sure that kids are helped in a timely fashion.

John Gunderson has provided years of wisdom and supervision. Mary Zanarini, Randy Auerbach, Joanna Chango, and Cynthia Kaplan have spearheaded many research initiatives that will continue to better define the nature of BPD in adolescents, its course, and the impact of treatment.

Marsha Linehan has truly underscored the role of mindfulness in treating BPD, and she has helped change the course, prognosis, and dialogue of BPD.

Perry Hoffman continues to educate the world about BPD through the National Education Alliance for Borderline Personality Disorder foundation.

Finally, I am certain that my fabulous editor Cara Connors is capable of reading my mind as she has the uncanny ability to succinctly decipher my ramblings into readable and sensible English, and without her we would never have been in on time! Thank you!

# About the Author

**Blaise Aguirre, MD,** is the founding medical director of 3East at the Harvard Medical School–affiliated McLean Hospital in Belmont, Massachusetts. This residential program treats young women exhibiting self-endangering behaviors and borderline personality disorder (BPD) traits using dialectical behavior therapy (DBT). He has been a staff psychiatrist at McLean since 2000 and is nationally and internationally recognized for his extensive work in the treatment of mood and personality disorders in adolescents. He is a board-certified psychiatrist and an assistant professor of psychiatry at Harvard University School of Medicine and lectures regularly in Europe, Africa, and the Middle East on BPD and DBT. He is a co-author of *Mindfulness for Borderline Personality Disorder (New Harbinger Publications, 2013)* and *Helping Your Troubled Teen* (Fair Winds Press, 2007).

# Index

oxytocin, 86

parents. *See also* attachment; relationships.
 adolescent development and, 61, 63
 adoption and, 216, 232, 235–236
 alexithymia and, 89
 arguments between, 111
 balance of discipline, 66–67
 balance of power and, 224
 "blame game," 88–89
 bond to child, 90
 communication and, 79–80
 dialectical behavior therapy (DBT) and, 66, 162
 diagnoses and, 66, 89, 113
 depression and, 89
 fearful feelings of, 51
 guilty feelings of, 27, 92, 111, 216
 independence and, 68–69
 manipulation of, 105, 106, 107–108, 109, 110–111, 130
 misdiagnoses and, 50
 nonverbal communication, 172–173
 perception of problem behaviors by, 67–68
 rage episodes and, 41–43
 recognition of symptoms, 46–47, 49
 self-injury and, 35, 38, 61, 66–67, 69, 73
 "splitting" behavior and, 36
 strategies for, 66–69
 suicide and, 35, 47, 51, 66–67
 teamwork, 111
 treatment and, 142–143, 144
 validation and, 151–154
 voices of, 216–219
parietal lobe, 82
Paris, Joel, 179
paroxetine (Paxil), 189
partial hospitalization, 177
patients, voices of, 209–215
Paxil. *See* paroxetine (Paxil).
PE therapy. *See* prolonged exposure (PE) therapy.
pets, 114
PFC. *See* prefrontal cortex (PFC).
Pfohl, Bruce, 168
physical abuse
 diagnoses and, 117
 frontal lobes and, 83
 post-traumatic stress disorder (PTSD) and, 44, 94, 126
 self-injury and, 70
 substance abuse and, 123
 suicide and, 125
pituitary gland, 85–86
post-traumatic stress disorder (PTSD)
 abuse and, 94, 119, 126–127
 anxiety and, 247
 comorbidities and, 95, 119, 126–127
 depression and, 247
 diagnoses and, 118, 126
 dissociation and, 127–128
 intensity of illness and, 127
 medications for, 186, 192, 193
 prefrontal cortex (PFC) and, 87
 prevalence of, 126

prognoses and, 247–248
 prolonged exposure (PE) therapy and, 127
 treatment and, 126, 136
Practice Guideline for the Treatment of Patients with Borderline Personality Disorder, 182–183
prefrontal cortex (PFC), 64, 87
Princeton University, 70
prognoses
 abuse and, 244
 adulthood and, 245
 current outcomes, 244–245
 dialectical behavior therapy (DBT) and, 250–251
 depression and, 242–243, 249
 future outcomes, 245–247
 historical outcomes, 243
 impulsivity and, 249
 international outcomes, 248–249
 lack of treatment and, 249
 long-term outcomes, 242–243
 post-traumatic stress disorder (PTSD) and, 247–248
prolonged exposure (PE) therapy, 118, 127
Prozac. *See* fluoxetine (Prozac).
psychodynamic therapy, 170–171
PTSD. *See* post-traumatic stress disorder (PTSD).
puberty, 49, 61

quetiapine (Seroquel), 186–187

rage episodes
 age and, 41
 calming skills, 42–43
 communication and, 43
 consequences for, 43
 friendships and, 42, 54, 87
 guilty feelings and, 43
 impulsivity and, 87
 intensity of, 212
 manipulation as, 108–109, 129–130
 prevention of, 42–43
 siblings and, 36
 timing of, 42
rapid cycling, 192
reactive attachment disorder (RAD), 56–57
reassurance-seeking behaviors, 19
relationships. *See also* families; parents; sexuality; siblings.
 abandonment, fear of, and, 19, 35, 110
 adolescent development and, 62, 63, 64
 adulthood and, 96
 cognitive-analytic therapy (CAT) and, 175
 cognitive-behavioral therapy (CBT) and, 169–170
 communication and, 79, 204
 essential fatty acids (EFAs) and, 194
 genetics and, 93
 Internet and, 97
 interpersonal dysregulation, 22
 interpersonal psychotherapy (IPT), 173
 manipulation in, 105
 medications and, 191
 mood and, 40, 54
 pets and, 114
 psychodynamic therapy and, 171
 rage episodes and, 87, 150